REBELS *and* DEMOCRATS

Elisha P. Douglass was graduated from Princeton and studied journalism at Columbia University before becoming a reporter for the *Hartford Times*. Later he received his Ph.D. in history from Yale and taught at the University of North Carolina, Chapel Hill, until his retirement. He is also the author of *The Coming of Age of American Business*.

REBELS *and* DEMOCRATS

The Struggle for Equal Political Rights
and Majority Rule
During the American Revolution

BY

ELISHA P. DOUGLASS

Elephant Paperbacks
Ivan R. Dee, Inc., Publisher, Chicago

First ELEPHANT PAPERBACK edition published
1989 by Ivan R. Dee, Inc., 1332 North Halsted
Street, Chicago 60622. Manufactured in the United
States of America.

Library of Congress Cataloging-in-Publication
Data
Douglass, Elisha P.
    Rebels and democrats.
    Reprint. Originally published: Chapel Hill, N.C.:
University of North Carolina Press, 1955.
    Bibliography: p.
    Includes index.
    1. United States—Politics and government—
Colonial period, ca. 1600–1775. 2. United
States—Politics and government—Revolution,
1775–1783. 3. Political rights—United States—
History—18th century. I. Title.
[JK57.P65D68   1989]   973.3   89-12000
ISBN 0-929587-12-X

PREFACE

IN 1925 Professor John Franklin Jameson, in a slender but tremendously important little volume, invited the historical profession to join him in viewing the American Revolution as a social movement. Since that time his invitation has been generally accepted, and accounts of the Revolutionary period have given due regard to aspects of the struggle which Jameson had in mind, such as the separation of church and state, the abolition of entail and primogeniture, the growth of the humanitarian spirit, and the expansion of commerce and industry in an environment freed from restrictions imposed from abroad. Yet one aspect of the social movement which marked the Revolution has as yet not been accorded the attention it deserves—the struggle of certain less privileged groups within the ranks of the Revolutionary party to obtain equal political rights for all adult males and a government in which the will of a majority of citizens would be the ultimate authority for political decision.

To many yeoman farmers and town artisans outside the

politically active classes, the Revolution was not an end in itself but a means of rebuilding society on the principles of the Declaration of Independence. Large numbers of those unable to vote or hold political office felt that the primary purpose of the struggle was to abolish the political institutions by which privilege had been maintained in the colonial governments. Thus when the question of home rule was succeeded by the question of who would rule at home, these groups of humbler rebels attempted to obtain equal consideration for themselves by demanding that democratic reforms be written into the new state constitutions.

It is with this phase of the Revolutionary movement that this book is concerned. The following pages will attempt to identify the various groups that sought reform, analyse their programs and those of their opponents, trace the course of the resulting struggles, and evaluate the achievements of both democrats and conservatives in the light of the general outcome of the Revolution.

The study is limited geographically to the thirteen original states and chronologically to a period beginning with the first evidence of democratic aspirations and ending with the adoption of the first state constitutions which outlived the Revolutionary period. Democratic agitation in frontier districts which contested the jurisdiction of the original states has not been taken into consideration, principally because the struggle for democracy in these regions belongs more properly to the post-Revolutionary period.

In any study which must make use of terms which do not evoke uniform responses, it is necessary to attempt definitions, even though such definitions will almost certainly not satisfy all readers. Outstanding among the many terms of indefinite content used today is "democracy" and its variant "democrat"—both of which will often be found on the following pages. Like all honorific terms they have been appropriated as a badge of respectability by aggressive political groups of the most diverse origins and objectives anxious to identify themselves with values commonly held in high regard. Books and articles describing democracy have flooded from the presses for nearly a century, and although such works have provided inspiration and guidance when such assistance was sorely needed, they have not made the task of definition any easier. The trouble is that theorists often confuse what democracy *is* with what it *should be,* and in the process transform the word into a symbol of value systems which sometimes have little in common. How are we to define democracy today when political leaders of such varying creeds as Harry S. Truman, Herman Talmadge, Harold J. Laski, Herbert Hoover, and the followers of Joseph Stalin all declare themselves to be standard bearers in its cause and roundly accuse each other of defection from the one true orthodoxy? No doubt all of us can be fairly sure where our sympathies lie even when we are confronted by such a mass of conflicting claims, but as long as the claims continue to have currency we are no closer to an objective definition of democracy. Unfortunately, the term as a word useful for designating a particular type of political system may be considered a casualty of party conflict and international cold war.

In the eighteenth century, however, before honorific connotations led to the pillage of its meaning, there were two conceptions of democracy—one explicit, traditional, based on Aristotelian logic, and the other implicit and empirical, never formulated into precise definition, but generally accepted within its limitations during the Revolutionary and early National periods. According to the explicit conception, democracy was power in the people as opposed to power in the best part of the people (aristocracy), or in a few people (oligarchy), or in one person (monarchy). The specific prototype of the democratic state was Athens, where the people

had exercised their power directly through the personal convention of all citizens. By the eighteenth century this element
of direct government by the people was held to be the chief
functional characteristic of democracy which set it apart
from all other types of government, particularly the republican form, which also lodged ultimate power in the people
but provided for the exercise of this power through representation. The difference between democracies and republics,
then, lay in the delegation of authority. Madison was expressing the common view of the matter when he stressed this
distinction in *The Federalist* (10).

It can readily be seen, however, that if the term democracy
meant no more in late eighteenth-century American than
direct popular government, its use would have been restricted
to treatises on political science and it would have dropped
out of the active vocabulary of the day. Actually representation was accepted as inevitable for any practical scheme of
government devised for geographical units larger than
towns. Although Madison and others might religiously re-
peat that democracy was direct popular government, the
definition had long since ceased to have any practical meaning, for it no longer expressed what most men of the time
had in mind when they used the word. What they were
thinking of was the implementation of the power in the
people by political equality and majority rule applied within
the forms of representative republican government. The crux
of the matter was whether representative government would
be merely a simple means of transforming the will of constituent majorities into law, or whether it would be a complex mechanism, weighted with checks and balances in such
a way as to block unwise or unjust action on the part of these
majorities or of any groups or individuals whose wills ran
counter to the general welfare. Reduced to its simplest terms,
then, democracy meant a political system in which all adult

males enjoyed equal political rights and in which the will of constituent majorities constituted the ultimate authority for political decision. As will be shown in the following pages, this conception of democracy first took form during the Revolutionary period. It received general acceptance during the nineteenth century. Although today democracy means more than political equality and majority rule, the peoples of the western world would probably agree that these factors are basic and indispensable to any democratic government.

If proper qualifications are considered, therefore, there seems to be adequate justification for applying the term "democrat" to those individuals and groups who sought equalitarian and majoritarian reforms during the Revolutionary period. Of course, not all democrats desired the same specific reforms, nor did they press their claims with the same degree of insistence. Except in Pennsylvania they had no party organization worthy of the name; their efforts tended to be sporadic, temporary, unguided, and usually ineffectual. Yet the common ideal of what they believed to be democratic government animated them all, and this ideal has today been transformed into normal political practice.

Since these Revolutionary democrats were to be found almost exclusively in the lower ranks of the Whig party, and since their conservative opponents who favored a republic in equipoise constituted almost the entire policy-making minority in the upper ranks, it seems not unreasonable to designate the opponents of majoritarian reform as "Whig leaders," or "Whigs," whenever a general term is needed. It should be understood, however, that the use of the term "Whig" in this connection does not imply that the democrats were in conflict with upper class Whigs regarding the separation from Britain. For the most part they loyally supported the party in the conduct of the war; they clashed with their leaders only over the nature of domestic institutions.

The present study cannot by any means be described as definitive. Within the general subject of Revolutionary democracy there are still geographical areas which invite further study and specific democratic reforms which might be investigated. I have attempted to write a useful book which might illuminate to some degree the origins of our democratic ideas and political institutions and stimulate further interest in the subject. If this volume is qualified or superseded by works to come it will have proved its usefulness and will have justified the efforts of writing it.

A book of this type which has gradually evolved from a doctoral dissertation in some respects resembles a cooperative work. Fortunately I have had the benefit of advice and criticism from many friends and associates. First and foremost I owe a deep debt of gratitude to Leonard W. Labaree, of Yale University, who has given me the benefit of his discernment and scholarly judgment nearly every step of the way. A. Whitney Griswold, now President of Yale but a member of the History Department while this study was being written, read the entire work and contributed many valuable suggestions on style and organization. Lester J. Cappon, Editor of Publications for the Institute of Early American History and Culture, and Douglass Adair, Editor of the *William and Mary Quarterly* were most helpful, and Lyman H. Butterfield, Director of the Institute, gave me the benefit of searching and detailed criticism of the whole manuscript. I am grateful to the Institute also for two grants-in-aid which enabled me to revise the original manuscript into its present form. My colleagues Fletcher M. Green and Hugh T. Lefler have read the entire manuscript and have given many helpful suggestions, and I have received similar assistance and encouragement from Richard Hofstadter and Henry F. Graff, of Columbia University, and from William Miller. Julian P. Boyd, of Princeton University, gave me the benefit of his vast knowledge of Jefferson in a criticism of my chapter dealing with the Sage of Monticello. It is only fair to those who have helped me to point out, however, that the interpretations and conclusions in the book are my own and do not necessarily represent their judgments.

The staffs of the various libraries and manuscript depositories where I worked have been unfailingly considerate. Dr. Christopher Crittenden, of the North Carolina Department of History and Archives, and Mr. Nicholas B. Wainwright, of the Historical Society of Pennsylvania, were particularly helpful. Finally, I owe a debt which I can never repay to my wife, who patiently typed and proofread the entire manuscript through two revisions.

CONTENTS

xiii

REBELS *and* DEMOCRATS

ONE

Conservatism and Radicalism

in the Revolution

IN RECENT years there has been considerable speculation about the causes of the American Revolution, but less, perhaps, about its essential characteristics. Was it primarily radical, a break from tradition which separated the destiny of America from that of Europe and ultimately produced a unique American character, or was it conservative, a reorientation of colonial and European experience to meet the needs of independence? Was the Revolution the result of a spontaneous upsurge of idealism seeking political and institutional expression, or was it a simple struggle over who, rather than what, should rule? Or if all these diverse elements were present, what were their proportions in the composition of the whole?

There are no simple answers to these questions because modern revolutions are complex and not simple phenomena. When any substantial portion of a population rises against lawful authority, its own internal conflicts are only temporarily shelved in the pursuit of a common objective. The various groups throwing their weight against existing government usually have different plans for the future; only the commonly shared oppression induces them to subordinate individual objectives for the main task at hand. But once the oppressor has been removed, group aims again become paramount. The chief cause of disagreement is usually the amount of change to be effected by the revolt. It suddenly becomes apparent that what were ends for one group are only means for another. Thus revolutionists naturally fall into classifications of conservative and radical. The simplicity of the revolutionary movement dissolves into the complexity inherent in the normal course of politics.

The American Revolution is no exception to the rule, but its complexity is not so apparent as that of many other revolutions, for its characteristics were predominantly conservative, as some students of the period have noted.[1] Yet it had a less conspicuous but important radical aspect. In many ways it represented the culmination of a desire for the abolition of political privilege on the part of groups outside the politically active classes who felt that in the past they had not received the consideration they deserved.

This desire for political reform did not suddenly come into being with the suppression of British authority. From the first days of settlement it had been a factor—although often a minor one—in the periodic outbreaks of violence directed against governors and royal officials. The gentlemen and the corporations who founded the first settlements, whether for profit or the glory of God, had all tried to reproduce the social system of England with only such variations as suited their special purposes. Such men as Penn and Calvert saw no incompatibility between applied philanthropy and a hierarchical society headed by themselves. The lords spiritual of Massachusetts had no intention of translating the equality of

---

1. A very able analysis of the conservative aspects of the American Revolution will be found in Daniel J. Boorstin, *The Genius of American Politics* (Chicago, 1953), ch. III.

all men before God into equality in civil society. The gentlemen who headed the Virginia Company and the Carolina
Proprietors subordinated any desires for self-expression on
the part of their settlers to the primary object of profit and
prestige for themselves. Yet in almost every instance the carefully laid plans of the founders were frustrated by the failure
of the settlers to cooperate and by the natural conditions of
America. Once possessed of freeholds, the former tenant
farmers of England exhibited a tendency to demand commensurate political privileges; a degree of economic independence promoted a desire to be consulted in the political
process.

Shortly after the founding of Massachusetts, for example,
the clergy were compelled to share their power with the
town delegates. Clerical authority waned further with the
adoption of the Half-Way Covenant which made church
membership, and consequently the franchise, easier to obtain
and suffered an even sharper reverse with the adoption of
the Charter of 1691 which divided political power between
the crown and the local freeholders. In the proprietary colonies the governors had all they could do to keep order, let
alone put their masters' elaborate political and social schemes
into effect. Royal governors were unable to realize more than
a pale reflection of crown, nobles, and commons in their
regimes patterned after the English system. Because of low
property qualifications for voting and officeholding and the
relative ease of acquiring land, the great majority of the
people lived in a condition of economic and social equality.
The few aristocrats who held high office were sometimes
hard-pressed to keep what measure of privilege and status
remained to them after the levelling process of natural conditions had done its work.

The sometimes hostile and uncooperative attitude of the
settlers toward their governments was usually not motivated

by a conscious desire for more democracy, although this may sometimes have been a factor. It would be a mistake to read into the tumultuous history of seventeenth-century America any continuing trend of class or sectional struggle. Usually specific grievances like the lack of protection from the government against Indians, unfair land distribution, high taxes, lack of a circulating medium, and extortion by officials were the cause of uprisings. The ease of acquiring land (except in New York), the wide dispersal of the population, the lack of communications, the remnants of a tradition of subordination, and the relative lack of class distinctions all conspired to retard the growth of conscious radicalism.

Yet in most of the periodic outbreaks against constituted authority there can be detected a thread of resentment against the few who had political privilege. Toward the end of the seventeenth century white servitude and the utilization of slave labor in the South, the expanding commercial activities in the northern towns, and the tremendous profits gained by privileged land speculation widened the gap between rich and poor. The raising of property qualifications for voting and officeholding, the close hold of the aristocracy on local government, and the under-representation of frontier districts gradually changed the assemblies from bodies truly representative of the people to political organs of the upper classes. This rise of a native aristocracy to a commanding position in politics apparently gave impetus to the occasional half-felt desire for the equalization of rights on the part of groups among the lower classes. The Land Bank incident in Massachusetts, the Paxton Riots of Pennsylvania, the "Great Rebellion of 1766" in New York, and the Regulator War in North Carolina all gave expression to a protest against privilege. On the eve of the Revolution, the dissatisfaction which had resulted in these outbreaks formed small but nourishing culture beds for the growth of democracy.

The appeals for freedom voiced by colonial leaders during the early years of the Revolution, the loosening of restraints which followed the suppression of British authority, and the necessity of redefining the relations of rulers and ruled in the succession governments all gave inspiration and opportunity for the transformation of latent resentment, where it existed, into a demand for political democracy. This development provoked immediate opposition from the Revolutionary leaders, for most of them were basically conservative and felt that majority rule and political equality constituted not only a threat to their dominant political position but a danger to the very freedoms for which the struggle against Britain had been undertaken. Circumstances divided the Revolutionary leaders into well-defined radical and moderate groupings regarding the separation from Britain; Whigs in colonies where assemblies had been dissolved and military operations were underway were usually more eager for separation than members of their party in colonies where reconciliation could be effected more easily. But in their ideas regarding the institutions and relationships to be included in the succession governments the Revolutionary leaders showed a rather surprising uniformity. All were agreed that the primary purpose of government was to protect rights and that the strongest possible barriers should be erected against the arbitrary use of power, but they did not conclude that the best way to effect these objectives was to place all power in the hands of the people. Far from it; as men of their age they feared that unchecked majorities of constituents or representatives would be as productive of tyranny as an unchecked despot.

In addition to these weighty considerations, the economic and political interests of the Revolutionary leaders led them to oppose democracy. Many of these men, particularly in the South, came from the high aristocracy and all were quite a social cut above the masses of the people. Possessing both property and power, they had much to lose and nothing to gain from a democratic reform of colonial institutions. Hence it is understandable that they resisted the attempts made by groups whose interests often conflicted with their own to seize the operative sovereignty in the state governments. In common with the possessors of wealth and power of every age, they considered the maintenance of their privileges to be an integral part of any political organization established in the name of liberty.

The Revolutionary leaders, therefore, were presented with two basic problems at the outset of the Revolution—the protection of rights against the arbitrary use of power, and the maintenance of their own superior position in the new state governments. The obvious solution was to establish constitutions which would include as many of the safeguards as possible utilized in colonial government. A revival of any semblance of the prerogative power was of course out of the question, but property qualifications for voting and office-holding and the principle of bicameralism had not been discredited by identification with British tyranny. These defenses against mobs and despots had been sanctioned by colonial experience and had become an integral part of the provincial governments; prudence dictated that they be included in the new state governments.

A political science devoted in part to frustrating majority will might at first glance seem inconsistent with the political philosophy of the Revolutionary leaders. From a modern point of view property qualifications seem incompatible with the doctrine of government by consent; the popular sovereignty emblazoned upon the Declaration of Independence appears in some measure to be qualified by the checks and balances of the first state constitutions. The men of '76 did not feel any conflict between their guiding principles and their political practice, however, because their principles contained many conservative assumptions which are often overlooked today. The rights they proclaimed were what they believed to be the traditional rights of Englishmen, not new and unprecedented privileges. The vocabulary of natural rights used in the Declaration of Independence did not indicate a sudden change to a more radical philosophy but was rather, as Carl Becker has indicated, an attempt to rephrase English rights in such a way that they would appeal to contemporary European intellectuals. The assertion of equality was not intended as a protest against the social distinctions, political privilege, and unequal distribution of wealth in the colonies but was rather a repudiation of hereditary status and the privilege derived from it in Britain and on the Continent. The assertion of the right of revolution, apart from its actual consequences, can scarcely be called a radical gesture in view of Locke's endorsement and the general acceptance of the proposition by previous generations of Englishmen. No one doubted the right of revolution; the only question was whether circumstances justified its invocation. Independence was for most of the Revolutionists a desperate measure of last resort. In their own minds they were defending the body of traditional English rights against an omnipotent, and therefore revolutionary, Parliament. Not accepting the Parliamentary supremacy implicit in the eighteenth-century British constitution, they considered themselves as counter-revolutionists rather than as rebels against lawful authority.

Any apparent discrepancies between the political philosophy and the political science of the Revolutionary leaders are therefore to a large extent reconciled by a pervasive conservatism which underlay the whole Revolutionary movement. The Whig leaders of 1776 could congratulate themselves after the struggle that their revolution, like that of 1688, was glorious as much for what it left untouched as for what it had altered. The traditional British institutions inherited from the empire had been remoulded into republican forms, traditional British rights were guaranteed to all American citizens, in most states the original leaders of the revolutionary party were firmly in control of the succession governments, and despite occasional shocks the colonial social system had weathered the levelling tendencies of the conflict.

Yet these felicitous results were not reached without occasional sharp conflicts with the less privileged groups among the rank and file who wanted to lower the center of gravity of political power. Both Whig and democrat were equally dedicated to the maintenance of human rights, both were equally opposed to arbitrary rule, but agreement on the fundamental postulates of a liberal philosophy could not settle the conflict over the location of political power. Thus the Revolution in some states acquired a dual nature. On one hand it was an uprising against British authority, on the other a movement for the democratic reform of all the institutions of provincial government whether tainted by the British connection or not. It would be a mistake, however, to assume from these instances that social upheaval was imminent throughout the country in 1776. As previously indicated, democratic agitation, although bitter and insistent, was localized, temporary, and unorganized. For the most part, the politically unprivileged came loyally to the support of the Revolutionary leadership and provided the sinews of the Continental armies. But the importance of historical events cannot always be determined by the standards of the age in which they occur. Seemingly insignificant at the time in comparison with the stirring military and political events which held the center of the stage, the democratic movement of the Revolution should have meaning for us today because it marks the beginning of the drive for political equality and majority rule which we have always associated with the age of Jackson and which has reached its culmination only in recent times.

TWO

The Conflict of Ideologies

THE groups who demanded equalitarian reform during the Revolution could find little support for their ideas in prevailing political philosophy. Since the time of Aristotle democracy had been recognized as a form of legitimate government, but it was usually considered so unstable as to be merely a prelude to anarchy. Yet outside of the politically active classes it had occasionally found advocates. The Levellers of the English Revolution, who resemble the American Revolutionary democrats from the standpoint of social class and program for reform, demanded from the Puritan oligarchy the substance of democratic, constitutional government.[1] John Locke, as a defender of the existing social and political order, was certainly no advocate of democracy as a form of government, but his description of how the social

1. Many fruitful comparisons can be made between the Levellers of 1645 to 1653 and American democrats of 1776 to 1783. See A. S. P. Woodhouse, *Puritanism and Liberty, being the Army Debates (1647-49) from the Clarke Manuscripts with Supplementary Documents Selected and Edited with an Introduction by A. S. P. Woodhouse; Foreword by A. D. Lindsay* (London, 1938); Theodore C. Pease, *The Leveller Movement* (Washington, 1916); William Haller (ed.), *The Leveller Tracts, 1647-1653* (New York, 1944); Don M. Wolfe, *Milton in the Puritan Revolution* (New York, 1941).

compact was formed and his unqualified assertion of popular sovereignty constituted the framework of a democratic philosophy.[2]

Although the Puritan oligarchy of Massachusetts denounced democracy as a form of government, nevertheless their acceptance of such equalitarian doctrines as Christian liberty and the priesthood of all believers and the existence of democratic procedures in Congregational polity made it possible for responsible men to advocate democratic principles in the political sphere. Thus John Wise, outspoken pastor of an Ipswich church from 1683 to 1725 and opponent of the Mathers' plan to introduce a semblance of Presbyterian polity into New England, made a spirited defense of democracy in his famous *Vindication of the Government of New England Churches.* According to Wise, democracy was "...a form of government which the light of nature does highly value, and often directs to as the most agreeable to the just and natural prerogatives of human beings." He felt that it gave the people a better guarantee against tyranny than any other political form.[3]

This tract, however, had little or no influence outside New England. Of more importance were the democratic implications in the writings of the Whig propagandists. Identifying their cause with universal principles of freedom, the Whigs often employed the language of democratic protest. This is particularly evident in the controversy over virtual representation. James Otis declared that absolute power "is *originally*

2. John Locke, *An Essay Concerning the True Original, Extent and End of Civil Government,* § 19, 87, 89, 95, 99, 122, 124, 168, 240, 242.

3. John Wise, *Vindication of the Government of New England Churches,* 3rd ed. (Boston, 1860), 54. For further details on Wise, see Paul S. McElroy, "John Wise: the Father of American Independence," Essex Institute Historical *Collections,* LXXXI (1945), 201-220; Clinton L. Rossiter, "John Wise: Colonial Democrat," *New England Quarterly,* XXII (1949), 3-32.

and *ultimately* in the people" and can be reclaimed by them if not exercised for their welfare.[4] Moreover, "No good reason can be given in any country why every man of sound mind should not have his vote in the election of a representative. If a man has but little property to defend and protect, yet his life and liberty are things of some importance." [5] Samuel Adams agreed. "The Acts of Parliament and the Constitution, consider every individual in the Realm as present in the high Court of Parliament by his Representative upon his own free Election. This is his indisputable Privilege —It is founded in the eternal law of equity—It is an original Right of Nature." [6] These generous professions did not indicate, however, that Otis and Adams favored an extension of the suffrage for the colonial assemblies or a more equitable apportionment of representation. Identifying the cause of liberty with provincial autonomy within the empire, both men simply failed to see any inconsistency between their political principles and assembly government. The two actually proved later to be opponents of political equality and majority rule. "When the pot boils, the scum will rise" was Otis's pungent comment on the group of radicals who agitated for reform of the Massachusetts government in the fall of 1776.[7] Sam Adams lent his personal popularity to secure the ratification of the plainly aristocratic constitution of 1780.[8]

4. Charles F. Mullett (ed.), *Some Political Writings of James Otis,* University of Missouri *Studies,* IV, 308-309.

5. James Otis, "Considerations on behalf of the Colonists in a Letter to a Noble Lord," in *ibid.,* 366. See also "A Vindication of the British Colonies," *ibid.,* 398-399.

6. Harry A. Cushing (ed.), *The Writings of Samuel Adams,* 4 Vols. (New York, 1904-1908), I, 46.

7. See below, pp. 156-157.

8. See below, p. 198.

Although democrats might have derived some aid and comfort from Dickinson's *Farmer's Letters,* John Adams' *Novanglus,* and Jefferson's *Summary View of the Rights of British America,* it was Thomas Paine who first identified the Revolution with democracy. The only Whig propagandist who was not a member of the colonial ruling class, neither merchant, lawyer, nor planter, Paine spoke in the language of the common people. *Common Sense* was a breath of fresh air to a propaganda literature which was beginning to suffocate on legalisms. The educated might be impressed by Dickinson's and Dulany's briefs for an equitable division of taxing power between colonies and mother country and by Jefferson's and Wilson's theory that the alleged expatriation of the colonists justified their claim for autonomy,[9] but argument on this level could have little meaning for the man on the street or at the plow. Everyone, however, could understand Paine's contention that America was an independent continent temporarily held in subjection by a vicious despot who derived his authority from a no less vicious system of government.

Paine conceived the Revolution as the means of establishing a new society based on equal rights. The struggle would be the symbolic labor pains attending the birth of a new order which would realize the heritage of freedom withheld for countless generations. "We have it in our power to begin the world over again," he announced. "The birthday of a new world is at hand, and a race of men, perhaps as numerous as all Europe contains, are to receive their portion of freedom from the events of a few months. Every spot in the old world is overrun with oppression. Freedom hath been hunted round the globe. Asia and Africa have long expelled her. Europe regards her like a stranger, and England hath

9. See below, p. 291.

given her warning to depart. O! receive the fugitive and prepare in time an asylum for mankind." [10]

This strain of utopianism, this vision of a better world as the object of the Revolution, is stronger in Paine than in any of his contemporaries. Once the prerogative power had been suppressed and the royal officialdom overthrown, most of the Revolutionary leaders were quite content to see a continuation of existing social and political relationships. For them the internal revolution was concluded by the summer of 1776. The task remaining was to insure the stability of society on its present basis; hence they turned for guidance in matters of government to colonial experience and to authorities who had already proved to be sound, such as Milton, Sidney, Bolingbroke, and Montesquieu. But Paine's conception of an adequate governmental framework owed nothing to authority or tradition. It represented only the minimum amount of machinery necessary to translate the will of majorities into legislation and insure unity among the colonies—unicameral assemblies in the states based on proportionate representation and subject to the Continental Congress.[11]

10. Phillip S. Foner (ed.), *The Complete Writings of Thomas Paine,* 2 Vols. (New York, 1945), I, 45, 31-32. Harry H. Clark argues that Paine's support of conservative fiscal policies in Pennsylvania during the early 1780's shows a basic conservatism which should be taken into account before labelling him a radical. See Clark (ed.), *Six New Letters of Paine* (Madison, 1939), introduction. It is true that Paine's economic ideas in this period are rather unexpected, but they in no way qualify his democratic political conceptions. His ideal government was always majoritarian democracy and he continually insisted on an equality of political rights. For illustrations of his thought, see his essays in defense of the Pennsylvania Constitution of 1776. *Writings,* II, 269-302. His democratic philosophy reached its fullest development during the period of his participation in the French Revolution, as evidenced by his "Dissertation on First Principles of Government," *ibid.,* 570-588, and *The Rights of Man.* Paine's importance as a democratic reformer has been emphasized by John C. Miller, *Origins of the American Revolution* (Boston, 1943), 504-505; *Triumph of Freedom* (Boston, 1948), 345.

11. "Common Sense," in Foner (ed.), *Writings of Paine,* I, 28.

An anonymous Massachusetts pamphleteer who wrote about the same time and whose ideas were reflected later among democrats during constitutional struggles in that state, was more openly critical of the plans of government supported by the Revolutionary leaders.[12] Asserting that the people "best know their wants and necessities and therefore are best able to govern themselves," he condemned upper houses armed with a veto and not directly responsible to the electorate as unworthy of a free state and declared that advocates of this type of bicameralism had designs against liberty. "The people are now contending for freedom; and would to God they might not only obtain, but likewise keep it in their own hands. There are many very noisy about liberty but are aiming at nothing more than personal power and grandeur. And are not many, under the delusive character of guardians of their country, collecting influence and honor only for oppression?"[13] He felt that representation should be in proportion to population, and that all adult free males should have the suffrage. Property qualifications for office he regarded as a source of corruption. "Social virtue

12. The People the Best Governors, or, a Plan of Government founded on the Just Principles of Natural Freedom (1776), reprinted as an appendix in Frederick Chase, History of Dartmouth College (Cambridge, 1891). The pamphlet was probably printed either in Boston, Worcester, or Hartford. Although mentioned by name only twice in 1776, nevertheless its spirit and specific recommendations reappear in scores of the political essays submitted by the Massachusetts towns to the General Court in reply to questions on constitutional issues. It summarizes the body of political thought which found expression in the instructions of Orange and Mecklenburg counties, North Carolina, to their delegates in the Provincial Congress, in the articles by democratic writers in Pennsylvania and Massachusetts newspapers, and in the public documents of the Pennsylvania Convention of 1776. The pamphlet is discussed briefly by Harry A. Cushing in American Historical Review, I (1895-1896), 284-287, and by William S. Carpenter in The Development of American Political Thought (Princeton, 1930), 66-68.

13. Chase, History of Dartmouth College, 662, 654.

and knowledge...is the best and only necessary qualification of [a representative]. So sure as we make interest necessary in this case, as sure we root out virtue....The notion
of an estate has the directest tendency to set up the avarisious
[sic] over the heads of the poor....Let it not be said in
future generations that money was made by the founders of
the American states an essential qualification in the rulers of
a free people." [14] By his plan of government the executive
and the judges would be selected by annual elections and
the executive denied a veto. In a unique provision he stipulated that an appeal from superior court decisions would
lie to the House of Representatives. "The judges, in many
cases, are obliged...to put such a construction on matters
as they think most agreeable to the spirit and reason of the
law. Now so far as they are reduced to this necessity, they
assume what is in fact the prerogative of the legislature, for
those that made the laws ought to give them a meaning
when they are doubtful." [15] The author apparently realized
that legal interpretation by the courts was often a disguised
form of legislation—a discovery usually attributed to the
twentieth century. In recommending the principle of legislative authority over judicial decisions he anticipated modern
critics of judicial review.

Common Sense and *The People the Best Governors* together illustrate the aspirations for a better world and the
desire to equalize political rights which characterized the
democratic groups in the Revolution. For them the preamble
of the Declaration of Independence was more than a collection of philosophical postulates; it was a set of principles to
be incorporated into political institutions. Popular sovereignty and equality were to be realized by manhood suffrage,
the abolition of property qualifications for officeholding,

14. *Ibid.*, 659-660.
15. *Ibid.*, 662.

representation according to population, and a government directly responsible in all its branches to the people as a whole.

The Whig leaders in the spring of 1776 were not slow to realize the threat to the established order in the confusion accompanying the Revolution. Wrote Paine, "I have heard some men say ... that they dreaded an independence, fearing that it would produce civil wars:..." [16] John Adams was one of these. "From the beginning," he declared, "I always expected we should have more difficulty and danger in our attempts to govern ourselves and in our negotiations and connections with foreign powers than from all the fleets and armies of Great Britain." [17] His kinsman, Sam Adams, found in 1776 that many Whig leaders felt the establishment of new governments would serve as a cloak for licentiousness. [18] Thus many representatives from colonies not already committed to war by the turn of events became almost desperate in their attempts to bring about a reconciliation with Britain. [19]

Before the suppression of royal government brought confusion to the colonies many Whigs had belittled the dangers

16. Foner (ed.), "Common Sense," *Writings of Paine,* I, 27.

17. Charles F. Adams (ed.), *The Works of John Adams,* 10 Vols. (Boston, 1850-1856), III, 13. Adams wrote his wife in the spring of 1776, "Such mighty revolutions make a deep impression on the minds of men and set many violent passions to work. Hope, fear, joy, sorrow, love, hatred, malice, envy, revenge, jealousy, ambition, avarice, resentment, gratitude,... were never in more lively exercise than they are now from Florida to Canada." Charles F. Adams (ed.), *Familiar Letters of John Adams and his Wife*... (Boston and New York, 1875), 168.

18. Cushing (ed.), *Writings of Samuel Adams,* III, 244.

19. The reluctance of the colonial ruling class as a whole to declare independence has been often noted. See Merrill Jensen, *The Articles of Confederation* (Madison, 1940), chs. 2 and 3; Arthur M. Schlesinger, *The Colonial Merchants and the American Revolution, 1763-1776* (New York, 1918), 593-606; Miller, *Origins of the American Revolution,* chs. 20 and 21.

to be anticipated from mob violence—at least in public. John Dickinson, replying to Tories who denounced the Stamp Act riots, had declared, "It was indeed a very improper way of acting, but may *not the agonies of minds not quite so polished as your own* be in some measure excused?" [20] Sam Adams, although exhibiting proper disapproval of the sacking of Lieutenant Governor Hutchinson's house in 1765, in 1769 described effigy burnings and riots as "joys of the Evening among the lower Sort, which, however innocent, are sometimes noisy." [21] When the Tory, Daniel Leonard, accused the Whigs of establishing a democratic despotism, John Adams, as "Novanglus," had replied magisterially, "The two ideas are incompatible with each other. A democratical despotism is a contradiction in terms," [22]—a position he was to reverse in a very short time.

But by 1776 the tolerant Whig attitude toward lawlessness underwent a transformation. The responsibilities of government gave them a new appreciation of the necessity for order, authority, and subordination. The rascals had been turned out; therefore good patriots should settle down and show a proper respect for authority. "How much soever I may heretofore have found fault with the powers that were I suppose I shall be well pleased now to hear submission inculcated to the powers that are," wrote John Adams.[23] Elbridge Gerry complained from Massachusetts that the people were feeling too strongly their new importance and

20. John Dickinson, *Political Writings,* 2 Vols. (Wilmington, 1801), I, 128.

21. Cushing, *Writings of Samuel Adams,* I, 406. Young Josiah Quincy, Jr., observed philosophically, "It is much easier to restrain liberty from running into licentiousness, than power from swelling into tyranny and oppression." *Memoir of the Life of Josiah Quincy, Jr., by his Son* (Boston, 1874), 304.

22. *Novanglus and Massachusettsensis* (Boston, 1819), 61.

23. Adams, *Works,* IX, 391.

needed a curb,[24] and James Warren, speaker of the Massachusetts House, dreaded the consequences of "the levelling spirit, encouraged and drove to such lengths as it is." [25] Sam Adams, to whom *vox populi* had been *vox Dei* when Hutchinson was in office, felt that there was "danger of errors on the side of the people" after the Whig leaders had seized control in Massachusetts. James Allen, a Pennsylvania Whig and a member of a wealthy family which had been a constant recipient of the proprietors' patronage, retired to his country seat in 1776 because the "mobility is triumphant." [26] The Whig leaders were particularly alarmed at the popular resistance to their plans to reopen the courts. As patriots they had been eager to drive royal judges off the benches, but as responsible administrators they were equally desirous to reestablish the judicial process as soon as possible.[27] The commissioning of courts, however, would amount to an assertion of sovereignty, a *de facto* declaration of independence. Thus the Whig leaders were placed in an uncomfortable dilemma: to continue without tribunals and legal government would be to invite chaos, but to establish authority equal to the exigencies of the hour would be open treason. It became apparent in some localities that debtors were using the glorious state of nature to prevent collection of their obligations. John Adams tells in his diary that a former client, whom he described contemptuously as a "horse

24. James T. Austin, *The Life of Elbridge Gerry*, 2 Vols. (Boston, 1828-1829), I, 78.

25. *Warren-Adams Letters*, 2 Vols. (Boston, 1917, 1925), Massachusetts Historical Society, *Collections*, LXXII, LXXIII, Vol. I, 219.

26. "Diary of James Allen," *Pennsylvania Magazine of History and Biography*, IX (1885), 186. He added that "The madness of the multitude is but one degree better than submission to Britain."

27. See Fletcher M. Green, *Constitutional Development in the South Atlantic States, 1776-1860; A Study in the Evolution of Democracy* (Chapel Hill, 1930), 56-58.

jockey," exclaimed to him with an enthusiasm which Adams could hardly share: "Oh, Mr. Adams, what great things you and your colleagues have done for us. We can never be grateful enough to you. There are no courts of justice in this province, and I hope there never will be another."[28] John Winthrop of Harvard, a pioneer American mathematician, physicist, and astronomer, informed Adams that the basic cause of opposition to the Revolutionary government of Massachusetts was "an unwillingness to submit to law and pay debts."[29]

When the course of events in the various colonies made it clear that there was no middle ground between capitulation to British demands and independence, the radical section of the Whig party firmly, if with misgivings, moved to seize the sovereign power. Thus Massachusetts established government under the provincial charter in order, among other things, to counter "the alarming symptoms of the abatement in the minds of the people of the sacredness of private property."[30] Edmund Pendleton, accepting the presidency of the Virginia Convention, observed, "It will become us to reflect whether we can longer sustain the great struggle we are making in this situation."[31] In Pennsylvania, many of the radical Whigs who had in 1774 done their best to discredit the proprietary government rallied to its support when the threat of internal revolution appeared imminent.

Lack of plans and procedures for the formation of succession governments as well as the gravity of seizing the sovereignty embarrassed the Whig leaders. Although *Common Sense* had received enthusiastic approval from radicals because of its castigation of Britain, its suggestions on govern-

---

28. Adams, *Works*, II, 420.
29. Massachusetts Historical Society, *Collections*, 5th Ser., IV, 307.
30. *American Archives* (Washington, 1837-1853), 4th Ser., II, 955.
31. *Ibid.*, VI, 1511.

ment elicited at best silence and at worst active opposition. Conservatives denounced the pamphlet in unmeasured terms. Landon Carter, a Virginia planter, could hardly restrain his rage. *Common Sense,* he asserted, was "repleat with art and contradiction ... rascally and nonsensical ... a sophisticated attempt to throw all men out of Principles ... which has drove all who espouse it from the justice of their contest." [32] Samuel Johnston of North Carolina called it "specious and dangerous," and Henry Laurens condemned "those indecent expressions with which the pages abound." [33] The North Carolina delegation to the Continental Congress at first refused to send copies home and only changed their minds at the insistence of the third delegate who had known democratic leanings.[34] Paine's *chef d'oeuvre* started a pamphlet war in Philadelphia—a type of slaughter not new to the city of brotherly love and one in which personal reputations and the English language had in the past been the chief sufferers. In Massachusetts the pamphlet was received enthusiastically by the radicals because of the tremendous assistance it afforded in drawing the other colonies into war. Nevertheless, some leaders realized the danger of its democratic ideas. "Don't be displeased with me," wrote Sam Adams to James Warren in a letter recommending the piece, "if you find the Spirit of it totally repugnant to your Ideas of Government." [35]

One of the most important effects of *Common Sense* was that in large part it stirred John Adams to write his famous

32. "The Diary of Landon Carter," *William and Mary Quarterly,* XVI (1907), 149-155.

33. Johnston to Hewes, March 3, 1776. Hayes Collection, North Carolina Department of History and Archives. David D. Wallace, *The Life of Henry Laurens* (New York and London, 1915), 22.

34. Hewes to Johnston, Feb. 20, 1776. North Carolina Letters from the Emmet Collection, North Carolina Department of History and Archives.

35. *Warren-Adams Letters,* I, 204.

Thoughts on Government, a pamphlet of almost equal importance in American history. Whereas *Common Sense* was the inspiration for independence and a new equalitarian society, *Thoughts on Government* erected the framework of American republicanism out of the solid materials of traditional institutions. The two stand as symbols of the democratic and conservative programs, the thesis and antithesis of the Revolution. Tom Paine, devastating as he was in his attack on hereditary government, had little of a practical nature to put in its place. Adams could never have matched Paine's fire and common-sense logic in presenting the case for independence, but his intellectual background made him much more able to construct a stable and practical government which would appeal to the ruling class.

Adams has given two versions of the circumstances surrounding the writing of *Thoughts on Government.* In a letter of April 20, 1776, he explained to Warren that the writer (the pamphlet was published anonymously) had been asked by two of the North Carolina delegates—William Hooper and John Penn—to put his ideas on paper for the benefit of their Provincial Congress, which would shortly draft a constitution. Adams complied, then on request made copies for other delegates whose colonies were on the point of establishing permanent governments—George Wythe, of Virginia, and Jonathan Dickinson Sergeant, of New Jersey. When still more copies were requested he gave permission to have one of the drafts printed.[36] In his autobiography however—written many years after the event—Adams claimed that he wrote the pamphlet to counteract the pernicious influence of Paine's political ideas. He "dreaded the effect so popular a pamphlet might have among the people,

36. *Ibid.,* 230-231.

and determined to do all in his power to counteract the effect of it." [37]

Although Adams' later statement of his motives in writing *Thoughts on Government* was undoubtedly influenced by his controversy with Paine during the era of the French Revolution, it is nevertheless plain that he regarded this "disastrous meteor" with some suspicion in the spring of 1776. "Sensible men think there are some whims, some sophisms, some artful addresses to superstitious notions, some keen attempts upon the passions [in *Common Sense*]," he wrote to his wife in March. Then noting that it had been bruited about that he was the author, he declared with candor, "although I could not have written anything in so manly and striking a style, I flatter myself I should have made a more respectable figure as an architect if I had undertaken such a work. This writer seems to have very inadequate ideas of what is proper and necessary to be done in order to form constitutions for single colonies as well as a great model of union for the whole." [38] Although Adams' account in later life exaggerates his antipathy for Paine in 1776, it is nevertheless clear that an important object of *Thoughts on Government* was to correct what he regarded as the dangerous heresies to be found in *Common Sense*.

The central theme of Adams' political architecture was the separation of powers, a device which he thought would check the drift toward social revolution. Since the separation of powers has had such a tremendous influence on American political thought and has been such a mainstay of conserva-

37. Adams, *Works*, II, 507. He considered Paine's ideas of government "as flowing from simple ignorance and a desire to please the democratic party in Philadelphia...." In the autobiography he mentions no solicitation from fellow delegates to write *Thoughts on Government* but stated that it was printed in response to a request from Richard Henry Lee.

38. Adams (ed.), *Familiar Letters of John Adams*, 146.

tism, it will be necessary to examine its assumptions, processes, and objectives.

Like Locke's theory of compact and natural law, separation of powers was a very old idea, even in the eighteenth century. It was discussed by Aristotle and was perhaps even known to Herodotus.[39] It may be defined as a political device designed to maintain stability in constitutional government by so balancing governmental organs and functions that power-seeking individuals and groups would automatically check each other before they could endanger the state. If democracy has always rested on an assumption that man is essentially cooperative, the theory of separation of powers in the eighteenth century was based on the premise that man is essentially unsocial, devoted exclusively to his own interests, and prepared to make war on his fellows at any time when advantage outweighed risk. According to the theory, government should not try to repress disruptive forces, for if it was strong enough to accomplish this it would be an oppressive force in itself. Rather it should direct these forces in such a way that they would neutralize each other. Like the balance of power in international affairs, the separation of powers was considered the only way to maintain stability and the moral order in an essentially unstable and immoral world.

There were three conceptions, or variants, of separation of powers in the eighteenth century. The first, and most primitive, was "balanced government" or "mixed monarchy." By this interpretation the medieval estates of the realm—crown, clergy, nobles, and commons—symbolized and represented the principal classes in society, and a balanced government kept them in equilibrium. Each estate was identified with a certain form of government—the king, monarchy; the

39. M. P. Sharpe, "The Classical American Doctrine of Separation of Powers," 2 *Chicago Law Review* (1935), 386.

nobles, aristocracy; the people, democracy. Each form had certain advantages and disadvantages. When it stood alone as a "simple" government, the disadvantages—or "weaknesses," as contemporary theorists preferred to call them— were greater than the advantages; but when the three forms were mixed together as in the British constitution, the disadvantages cancelled each other out by some mysterious metaphysical process never explained but never doubted.[40] The second conception of separation of powers was the separation of the organs or departments of government. This interpretation was partially a functional abstraction of balanced government and partially an attempt empirically to analyse the processes of government as a whole. Prior to 1776 colonial leaders thought of the separation of powers as mixed monarchy; when monarchical institutions became discredited they viewed crown, nobles, and commons functionally as executive, senate, and house of representatives. The third conception of the separation of powers was the equal distribution of the multitude of political functions performed by any government. This view predominated in the Federal Convention of 1787. Nomination, veto, appropriation, impeachment, trial of impeachment, judgment, treaty making, and the like were assigned to the different departments in such a way that each department would have equal weight. This was the most effective application of separation of powers, for only the proper distribution of functions could give the balance which was the object of

40. The two best treatments of balanced government are: Stanley Pargellis, "The Theory of Balanced Government," in Conyers Read (ed.), *The Constitution Reconsidered* (New York, 1938), 37-50; Leonard W. Labaree, "A Balanced Government," *Conservatism in Early American History* (New York, 1948), ch. 5. Pargellis traces the idea through English history of the seventeenth and eighteenth centuries. Labaree discusses the views of colonial conservatives concerning it.

separation.[41] Separation without the balance of power would be of little help in maintaining stability.

The separation of powers derives its essential character from the type of institutions it is designed to protect. Applied to a democratic government it brings stability and efficiency without loss of responsiveness to the people, but applied to the essentially hierarchical institutions of the eighteenth century it became a means of blocking popular expression and insuring the continuance of classified citizenship. Both the democrats and the conservatives of the Revolution, appreciating its value, included it in their programs, but in somewhat different forms and with quite different objectives. Democrats, viewing it primarily as a safeguard against a monopoly of political power by the upper classes, made it the basis of their demands for the abolition of plural office-holding; conservatives, conceiving it as a safeguard against arbitrary rule by mob or despot, gave it institutional expression in their plans for bicameral legislatures.

It is entirely understandable, therefore, that Adams, in combating what he felt to be the drift toward social revolution, should seize on the separation of powers institutionalized in bicameralism as the best hope for maintaining stability, human rights, and the leadership of the Whig revolutionaries in the succession governments. And in so doing he made Montesquieu, not Locke, the chief luminary among political philosophers, for Montesquieu had conceived—wrongly, of course—that separation of powers was the guiding principle of the eighteenth-century British constitution and the only way to avert tyranny from either mob

41. Separation of powers as separation of organs and distribution of functions is discussed by Sharpe, "The Classical Doctrine of Separation of Powers" in *Chicago Law Review*, and by B. F. Wright Jr., "The Origins of the Separation of Powers in America," *Economica*, XIII (1933), 169-185, but the distinction between the two variants is not made clear by either author.

or despot.[42] With the Revolutionary congresses, conventions, and committees in mind, Adams declared that single assemblies were capricious, avaricious, and ambitious. They "would make arbitrary laws for their own interest, execute all laws arbitrarily for their own interest, and adjudge all controversies in their own favor." [43] In order to secure stability and the rule of justice, therefore, Adams would create a second house, independent alike of the people and their representatives, to act as a check upon the lower. The executive power he would place in the hands of a governor assisted by a council, and, as a further check upon the legislature, he suggested for the executive an absolute veto. In later writings Adams treated the two houses as representative of the democratic and aristocratic elements in society. They would be perpetually in conflict, he felt; a victory of either would bring despotism. Therefore the governor occupied a key position in maintaining a balance. In this tripartite system Adams recreated the elements of mixed monarchy in the form of a "regal republic." [44]

42. Locke, as well as Montesquieu, had advocated separation of powers, but the two philosophers had different views of the device which in some ways resembled those of the Revolutionary democrats and conservatives respectively. For Locke, separation of powers was primarily a means of promoting efficiency in government. The ultimate guarantee of liberty was popular sovereignty. *Second Essay*, § 242, 240, 168. Montesquieu, whose essential aim was to strengthen the power of the nobility against the capricious authoritarianism of the Bourbon monarchy, saw it as the sole guarantee of liberty. "The liberty he preached was the liberty of the aristocracy. His *Spirit of the Laws*, from this point of view can be considered a handbook of aristocratic belief," writes Georges Lefebvre. *The Coming of the French Revolution, 1789* (Princeton, 1947, tr. by R. R. Palmer), 20. For a concise statement of Montesquieu's aims, see E. Carcasonne, *Montesquieu et le problème de la constitution française au XVIIIᵉ siècle* (Paris, n. d.), 84-85.

43. Adams, *Works*, IV, 196.

44. This apt phrase was apparently coined by Joseph Dorfman in his article, "The Regal Republic of John Adams," *Political Science Quarterly,*

If the common people were to have only a one-third interest in government under the Adams scheme, the lower house at least was to be their very own. "It should be in miniature an exact portrait of the people at large. It should think, feel, reason, and act like them." [45] But Adams did not implement this logic by advocating manhood suffrage for the lower house. Instead he called on the states "to agree on the number and qualifications of persons who shall have the benefit of choosing ... representatives." In his view, the propertyless should be classified with women and children as inherently unfit to vote. "Is it not true," he wrote to James Sullivan, "that men in general, in every society, who are wholly destitute of property, are also too little acquainted with public affairs to form a right judgment and too dependent on other men to have a will of their own? If this is a fact, if you give to every man who has no property a vote, will you not make a fine encouraging provision for corruption by your fundamental law? Such is the frailty of the human heart that very few men who have no property have any judgment of their own." [46]

LIX (1944), 227-248. In his *Defense of the Constitutions ... of the United States* ... (1787), Adams laid great stress on the need for an independent executive because he felt that bicameralism alone had proved unequal to protecting conservative interests. Lower houses of the legislatures often dominated senates in the same manner as colonial assemblies sometimes dominated royal councils. Governors, almost devoid of power under the terms of most state constitutions, were unable to maintain a balance. Adams never departed from the basic rule of three laid down in *Thoughts on Government*. Subsequent changes in his ideas were only ones of emphasis. For an extended analysis of Adams' thought, see Correa M. Walsh, *The Political Science of John Adams* (New York and London, 1915). Edward S. Corwin discusses the general problem to which Adams addressed himself in "The Progress of Political Theory from the Declaration of Independence to the Federal Convention," *American Historical Review*, XXX (1924-1925), 511-536.

45. Adams, *Works*, IV, 195.
46. *Ibid.*, IX, 376.

Adams' fear of manhood suffrage was based primarily on English rather than American experience. In Parliamentary elections, tenant farmers had proved to be very susceptible to bribery and corruption, primarily because they did not have the economic security to afford independent judgment. Therefore eighteenth-century conservatives perhaps had some justification for fearing that if the suffrage were broadened under similar circumstances, impecunious voters might become the willing tools of demagogues. Quite possibly infatuated majorities might demand a redistribution of wealth or an overthrow of the constitution. General Ireton had put it bluntly in the Army debates of 1647. If suffrage were given to all adult males, as the Levellers demanded, "... we shall plainly go to take away all property and interest that a man hath either in land or by inheritance, or in estate by possession or anything else.... All the main thing I speak for, is because I would have an eye to property." [47] James Wilson, much admired by Lord Bryce and often considered a democrat because of his advocacy in the Federal Convention of a popularly elected senate and executive, expressed the prevailing justification for limitations on the right to vote when he wrote in his *Considerations on the Nature and Extent of the Legislative Authority of the British Parliament:* "In Britain, all those are excluded from voting whose poverty is such that they cannot live independent, and therefore must be subject to the undue influence of their superiors. Such are supposed to have no will of their own; and it is judged improper that they should vote in the representation of a free state.... Thus is the freedom of elections secured from the *servility*, the

47. Woodhouse, *Puritanism and Liberty*, 55, 57. The argument over the extent of the suffrage between Ireton and Rainborough during the Putney debates of October 29, 1647, is one of the most revealing illustrations in print of the perennial clash between conservatives and democrats on majority rule. *Ibid.*, 52-86.

ignorance, and the *corruption* of electors; and from the inter-
positions of officers depending immediately upon the crown.
But this is not all. Provisions, equally salutary, have been
made concerning the qualifications of those who shall be
elected. All imaginable care has been taken that the Commons of Great Britain may be neither awed, nor *allured,*
nor *deceived* into any nomination inconsistent with their
liberties." [48]

Forecasts of the consequences of manhood suffrage and
the abolition of property qualifications for office varied. Some
conservatives—like Ireton—were particularly anxious for the
safety of property. Others—like Adams—while not ignoring
this threat felt that the danger of dictatorship and the loss of
constitutional liberties was greater. But few, if any, of the
Whig leaders evidenced any awareness of the basic contradiction between a limited suffrage and their equalitarian philosophy. Hence a double paradox: to preserve their own liberty,
the unprivileged masses must be prevented from infringing
on the privileged few; to maintain a government based on
consent, a large proportion of the people must be deprived of
the ability to extend or withhold consent.

The effect of Adams' pamphlet, *Thoughts on Government,* can hardly be overestimated. Most Whig leaders,
although worried by the growing anarchy and disregard for
private property exhibited by their more humble followers,
had not yet realized that permanent stability could be
reached only by abolishing the dictatorship of the Revolutionary congresses and committees.[49] Regarding royal gov-

48. Randolph G. Adams (ed.), *Selected Political Essays of James Wilson*
(New York, 1930), 51-53.

49. In 1775 Adams had decided against urging the Continental Congress to recommend a form of government for all the colonies because "all
those who were most zealous for assuming governments, had at that time
no idea of any other government but a contemptible legislature in one
assembly with committees for executive magistrates and judges." Adams,

ernors and councils as the greatest threat to freedom, they
were determined above all else to avoid a re-establishment of
anything which resembled the prerogative. So strong was
the obsessive fear of executive power that even in 1787 it
constituted the greatest obstacle which the Federalists had to
face in their drive for a balanced government. But if Adams
could not persuade the Whig leaders to establish strong governors, he at least convinced them of the need for bicameral
legislatures. Only Pennsylvania, Georgia and Vermont stub-
bornly adhered to democratic unicameralism. *Thoughts on
Government* was not only discussed in the committee drafting
the North Carolina constitution but was written verbatim into
the executive letter book.[50] Arriving in Virginia at the moment the constitution was under discussion, it was enthusiastically received by Patrick Henry.[51] Jonathan Dickinson
Sergeant adopted some of its provisions for the constitution
of New Jersey,[52] and—according to Adams—the constitution
of New York was modelled on his plan.[53] Finally, he was
able literally to translate *Thoughts on Government* into
political reality when he drafted the Massachusetts Constitu-

---

Works, III, 22. Even Sam Adams and Thomas Cushing "were inclined to
the most democratical forms." Their inclination was only temporary, however. Cushing later became a mainstay of the conservatives and Adams
used his personal popularity to insure the ratification of the obviously anti-
democratic Massachusetts Constitution of 1780.

50. Walter Clark (ed.), *The State Records of North Carolina,* Vols. 11
to 26 (Winston, Goldsboro, Charlotte, 1895-1905), XI, 321.

51. "I have two reasons for liking the book," wrote Henry. "The sentiments are precisely the same I have long since taken up, and they come
recommended by you." Adams, *Works,* IV, 201.

52. Adams and Sergeant were close friends. For a discussion of their
relations and the influence of *Thoughts on Government* on the New Jersey
constitution, see Charles R. Erdman, Jr., *The New Jersey Constitution of
1776* (Princeton, 1929), 36, 50, 57.

53. Adams to Mercy Warren, July 11, 1807. Massachusetts Historical
Society, *Collections,* 5th Ser., IV, 326.

tion of 1780. Thus in five states his proposals were possibly the paramount guide in composing the first instruments of government, and, when it is considered that the state constitutions—particularly that of Massachusetts—were the greatest single influence on the Federal Constitution, the full importance of the pamphlet should be evident. In the words of one authority, "Adams' ideas, more than those of any other single person, guided and pervaded the movement which established republican government in America, and therefore in the modern world." [54]

Common Sense, The People the Best Governors, and Thoughts on Government made clear in 1776 what the issues were to be in the forthcoming struggle between democrats and conservatives to write their political ideas into the first state constitutions. Although the necessity for compromise made both groups relinquish their extreme demands, the democratic ideal continued to be a simple government with a sovereign legislature—preferably unicameral—directly dependent upon an electorate which included all adult, free males. In contrast to this equalitarianism, the Revolutionary leaders were to press for complex governments based on the separation of powers and traditional institutions which would preserve the existing social system, guard the existing distribution of wealth, preserve human rights, and secure the dominance of the Revolutionary party in the new regimes.

54. George M. Dutcher, "The Rise of Republican Government in the United States," Political Science Quarterly, LV (1940), 211.

THREE

The Transition from Colonies to Conservative
Commonwealths: South Carolina

B EFORE entering upon an examination of the democratic movement during the Revolution, it is necessary to describe briefly the transition from a colonial to an independent status in the states where the regimes of the Revolutionary leaders encountered little challenge from advocates of democratic reforms. Since Revolutionary democracy was in large measure a reaction against the pervasive conservatism which characterized the Revolutionary movement as a whole, an understanding of the one necessarily entails an analysis of the other. In South Carolina a small group of very wealthy planters in and near Charleston completely controlled the political affairs of the province. The back country, which contained almost four-fifths of the white population,[1] was largely unrepresented in the assembly, the lower house of which was called the Commons House of Assembly. The Scotch-Irish and German farmers were regarded by the Charleston elite as "strangers to our interests, customs, and

1. William A. Schaper, *Sectionalism and Representation in South Carolina,* American Historical Association Annual *Report,* 1900 (Washington, 1901), 251.

concerns." [2] Although compelled to bear their share of taxes, the back-country settlers were denied most of the services of government. There were no courts or effective agencies of law enforcement. Litigants were compelled to travel perhaps hundreds of miles to Charleston. The right to vote, for those who had it, could only be exercised at parish churches near the seacoast.

The apparent indifference of the Charleston government to the welfare of the back country aroused considerable resentment during the years preceding the Revolution. In the absence of courts, groups of vigilantes attempted to round up the brigands who infected the country and enforced expeditious but unauthorized frontier justice. When Charleston officials objected, civil war was on the point of breaking out. Peace was restored by a Circuit Court Act in 1769, but sectional antagonisms remained.[3]

If the lack of units for representation disqualified the back-country farmers from participation in political affairs, the same effect was produced within the eastern parishes by high property qualifications for voting and officeholding. After 1759, when the qualifications were raised, voters were required to own either a "settled" plantation of at least 100 acres, personalty of £60 value, unsettled land paying taxes, or they could qualify by paying ten shillings in taxes a year. Members of the Commons House must possess a settled freehold of at least 500 acres with at least twenty slaves, or personalty to the value of £1000.[4]

The leaders of the Revolutionary movement were almost exclusively members of the tidewater aristocracy which had

2. *Ibid.*, 280.

3. Max Farrand, "The West and the Principles of the Revolution," *Yale Review*, XVII (1909), 49. Charles Woodmason, *The Carolina Backcountry on the Eve of the Revolution*, ed., Richard J. Hooker (Chapel Hill, 1953), 166, 184-185, 188-189.

4. Schaper, *Sectionalism and Representation in South Carolina*, 350-351.

dominated colonial politics. For example, William Henry Drayton, the most radical of all the Whigs, was a descendant of one of the founders of the province and a nephew of Lieutenant Governor William Bull. After studying at Oxford and Middle Temple he was appointed a royal councillor in 1772 at the age of thirty and occupied a seat beside his father, John, and his uncle, Thomas Drayton. Suspended from the Council in 1775 for his anti-British bias, he became a member of nearly all the Revolutionary bodies, did his best to promote armed resistance, and was one of the few South Carolina Whigs to advocate independence. Another extremist, Arthur Middleton, received the same education as Drayton but topped it off with a grand tour of the continent. Returning to South Carolina in 1763, he was elected to the Commons House at the age of twenty-one. Active in the Revolutionary bodies, he represented South Carolina in the Continental Congress where he was considered "warm," even by New Englanders.

The brothers John and Edward Rutledge, who also received an English education, were outstanding conservative Whigs. Although they opposed the movement for independence, both were active in the drafting and adoption of the Constitution of 1776 and both later became outstanding Federalists. Charles Cotesworth Pinckney, after finishing his law studies at Middle Temple, studied botany in France under Charles, chemistry under Fourcroy, and military science at the Royal Academy of Caen. Known as a radical at the outbreak of the Revolution, he became a noted militia leader in addition to his work in the Revolutionary bodies. Federalist candidate for president in 1804 and 1808, his career subsequent to the Revolution is a part of the history of the nation.

The same pattern of class and education, which transcended distinctions of radicalism or conservatism regarding resistance to Great Britain, will be found in the other leaders —among them Henry Laurens, Christopher Gadsden, Miles Brewton, Thomas Heyward, Jr., Rawlins Lowndes, and Thomas Lynch. All had been members of the Commons House or the Council, most were lawyers, and all were surprisingly young. In 1776 Middleton was thirty-three, Heyward thirty, Edward Rutledge twenty-seven, Lynch twenty-seven, Pinckney thirty, Drayton thirty-four, and John Rutledge thirty-seven.[5]

The method by which the South Carolina group seized power was typical of the revolutionary process throughout the colonies. When the Charleston Committee of Correspondence received the Boston circular letter of 1774 asking for cooperation in measures of retaliation against Britain, a number of "principal gentlemen" of the town called a public meeting which passed resolutions of sympathy for Boston and censure for Britain. It dispatched requests to the "principal gentlemen" of the parishes to hold elections for a Provincial Congress whose primary aim would be to elect delegates to the Continental Congress.[6] There was no limit to the number of representatives a parish could send, and gentlemen not so fortunate as to be elected were invited to attend and vote anyway. Thus the Congress was not really a representative body at all, but a convention of what was to become the Whig party. Nearly all the members of the Commons House attended; in its later sessions the Provincial Congress became in reality the Commons acting in a revolutionary capacity.

Before disbanding, the Congress nominated an interim committee which undertook to provide representation for

5. Biographical details on South Carolina leaders are taken from the *Dictionary of American Biography*.

6. Edward McCrady, *South Carolina under the Royal Government, 1719-1776* (New York, 1899), 733-734.

the back country at the next meeting. This act of belated justice, while doing credit to the Charleston leaders, was probably motivated to some extent by a desire to bring their influence to bear on the back-country farmers. As one Whig observed, "It was thought politic and right to give these large districts ten representatives, the better to unite them with the lower country...by which their constituents might be better informed about the nature of the dispute with Great Britain and America...."[7] The extension of representation was more apparent than real, however. As was the case in the parishes, the elections were presided over by "principal gentlemen," and most of the delegates elected were tidewater aristocrats. Among them were Edward Rutledge, Arthur Middleton, and William Henry Drayton. Considering the economic and social, as well as geographic, distance between these men and their constituencies, their representative capacities were doubtful.[8]

After the receipt of the news of Lexington and Concord, so great was the military ardor among the gentlemen of the colony that there were four times as many candidates for commissions as could be employed. Apparently the policy of the Whig leaders was to equate military with social rank. Commissions were granted on grounds of "natural qualifications...in addition to...an influential rank among their fellow citizens."[9] Yet the excitement did not interfere with the amenities. When Lord William Campbell arrived to take over the royal administration from Lieutenant Governor Bull, he was assured in a cordial address by the Provincial Congress that "no love of innovation, no desire of altering

7. *Ibid.*, 759.

8. Rutledge, Middleton, and Drayton represented respectively the districts of Ninety-Six, Saxe-Gotha, and the region between the Broad and Catawba Rivers. *Ibid.*, 761.

9. David Ramsay, *History of South Carolina, 1670-1808* (Newberry, S.C., 1858), 135.

the constitution of government, no lust for independence has the least influence upon our counsels." [10] This attitude gives point to the statement by Ulrich B. Phillips that the Revolutionary movement in South Carolina "was controlled by the aristocracy and had little concern with the doctrine of natural rights. It was merely a demand for home rule, with few appeals to theory of any sort." [11] Until other accommodations could be arranged for Campbell and his family, he was entertained at the splendid home—still in existence—of Miles Brewton, then a member of the Council of Safety. The governor responded to this courtesy by signing the commissions of militia officers recommended by the popular leaders.[12] In 1775, when unpleasantness became unavoidable and the governor thought it wise to establish his headquarters aboard a British warship in the harbor, the Council of Safety informed him that if an attack were planned on the ship he would be notified in time to secure other accommodations.

During the summer of 1775 the martial spirit cooled among the gentry of Charleston but increased proportionally in the lower class Committee of Mechanics. As in New York and Philadelphia, this organization of "carpenters, cobblers, and butchers" which had taken upon itself the enforcement of the Continental Association, suspected that some of the Whig gentlemen were not firm in their support of non-intercourse.[13] The Committee declined in importance after 1775

10. *Ibid.*, 136.

11. Ulrich B. Phillips, "The South Carolina Federalists," *American Historical Review*, XIV (1908-09), 531.

12. Ramsay, *History of S.C.*, 141.

13. In January, the Committee of Inspection caused a clamor when it gave permission to a family returning from Britain to land horses and personal effects. The cry was raised—so often heard in Boston, New York, and Philadelphia—that the gentlemen were breaking the Association. So serious was the resentment that the order was rescinded. McCrady, *South Carolina under Royal Government*, 775-778.

and it apparently exercised no influence on the deliberations preceding the adoption of the Constitution of 1776.

A more immediate reason for caution on the part of the Whig aristocracy might have been the increase of Tory sentiment in the back country. Lord Campbell found many of the yeomen farmers receptive to his overtures for support. Many were impressed by his warning that the local associations were preparing to stop the importation of salt—so important for the preservation of food—question their land titles, and tax them heavily for the maintenance of troops.[14] To counter this disaffection, the Provincial Congress sent Drayton and the Presbyterian minister, William Tennent, into the western districts to explain the Whig cause. The two held scores of meetings in the back country, but Tory partisans were able to work up hostility against the "gentlemen" from the seacoast and the trip ended in failure.[15] The farmers of the western districts may well have felt themselves to be exploited colonists of Charleston since they were subjected to virtual representation, were taxed without their consent, and were given no voice in the administration of local affairs. Back-country loyalism was in a very real sense a revolution within the Revolution.

The proposal to draft a constitution came from John Rutledge while acting as a delegate to the Continental Congress. At first sight it might seem inconsistent for the colony's leading conservative to advocate a repudiation of British sovereignty, particularly after declaring that "he would ride post day and night to Philadelphia to prevent a separation

14. Ramsay, *History of S.C.,* 143; Edward McCrady, *The History of South Carolina in the Revolution, 1775-1780* (New York, 1901), 34-39.

15. Philip Davidson, *The Southern Backcountry on the Eve of the Revolution,* in Avery O. Craven (ed.), *Essays in Honor of William E. Dodd* (Chicago, 1935), 12-13.

from the mother country." [16] Yet his proposal of a constitution was in the truest sense an expression of his conservatism.[17] Convinced that the threat of anarchy at home was as dangerous as the possibility of war with Britain, he conceived the seizure of sovereignty as the only alternative to chaos. Hence, with the enthusiastic cooperation of John Adams, Rutledge prevailed upon the Congress to recommend that South Carolina call a "full and free representation of the people, and that this said representation, if they think it necessary, shall establish such a form of government as in their judgment will produce the happiness of the people and most effectively secure peace and good order in the colony during the continuance of the present disputes between Great Britain and her colonies." [18]

If Rutledge the conservative desired a constitution in order to stabilize conditions within South Carolina, Adams the radical pressed for it because he thought it would amount to a tacit declaration of independence.[19] The Provincial Congress, however, was determined to avoid this implication. When Christopher Gadsden read portions of *Common Sense* during the debate on the question of a constitution and identified the establishment of regular government with independence, he was rebuked by a large majority of the mem-

16. David D. Wallace, *The Life of Henry Laurens* (New York and London, 1915), 221.

17. The character of Rutledge's political ideas is indicated by the fact that he was one of the delegates to support the plan of union which Joseph Galloway, who later became a Tory, proposed in the First Continental Congress. Richard H. Barry, *Mr. Rutledge of South Carolina* (New York, 1942), 162.

18. Worthington C. Ford (ed.), *Journals of the Continental Congress, 1774-1789*, 29 Vols. (Washington, 1904-1933), III, 326-327.

19. During debate on the motion, he attempted to have the word "colony" struck out and replaced with "state." Congress refused, however, realizing the implication of such an alteration. "The child was not yet weaned," Adams observed in his autobiography. Adams, *Works*, III, 21-22.

bers, and Rutledge pointed out that the careful wording of
the resolution by the Continental Congress made it plain
that any instrument to be adopted would be in effect only
until a reconciliation with Britain could be accomplished.

Thus in what was essentially an attempt to gain the benefits without suffering the consequences of an assertion of
sovereignty, the Provincial Congress in February, 1776, nominated a committee of eleven to prepare a plan of government. It is significant that no attempt was made to call "a
full and free representation of the people" as the Continental
Congress had recommended. Without hesitation the Provincial Congress, although now so sparsely attended that it
was scarcely more than a caucus of the Whig party, declared
itself to be "a full and free representation" and assumed
constituent powers. In Massachusetts, New Hampshire, and
New York, the assertion of constituent powers by the revolutionary bodies was vigorously contested by groups with
democratic leanings on the grounds that fundamental law
should be drafted only by a convention elected for the purpose. South Carolina conservatives also questioned the propriety of allowing their legislative body to write a constitution, but for an entirely different reason: they hoped to delay
any radical move which would further embroil the colony
with Britain.[20]

The drafting committee was composed of the leading
Whigs of the colony, among them John Rutledge, Pinckney,
Laurens, Lowndes, Middleton, Gadsden, and Lynch.[21] The
instrument they reported was adopted March 26 after
amendment and a good deal of debate on the propriety of

20. McCrady, *South Carolina in the Revolution*, 110-112. The calling of
the Convention is discussed in Fletcher M. Green, *Constitutional Development in the South Atlantic States, 1776-1860; A Study in the Evolution of
Democracy* (Chapel Hill, 1930), 60-62.

21. McCrady, *South Carolina in the Revolution*, 110.

exercising constituent powers. The document itself is mute testimony to the antipathy of the Whig leaders for innovation. Most of the colonial institutions and procedures were retained and the relationships between rulers and the ruled were not radically altered. The Congress, after declaring itself to be the legal General Assembly, chose an upper house, then both bodies jointly selected a president and a vice-president from among their own members. Both houses also chose a Privy Council with the administrative and judicial but not the legislative duties of the old royal council. Colonial politicians were motivated by the same desire to insure the independence of the legislature from executive agencies which characterized the seventeenth-century English Parliamentarians. This tendency, very evident in the Convention of 1787 and in the Federalist administrations which followed, obviated the possibility of evolution into cabinet government and gave our national constitution its essential characteristic of separated functions.

The president was given a legislative veto (Sect. VII),[22] but almost the entire executive patronage of the royal governors was lodged in the Assembly. The qualifications for suffrage and officeholding were the same as under the colonial regime. The western districts were given sixty-four delegates in all, but the ratio of representation was still less than that of the Eastern parishes, which had six apiece, or Charleston, which had thirty (Sect. XI).[23] John Rutledge was elected president and Henry Laurens vice-president.

The constitution aroused considerable dissatisfaction because of: (1) the hasty manner of its adoption and the lack of a popular mandate; (2) the presidential veto, which

22. Francis N. Thorpe, *Federal and State Constitutions,* 7 Vols. (Washington, 1909), VI, 3241-3248.
23. McCrady, *South Carolina in the Revolution,* 114; Schaper, *Sectionalism and Representation in South Carolina,* 364-365.

smacked of royal prerogative; (3) the election of the upper house by the lower instead of by the people; (4) the lack of any guarantee of religious freedom. The temporary nature of the instrument seemed to justify a thorough revision, particularly after the Declaration of Independence made it plain that there would be no reconciliation with Great Britain. Hence the Assembly in 1777 drafted an entirely new constitution, which included some of these reforms desired by a large part of the population, and presented it to President Rutledge for approval as a legislative act. Rutledge vetoed it on the surprising grounds that a reconciliation was still possible, that the existing constitution represented the will of the people, and that constituent matters were *ultra vires* for the legislature.[24] The increased powers of the electorate probably constitute the underlying reasons for his action. Unwilling to cause further controversy, however, he resigned following his veto, and a successor allowed the Constitution to be adopted.

By the new instrument senators were to be directly elected as well as representatives, and the suffrage qualifications were lowered to a fifty-acre freehold, a town lot, or payment of taxes on an equivalent valuation (Sect. XIII).[25] But as if to compensate for this concession, the value of the requisite freehold for the governor was raised to £10,000, and for senators to £2,000. There was no residence requirement for senators or representatives, but nonresident delegates in both categories had to meet higher property qualifications. Thus tidewater aristocrats could continue to "represent" the back country. The unfair apportionment of delegates which dis-

24. McCrady, *South Carolina in the Revolution*, 236-240. Green, *Constitutional Development in the South Atlantic States*, 112. The constitution had been adopted by legislative act and Rutledge himself had signed legislation altering constitutional provisions. Obviously the legislature had the power to undo its own handiwork.

25. Thorpe, *Constitutions*, VI, 3248-3257.

criminated against the West was again written into the fundamental law of the state, but a reapportionment was to be made at the end of seven years and thereafter at intervals of fourteen years "in the most equitable and just manner on a basis of both numbers and taxable property"—whatever that might mean.

The Anglican church was disestablished, and all sects were declared equal before the law, but "The Christian Protestant religion" was declared the established religion of the state. All churches were required to incorporate and subscribe to a creed which was possibly unacceptable to Catholics and certainly to Jews (Sect. XXXVIII). As corporations the churches were subject to state control and the wording of the article would even permit support by public taxation.

Thus the aristocracy of South Carolina succeeded in entrenching itself in power and in prolonging the existence of political privilege. But it was to pay dearly for its success in protecting its interests in the new state government. The strong Loyalist movement in the back country was without doubt motivated to some degree by a protest against the domination of politics by the tidewater planters, and the years following the war were to be marked by increasingly intense efforts on the part of the unprivileged to secure their right to equal consideration.

FOUR

The Conservative Transition: Maryland

IN MARYLAND the Revolution was accomplished and a conservative constitution adopted without civil war. Here,
because of the great unpopularity of the Proprietor and his
officials, the Assembly came to be looked upon as the guardian of the people's liberties. As absentee landlords, the suc-
cessive Proprietors had no other interest in their fief than the
enhancement of its value and the extraction of revenue. At
the time of the Revolution, they received about £12,000 a
year from rents, taxes, fines, and duties, and their placemen
who administered the government and served the established
church cost the colonists about £20,000 more. Only about
£18,500 of the colony's gross revenue went to support local
services.[1] Maryland was saddled with possibly a more expensive government than any of the other British colonies,
great or small, with a corresponding drain on its prosperity.[2]

Opposition to the coterie of proprietary favorites who

1. Charles A. Barker, *The Background of the Revolution in Maryland*
(New Haven, 1940), 143, 151.
2. *Ibid.,* 144, 125. "The great officials at the top (numbering about 120),
were the guardians of the land system and of the proprietor's revenues;
they were the keepers of order in a province where quitrents, fees, and
duties were sacrosanct."

waxed fat at the trough of public service was led by the "country party" in the Assembly. The differences between the proprietary and Assembly factions were political rather than social and economic, however. One member of the country party owned 17,000 acres of land, and many others possessed from 3,000 to 5,000 acres, which was the average holding of the Proprietors' councillors. "Both houses were composed of large planters," concludes Dr. Barker.[3]

In the minds of most of the colonists, the issue of British taxation tended to be merged with the exactions of proprietary officials, and the magnitude of the combined grievances united behind the Assembly all classes not profiting from the proprietary system. Yet the tone of the resistance was conservative. It was well characterized by Daniel Dulany's pamphlet, *Considerations on the Propriety of Imposing Taxes in the British Colonies.* An outstandingly successful land speculator and lawyer, the younger Dulany was one of the wealthiest men in the province. Although generally remembered for his argument against internal taxes, his discussion of virtual representation is equally significant as an illustration of Whig views on suffrage. He attacked virtual representation not in principle but in its application by Parliamentary policy makers. It was justified, he said, when there was a community of interest between persons actually and those virtually represented but unjust when no such common interest existed. Thus the virtual representation of America in Parliament was contrary to the principles of free government because the distance between America and England precluded common interests. But if persons without a vote had friends and neighbors who elected a delegate to a law-making body, there could be no objection to virtual representation. The interests of nonvoters were theoretically

3. *Ibid.,* 181-182.

identical with those of persons who possessed the right of suffrage, therefore the nonvoters received representation as effective, if not as direct, as those who actually cast ballots. Although Dulany did not state it, his rationale made it plain that there was no necessity for manhood suffrage in a truly representative government.[4]

As in South Carolina, the leadership of the Whig party was assumed by planters and lawyers of means and well-established social positions who had been influential in the Assembly, among them Matthew Tilghman, Edward Lloyd, Robert Goldsborough, Charles Carroll of Carrollton (who had inherited an estate worth £88,000), Charles Carroll the barrister, William Paca, Thomas Johnson, Daniel of St. Thomas Jenifer, and Samuel Chase.[5] These men "were more than representative of the ruling class; they were almost identical with it." [6] It was they who formed the committees of correspondence at Baltimore and Annapolis, called and dominated the Provincial Conventions, and raised the military forces which swept away the hated proprietary government.

In contrast to South Carolina, however, the western portions of the state tended to be stronger in radical sentiment than the East. The reasons for this are obscure and deserve a more thorough examination than has been given heretofore. Perhaps the West, as a debtor region, suffered more from the exactions of proprietary government than the more affluent tidewater counties. In any case, when the radicals Samuel Chase and Charles Carroll made an expedition into the western country in the spring of 1776 to gain support for

4. Daniel Dulany, *Considerations on the Propriety of Imposing Taxes in the British Colonies* (London, 1765), 4-5.

5. Philip A. Crowl, *Maryland During and After the Revolution* (Baltimore, 1943), Johns Hopkins *Studies* in History and Political Science, LXI, 22-29.

6. *Ibid.,* 29.

independence, they had much more success that did Drayton and Tennent on a similar mission in South Carolina. Many of the local committees adopted resolutions favoring separation from Britain.[7]

But as radical sentiment burgeoned near the frontier, an undercurrent of hostility toward the eastern-dominated Convention became apparent. Committees in Frederick County complained of the secrecy of debates in that body and declared that "where the power to make laws and the power to enforce such laws is vested in one man or in one body of men, a tyranny is established." [8] In part, this hostility may have been caused by the underrepresentation of the West, so characteristic of the southern colonies,[9] but a more immediate reason, as illustrated by the course of the Revolution in Pennsylvania, was the continuing desire on the part of many leading Maryland Whigs for a reconciliation with Britain. One committee in Frederick County invited internal revolution by declaring the Convention "incompetent to the exigencies of the Province and dangerous to our liberties." [10] Similar declarations made by Philadelphia radicals provided the justification for overthrowing the proprietary government of Pennsylvania after its Assembly likewise refused to sanction independence. Possibly there was some communication between radical groups in Maryland and Pennsylvania,

7. Bernard C. Steiner, *Western Maryland in the Revolution* (Baltimore, 1902), Johns Hopkins *Studies* in History and Political Science, XX, 19.

8. *Ibid.,* 20.

9. In Maryland, one-third of the population lived in the back country, over 14,000 in Frederick County alone; yet all counties had the same number of Assembly delegates regardless of population. "The whole frontier area of the province, from the upper Potomac to the Elk, stood in a kind of colonial relationship to the old Maryland of the proprietary government and the tobacco plantations." Barker, *Background of the Revolution in Maryland,* 22.

10. Steiner, *Western Maryland in the Revolution,* 22.

for Benjamin Rush, the Philadelphia physician and radical leader, reported a rumor May 29, 1776, that 7,000 men from the back country of Maryland "have risen in arms to compel their Convention to declare independence." [11]

On June 28 the Convention bowed to the wishes of the West and ordered its delegates at Philadelphia to join in a declaration of independence. At the same time it called for a meeting August 1 to draft a state constitution.[12]

Representation at this Convention was to be made more proportionate to population by dividing Frederick County into three districts, each with four delegates, and by allowing Baltimore and Annapolis two delegates apiece. The property qualification for voting was to be the same as under the proprietary government, however—a fifty-acre freehold or personalty worth £40.[13] This latter provision evoked protest in some sections, particularly among militiamen who could not meet the qualifications. When election judges in Prince George County refused to recognize the plea "that every taxable bearing arms, had an undoubted right to vote for representatives at this time of public calamity," the people chose new judges who carried on the elections without regard for suffrage qualifications. In Kent County the judges closed the polls when unqualified persons asserted the right to vote, but in the lower district of Frederick County, delegates were elected by "all who had armed in defense of the country" regardless of property qualifications.[14] In Pennsylvania,

11. Lyman H. Butterfield (ed.), *The Letters of Benjamin Rush*, 2 Vols. (Princeton, 1951), I, 100.

12. Crowl, *Maryland During and After the Revolution*, 29.

13. John A. Silver, *The Provisional Government of Maryland, 1774-1777* (Baltimore, 1895), Johns Hopkins *Studies* in History and Political Science, XIII, 521-522; Crowl, *Maryland During and After the Revolution*, 29-30.

14. *Ibid.*, 30.

the military "associators" insisted on the right to vote for the same reason as the Maryland militia.[15]

These instances of democratic aspirations were apparently not numerous, however. "The masses of the inarticulate citizens remained, on the whole, inarticulate. When they did raise their voices to demand a share in state making, they were disregarded or squelched." [16] The Convention, refusing to acknowledge that those who were willing to fight for their country deserved the right to participate in its political life, would not seat the delegates from Frederick who had been irregularly elected and had new elections held with a proper regard for property qualifications. When a group of voters in Ann Arundel County attempted to force their representatives to support a plan of government they had drawn up reputed to be "democratical in the extreme," three of the representatives—Chase, Carroll the barrister, and Brice Worthington—resigned their seats in protest. Worthington and Chase subsequently returned, presumably after new elections, but not Carroll.[17] Nothing more was heard of the democratic plan.

The committee to draft the constitution was made up of the outstanding Whig leaders—Tilghman, Carroll of Carrollton, Carroll the barrister, Paca, George Plater, Chase, and Goldsborough.[18] The document they framed, and which was subsequently adopted by the Convention, was basically as conservative as either of the South Carolina constitutions, but it also incorporated some concessions to the back-country population.

The Constitution was preceded by a comprehensive bill of

15. See below, pp. 250-252.

16. Crowl, *Maryland During and After the Revolution*, 18-19.

17. Kate M. Rowland, *The Life of Charles Carroll of Carrollton, 1737-1832* (New York and London, 1898), 187. Allan Nevins, *The American States During and After the Revolution, 1775-1789* (New York, 1924), 157.

18. Crowl, *Maryland During and After the Revolution*, 31.

rights which declared all persons invested with legislative power to be "trustees of the public" (Sect. IV).[19] The conception of relations between government and people as trustee-beneficiary rather than agent-principal is typical of Whig thinking. Public officials, as trustees, were primarily responsible not to their beneficiaries but to a higher moral law which governed them both, and they were bound to administer their trust according to the dictates of the moral law rather than the will of the beneficiary. By the agent-principal conception of political society, however, the will of the delegate is considered only an extension of the will of the electorate; the moral considerations of policy are exclusively the province of the constituency. Although democratic government is today considered an agency rather than a trust, both conceptions hold dangers when carried to their logical extremes. The Whig leaders who looked on representation as a trust, although dedicated to the maintenance of human rights, tended to equate the economic and political welfare of their class with moral law, and thus justified an aristocratic system of government which would keep the people permanently in tutelage. When representatives today regard themselves as agents whose sole duty is to accomplish the will of their constituents, they intensify sectional differences, overlook ethical principles, and hinder the formulation of national policies. Hamstrung by the conflict of local interests, the legislature loses its capacity for leadership and becomes a center of weakness for a democratic nation rather than a source of strength.

Section V declared, "The right of the people to participate in the legislature is the best security of liberty and the foundation of all free government." But suffrage was to be given only to those "having property in, and a common in-

19. Francis N. Thorpe, *Federal and State Constitutions*, 7 Vols. (Washington, 1909), III, 1686-1712.

terest with, and an attachment to, the community." Why did the Whig leaders see no inconsistency between these two propositions, both of which were commonplaces of their political thought? The reason is that they considered the state as a vast corporation, much like our industrial corporations today, in which political privileges were commensurate with equity in the corporate assets. They felt that persons without equity would not have enough interest in the welfare of the corporation to merit a voice in its administration. Indeed, if given a voice they would probably use it to seize the equity of others. Manhood suffrage and the dominance of majority will seemed just as dangerous to the eighteenth-century Whigs as would today a policy of allowing industrial workers to attend and vote in stockholders' meetings. Government by compact, as conceived in the seventeenth and eighteenth centuries, meant rule by the stockholders in the visible assets of the nation. The equalitarianism inherent in Locke was an idealization which no proper Whig ever expected to put into practice. It was a symbol of the eighteenth-century republic rather than its governing principle.

The drafters of the Constitution set the price of a share of voting stock in the corporation of Maryland at a fifty-acre freehold or a £30 estate—slightly lower than under the proprietary government. For officers the requisite equity was of course higher. Assemblymen must be worth, in real and personal property, £500; senators, councillors, and congressional delegates £1000 (Sects. II, XIV-XIX, XXVI, XXVII). The Senate was selected by an electoral college and could fill vacancies by its own appointment, thus effectively insulating it from popular control. This method of choosing the upper house, suggested by Carroll of Carrollton, elicited considerable admiration from contemporaries and later observers. Samuel Chase described it as "virgin gold," and the historian Ramsay and Roger B. Taney both heartily endorsed it.[20] Jefferson included it in his draft of a constitution for Virginia drawn up in 1783.[21] Madison, who particularly liked the fact that the Senate could fill its own vacancies, declared in *The Federalist* (No. 63) that the Maryland constitution "is daily deriving, from the salutary operation of the indirectly-elected senate, a reputation in which it will probably not be rivalled by that of any state in the Union."

An upper house so elected was admired because it could afford to be independent of both the people and the lower house. If directly chosen by the people, it might become an agency of their will; if chosen by the lower house, it might become a creature of the people's delegates. In either case the delicate balance of powers supposedly necessary for good government would be lost. The device of an electoral college made it possible to secure a body of trustees for the public welfare which could not be swayed by either the public or its representatives.

The Anglican church was theoretically disestablished, yet, "The legislature may, at their discretion, lay a general and equal tax for the support of the Christian religion, leaving to each individual the power of appointing the payment of the money" (Sect. XXXIII). Thus, as in South Carolina, the state would become the protector of religion if not of any specific church.

But if the property qualifications insured a government by the wealthy and well-born, checked by the well-to-do, the Constitution nevertheless incorporated certain reforms which had been demanded by the common people. There were stringent prohibitions against plural officeholding, particu-

20. Rowland, *Charles Carroll*, 192; Bernard C. Steiner, *The Electoral College for the Senate of Maryland and the Nineteen Van Buren Electors*, American Historical Association *Report*, 1895, 132-133.

21. Paul L. Ford (ed.), *The Works of Thomas Jefferson*, 12 Vols. (New York and London, 1904-1905), IV, 151.

larly on the part of members of the legislature (Sects. XXXVII, XXXIX, LIII). Sheriffs were to be elected in the counties instead of being nominated by the governor, as was the case in most states; residence was required for all county delegates, rotation in office was provided for, poll taxes were declared oppressive, and the principle of progressive taxation was endorsed. Although popular ratification was not specified, the Constitution and the Bill of Rights were printed for public perusal before discussion by the convention. The body then adjourned for two weeks, presumably to ascertain public reaction to the documents. Apparently there were no serious objections from constituents, for the Convention voted the drafts into fundamental law upon reassembling.[22]

Certain desired reforms were voted down by the Convention, however. Among them were lower property qualifications and a provision that militia companies be allowed to choose their own officers.[23] Only about 55 per cent of the free adult male population enjoyed the right to vote.[24]

Thus the pattern of conservatism established in South Carolina was followed in its essentials by Maryland. Both states adopted constitutions which secured the rights which were a primary objective of the Revolution and erected barriers against arbitrary government. But these constitutions also protected the economic interests and political privileges of the aristocracy by excluding large numbers of the common people from participating in political processes and by denying authority to majorities. The people of Maryland and South Carolina could look forward to honest, efficient, and equitable government in their new condition of independence, but not to popular rule.

22. Silver, *Provisional Government of Maryland*, 526.
23. Crowl, *Maryland During and After the Revolution*, 34-36.
24. *Ibid.*, 36.

FIVE

The Conservative Transition: New York

IN SOUTH CAROLINA and Maryland, what resistance there was to upper-class domination of the Revolutionary movement came from yeoman farmers of the West, but in New York the Whig leaders were also confronted by a lower middle-class city population which demanded a voice in their councils. Parties had formed periodically over local issues in the seaport towns of the colonies during the early eighteenth century, but after 1765 they became permanent. In New York the wealthiest merchants and lawyers, the Anglican clergy, and the great landholders such as the Philipses, Schuylers, De Lanceys, Van Cortlandts, Van Rensselaers—all united themselves into a fairly cohesive conservative party. Against them formed a more radical group of substantial, ambitious, generally younger merchants and lawyers who hoped to increase their influence and their fortunes. In this group were John Morin Scott, Isaac Low, William Livingston, John Jay, Gouverneur Morris, and James Duane. On the left wing of the party were Isaac Sears, John Lamb, and Alexander McDougall—self-made men of humble origins who were regarded as popular leaders.

The Stamp Act temporarily united all classes against the British government from the great landlords, lawyers, and merchant princes to the lowest dock wallopers. But when rioters paraded the streets of New York, stoned the Battery, and burned Lieutenant Governor Colden in effigy, then—in the words of Carl Becker—"This sort of thing brought men of property to a realization of the consequences of stirring up the mob. A little rioting was well enough, so long as it was directed to the one end of bringing the English government to terms. But when the destruction of property began to be relished for its own sake by those who had no property, and the cry of Liberty came loudest from those who were without political privilege, it was time to call a halt. These men might not cease their shouting when purely British restrictions were removed. The ruling classes were in fact beginning to see that 'liberty and no taxation' was an argument that might be used against themselves as well as against the home government. The doctrine of self-government, which for so many years they had used to justify resistance to colonial governors, was a two-edged sword that cut into the foundations of class privilege within the colony as well as into the foundations of royal authority without. Dimly at first, but with growing clearness, the privileged classes were beginning to realize the most difficult problem which the Revolution was to present to them: the problem of maintaining their privileges against royal encroachment from above without losing them by popular encroachments from below. It was this dilemma which gave life and character to the conservative faction." [1]

The Stamp Act riots not only drove the party of the great landlords into Toryism, it also split the Whig party into distinct radical and conservative factions. Men like Jay, Duane, Livingston, and Scott began to realize that they were riding the whirlwind when directing a rank and file from the lower

1. Carl L. Becker, *The History of Political Parties in the Province of New York, 1760-1776* (Madison, Wisconsin, 1909), 31-32.

middle class under the influence of parvenus like Sears and
McDougall. The problem was how to rein in without being
thrown off. Some leaders of the conservative Whigs made no
secret of their fear that the Revolution would result in sweep-
ing social changes. "The mob begin to think and reason,"
wrote Morris. "Poor reptiles, it is with them a vernal morn-
ing, they are struggling to cast off their winter's slough, they
bask in the sunshine, and ere noon they will bite.... I see
and I see it with fear and trembling, we will be under the
worst of all possible dominions...—a riotous mob." [2] John
Jay found himself in the paradoxical position of being forced
to become a radical in order to counsel moderation,[3] and
James Duane, styled by his biographer "a rebel through
necessity," expostulated, "God forbid that we should ever be
so miserable as to sink into a republic!" [4]

If the Stamp Act disturbances were disconcerting, on their
heels came agrarian riots upstate of such proportions as to
cause serious alarm. When the British took over the colony
in 1664, they fell heirs to the semi-feudal patroon system of
the Dutch. Although the Board of Trade tried to prevent the
engrossment of land by speculators, the leading New York
families, in collusion with the royal governors, secured im-
mense grants and over a period of years built up baronial
estates tilled by tenant farmers.[5] On all of these the landlords
held a privileged position. In some instances they administered justice through private courts baron and leet, and could
legally prohibit the governor's constable and tax collector

2. Jared Sparks, *The Life of Gouverneur Morris*, 3 Vols. (Boston,
1832), I, 25.
3. Frank Monaghan, *John Jay* (New York, 1935), 66.
4. E. P. Alexander, *A Revolutionary Conservative, James Duane of New
York* (New York, 1938), 121.
5. Irving Mark, *Agrarian Conflicts in Colonial New York, 1711-1775*
(New York, 1940), chs. I and III; E. Wilder Spaulding, *New York in the
Critical Period, 1783-1789* (New York, 1932), ch. III.

from setting foot on their property. Three eighteenth-century manors—Van Rensselaer, Livingston, and Van Cortlandt— each sent a representative to the Assembly.[6] Land tenures sometimes carried a few of the ancient servile dues of the feudal age such as personal service for the lord and alienation fines.[7]

It was not difficult for the great landlords to control the politics of the province. Although many of the tenants were able to meet the £40 freehold qualification for voting,[8] the lack of the secret ballot prevented them from utilizing the suffrage to their advantage. Since *viva voce* voting was always the rule, few tenants would risk antagonizing their landlords by not supporting the candidate of his choice. For the great families, the manors and patents were "pocket boroughs" which guaranteed them a personal representation in the Assembly. Livingston Manor, for example, was always represented in the Assembly by a Livingston.

The steady engrossing of land by the leading families, high rents and precarious tenures led to the so-called "Great Rebellion of 1766." Demanding that their short-term lease-holds be turned into freeholds, tenants in Westchester and Dutchess counties, numbering perhaps 2000 in all, refused to pay rent until the demand was met. When the landlords countered with evictions, the farmers turned to violence. They expelled local officers, broke open the Poughkeepsie jail, and even threatened to march on New York and burn

6. *Ibid.,* 59.
7. *Ibid.,* 61-62.
8. Albert E. McKinley, *The Suffrage Franchise in the Thirteen English Colonies in America* (Philadelphia, 1905), The University of Pennsylvania *Publications,* Series in History, II, 212. The limits of the term "freehold" were vague in colonial New York. Apparently leaseholds for life or lives were regarded as freeholds, but leaseholds for under twenty-one years were not. Spaulding, *New York in the Critical Period,* 60-61.

down the homes of Pierre Van Cortlandt and Lambert Moore.[9] Calling themselves Sons of Liberty, they confidently expected support from the Whigs of New York City, who only a few months before had so enthusiastically nullified the Stamp Act. But the conservative leaders did not regard violence against vested property in the same light as infractions of imperial legislation. Dubbing the farmers "Levellers" (a term of opprobrium in the eighteenth century), the Liberty Boys joined forces with the great landlords and called loudly for royal troops to put down the insurrection. One observer commented caustically that the substantial Whigs of the city "are of the opinion that no one is entitled to Riot but themselves."[10] The disturbances were eventually suppressed by British regulars, and the New York Supreme Court, dominated by the landlords and numbering among its judges John Morin Scott and Robert R. Livingston, meted out severe sentences to the ringleaders. Like the Regulators of North Carolina the New York farmers bitterly resented the summary treatment they received from the alleged standardbearers of liberty. Lieutenant Governor Colden, who had also suffered at the hands of the Whigs, sympathized with the rioters as much as his position would allow. What impelled them to violence, he felt, was their conviction that they could get no justice in the courts. Perhaps the most significant comment on the riots was made by General Gage, in command of the troops. "They [the Whigs] certainly deserve any losses they may sustain, for it is the work of their own hands. They first sowed the seeds of Sedition amongst the People and taught them to rise in Opposition to the Laws. What now happens is a consequence that might be easily foreseen after the Tumults about the Stamp Act, and I

9. Mark, *Agrarian Conflicts*, 134-145.
10. *Ibid.*, 138.

could wish that this uneasiness amongst the People had happened just at that Time." [11]

The most notable aspect of the Revolutionary movement in New York was the competition for control between the left and right wings of the Whig party. By 1776, however, the conservatives had gained an ascendency in the Provincial Congress and in the New York City Committee. Little was heard from the Mechanics group which had exercised considerable influence in the earlier phases of the movement. The presence of British ships in the harbor, financial stringency, an increasing number of Loyalists—particularly in the Hudson valley counties—and the departure of the hot patriots to war all served to weaken the radical position. As in South Carolina and Maryland, the Provincial Congress drew back when faced with the question of independence and a constitution. Duane probably expressed the mind of a majority of the delegates when he wrote, "There seems no necessity why our colony should be too precipitate in changing the present mode of government. Let the people be followed rather than driven." [12] But Jay, echoing the sentiments of Rutledge in South Carolina, declared that a new government was necessary because the present one "will no longer work anything but mischief," and Gouverneur Morris, advocating independence in a long speech before the Provincial Congress, warned that it would not be "quite proper for us all to abandon the Senate House, and leave the business to entire new men, while the country continues in its present dangerous situation." [13]

There was general agreement, however, that the existing Congress should not undertake to write a constitution. Some

11. *Ibid.*, 151.
12. Becker, *Political Parties in New York*, 266.
13. Sparks, *Morris*, I, 106.

radicals feared that men like Jay, Duane, and Livingston would subject the colony "to a tyranny not much better than that of Britain," [14] and many conservatives, hoping for delay and anxious to diffuse responsibility for an act of treason, wanted a special mandate from the people before seizing the sovereignty. Therefore the Provincial Congress resolved May 31 that elections be held for a new Congress empowered to establish permanent government, if the new body considered such a move necessary. This Congress would exercise legislative as well as constituent powers, and would have the authority to put the constitution in force without popular ratification.[15]

This last provision provoked an outcry from the Committee of Mechanics, which had always been restive under the leadership of the gentlemen. The "carpenters, cobblers and butchers" demanded that any constitution drafted by the Congress be submitted to popular referendum for ratification. In an open letter to the Congress the Committee declared: "We could not, we never can believe that you intended...to deny...that...right which God has given [the people of New York] in common with all men, to judge whether it be consistent with their interest to accept or reject a Constitution framed for that State of which they are members. This is the birthright of every man.... Whatever the intended supporters of oligarchy assert to the contrary, there is not, perhaps, one man nor any set of men upon earth, who, without the special inspiration of the Almighty, could frame a constitution which, in all its parts, would be truly unexceptional by a majority of the people." Popular referendum was

14. Becker, *Political Parties in New York*, 267-268.
15. Although the first draft of the resolution would have allowed all inhabitants to vote for the Congress, as finally passed it allowed only the qualified voters to go to the polls. *American Archives*, 4th Ser., VI, 1338; 1351-1352.

"the only characteristic of the true lawfulness and legality that can be given to human institutions." The people should also have the power to initiate special procedures for amending the constitution.[16]

This protest of the Mechanics is one of the first indications of a recognition during the Revolutionary period of the differences between fundamental law and statute law, legislative and constituent powers. As will be shown in the discussion of the democratic movement in Massachusetts, these distinctions, so basic in American constitutionalism, were often a by-product of the democratic protest against aristocratic domination of politics. The objective of democrats was to institutionalize the concepts of popular sovereignty and natural law in Whig political philosophy.

The Convention met in White Plains on July 9. All but 6 of the 107 delegates had served in at least one of the Provincial Congresses, which may be taken as an expression of confidence in the Whig leadership. Although the Convention in July appointed a drafting committee which included Jay, Morris, William Duer, Robert R. Livingston, John Morin Scott, and James Duane, a document was not ready for discussion on the floor until March, 1777. The delay was caused in part by the peregrinations which the body was compelled to undertake in order to escape the British, who had occupied New York City. The members also had their hands full running a war. Many of them were anxious to postpone the drafting of a constitution until conditions were more settled. Jay thought it advisable "to secure a state to govern before they discussed a form to govern it by." [17]

The draft reported by the committee was consistent with the Whig constitutional pattern. Suffrage for the lower house was limited to freeholders of the state and taxpayers

16. *Ibid.*, 895-898.
17. Monaghan, *Jay*, 86; Sparks, *Morris*, I, 120.

resident in the counties. There were property qualifications for officeholding, and the senate was to be chosen by an electoral college.[18] The draft was unique, however, in that it stipulated the use of the secret ballot in elections for assemblymen and laid down detailed rules to prevent interested persons from bringing pressure to bear on the voters. In New York, because of the prevalence of tenantry, *viva voce* voting was a serious grievance because the tenant farmer who raised his hand to vote against his landlord's candidate might pay with his lease for such temerity. Thus, as James Harrington pointed out so cogently in *Oceana,* the secret ballot was an absolute necessity to maintain freedom of elections in any state where tenantry was the usual method of landholding. The provisions on election procedures are strong evidence that there was considerable opposition within the Convention to the landed aristocracy.

The conservative element proved to have the usual ascendency, however. Robert R. Livingston and Gouverneur Morris prevailed on the Convention to raise the suffrage requirement to a leasehold for resident voters and a £20 freehold for nonresident voters, and on Morris's motion the provisions for ballot voting and the supervision of elections were stricken from the draft. Here the matter might have rested had not Jay, in a somewhat surprising move, persuaded the convention to include in the constitution a provision which endorsed ballot voting in principle and kept the door open for its ultimate adoption. For the present, elections for the Assembly would be carried on as usual, but the legislature was enjoined to inaugurate the use of the ballot as soon as possible after the war. If the innovation should appear, on experience, "to be attended with more mischief and less conducive to the safety and interests of this state than the

18. Charles Z. Lincoln, *The Constitutional History of New York,* 5 Vols. (Rochester, 1906), I, 514-519.

method of voting *viva voce*," the legislature could abolish it
by a two-thirds vote.[19] Jay also succeeded in having the franchise widened to include city freemen.[20] The great landlords
were able to postpone the use of the ballot until 1787, however, and secret voting did not become a part of fundamental
law until 1821.

Other elements of the Constitution indicate that the Convention as a whole was more democratically inclined than
some of the conservative leaders. In the final draft property
qualifications for assemblymen, senators, and the governor
were lowered to a mere freehold, and the electoral college
for senators was dropped in favor of direct election. But apparently by way of compensation the possession of a £100
freehold was required for senatorial and gubernatorial electors (Sects. VII, X, XII, XVII). The upper house was thus
evidently designed to represent the wealthier citizens. A
bicameral legislature established on the New York plan entailed a classified citizenship but it came closer to the ideal
of representative government than the plan adopted in Maryland because members of the upper house were responsible
to constituencies. Under the indirect method of election the
upper house was unrepresentative and "independent." Both
senators and assemblymen were to be apportioned on the
basis of population (Sects. IV, V). When conservatives and
their opponents clashed on whether the patronage would be
given to the governor or the legislature, Jay worked out a

19. *Ibid.*, 513.
20. City freemanship was a status given to merchants, artisans, and
some professional men of New York City and Albany during the colonial
period which enabled them to vote without meeting the freehold requirement. Apparently it was not conferred lightly, for at the outbreak of the
Revolution only one-ninth to one-fourteenth of the total population of
New York City possessed the suffrage right. McKinley, *Suffrage Franchise*,
218-221.

compromise whereby the governor and four senators nominated by the Assembly constituted a Council of Appointments (Sect. XXIII).[21] This body eventually controlled the
nominations to almost 15,000 offices bringing nearly $2,-
000,000 annually. Inevitably it became a center of intrigue
and corruption.[22]

The question of an executive veto provoked controversy
along the same lines as did the location of the patronage.
Morris, who had pressed strongly for extensive appointing
power in the governor, was equally desirous of giving him
the legislative veto. Morris's opponents, on the other hand,
feared anything resembling the royal prerogative. Again a
compromise was worked out by dividing the contested power
among several officeholders who could be expected to act as
a check on each other. The governor, the chancellor, and the
judges of the Supreme Court were named as a Council of
Revision with power to alter bills passed by the lower house
and send them back for further consideration. The Council
might also impose a veto which could be overridden only by
a two-thirds vote of both houses (Sect. III). This provision
of the Constitution is most significant in the history of
judicial review for it suggested, by its inclusion of the judicial
branch, that the legislative veto was as properly a function of
law as of administration. The New York Council of Revision was in the minds of the members of the Federal Convention when they discussed the executive veto, and it was
in part at least the inspiration for Hamilton's famous *Federalist* (78).

The validification by the Constitution of royal land grants
conferred before 1775 is an indication of the power of the
landlords. The instrument provided for complete religious

---

21. Lincoln, *Constitutional History of New York,* I, 531-535.
22. Sparks, *Morris,* I, 123n.

freedom, but the Convention would not include a provision for the abolition of slavery desired by Jay and Morris.[23]

The New York Constitution of 1777 perhaps deserves Monaghan's description, "A victory for the minority of stability and privilege,"[24] but it was not an easy triumph. Unfortunately we know little or nothing about the political maneuverings in the Convention, but the compromises at crucial points in the Constitution suggest the existence of a party holding democratic ideas. The aristocracy, whose dominance in New York had been unquestioned until the Revolution, went into a steady decline under the new state government. The Clinton machine conducted a campaign to democratize the fundamental law of the state in the arena of practical politics which carried on to final victory in the mid-nineteenth century.

The transition from colony to commonwealth in South Carolina, Maryland, and New York provides sufficient illustration of the conservative forces at work in the Revolution to make unnecessary a further examination of the movement in the other colonies where conservatism was generally successful. In New Jersey and Delaware the adoption of constitutions on the Whig model apparently evoked no protest and was not accompanied by significant incident.[25] In Vir-

23. *Ibid.*, 125-127; Monaghan, *Jay*, 95.

24. *Ibid.*, 97. The constitution was better than most of its contemporaries, however, in that it was the first to give adequate powers to the governor and effectively balance the departments of government. "At the time, and with reason, it was widely regarded as the best of the organic laws, and it exerted a considerable influence on the Federal Constitution." Allan Nevins, *The American States During and After the Revolution, 1775-1789* (New York, 1924), 161.

25. The course of the Revolution in New Jersey culminating in the writing of the constitution can best be followed in the following works: Edgar J. Fisher, *New Jersey as a Royal Province, 1738-1776* (New York, 1911); Donald L. Kemmerer, *Path to Freedom, The Struggle for Self-*

ginia the drafting of organic law produced a sharp conflict between a liberal and an "aristocratic" faction of the Revolutionary party. The latter, who hoped to obtain institutional recognition for their status, pressed for a government which would to some degree acknowledge hereditary claims. The liberal group, led by Richard Henry Lee, Patrick Henry, and George Mason, desired the republic outlined by Adams in *Thoughts on Government*. They were ultimately successful; the first Virginia Constitution was much like the instruments adopted elsewhere in the South.[26] In Connecticut radicalism was strong among farmers and speculators anxious to settle the colony's western land claims and there was a good deal of antagonism against the established Congregational church,

---

Government in Colonial New Jersey, 1703-1776 (Princeton, 1940); Leonard Lundin, *Cockpit of the Revolution, The War for Independence in New Jersey* (Princeton, 1940); Charles R. Erdman, Jr., *The New Jersey Constitution of 1776* (Princeton, 1929). The following works cover the Revolution in Delaware: Ignatius C. Grubb, *The Colonial and State Judiciary of Delaware,* Historical Society of Delaware, *Papers,* II, No. 17; William T. Read, *The Life and Correspondence of George Read* (Philadelphia, 1870); George H. Ryder (ed.), *Letters to and from Caesar Rodney* (Philadelphia, 1933); Roberdeau Buchanan, *Genealogy of the McKean Family of Pennsylvania* (Lancaster, 1890); Max Farrand, "The Delaware Bill of Rights," *American Historical Review,* III, (1897-1898), 641-650.

26. The struggle between the liberal and "aristocratic" factions in Virginia has been ably described in Nevins, *American States During and After the Revolution,* 124-125, 143-149, and by Fletcher M. Green, *Constitutional Development in the South Atlantic States, 1776-1860; A Study in the Evolution of Democracy* (Chapel Hill, 1930), 62-65. For other materials bearing on the Constitution see Robert L. Hilldrup, The Virginia Convention of 1776 (Doctoral dissertation, University of Virginia, 1935); Hugh B. Grigsby, *The Virginia Convention of 1776* (Richmond, 1855); Charles R. Lingley, *The Transition in Virginia from Colony to Commonwealth* (New York, 1910); Hamilton J. Eckenrode, *The Revolution in Virginia* (Boston and New York, 1916); James M. Leake, *The Virginia Committee System and the American Revolution* (Baltimore, 1917), Johns Hopkins *Studies* in History and Political Science, XXXV. Much useful material on Virginia in this period will also be found in biographies of Jefferson, Madison, Patrick Henry, Randolph, Mason, and Pendleton.

but the adoption of the colonial charter as the state constitution removed most of the opportunity for reform of existing institutions. Likewise radicalism in Rhode Island, which manifested itself primarily in debtor-inspired legislation to cheapen the currency, did not extend to basic political relationships because the charter was again accepted as the state constitution.[27] Elsewhere democratic movements were of such importance that each will be considered separately in the following chapters.

Now that political equality and majority rule have become accepted as norms for free government, it is easy to underestimate the importance of the reforms embodied in even the most conservative of the first state constitutions. If these instruments were far from democratic and if they maintained the framework of traditional institutions, they nevertheless inaugurated the freest governments that the world had seen since ancient times. First among their contributions to a liberated society was the abolition of the prerogative. Although to some extent circumvented by the assemblies, this power, as exercised by governors under instructions from a British regime which was often indifferent to the welfare of the colonies, usually badly informed as to conditions there, and always motivated by the mercantilist ideal, checked

27. The most useful works for the study of the Revolutionary period in Connecticut are: Edith A. Bailey, *Influences Toward Radicalism in Connecticut, 1754-1775* (Northampton, 1920), Smith College *Studies* in History, V; Oscar Zeichner, *Connecticut's Years of Controversy, 1750-1776* (Chapel Hill, 1949); Richard J. Purcell, *Connecticut in Transition, 1775-1818* (Washington, 1918); Lawrence H. Gipson, *Jared Ingersoll* (New Haven, 1920); M. Louise Greene, *The Development of Religious Liberty in Connecticut* (Boston and New York, 1905). The following contain material on the Revolution in Rhode Island: Irving B. Richman, *Rhode Island, a Study in Separatism* (Boston and New York, 1905); Rhode Island *Colonial Records*, 10 Vols. (Providence, 1856-1865), VIII; Rhode Island Historical Society, *Collections*, 34 Vols. (Providence, 1827-1940), VI.

normal development in many phases of colonial life. Although the colonies did derive certain economic and political advantages from the British connection, the assemblies were certainly justified in resenting permanent political tutelage.

Of scarcely less importance was the general acceptance of the principle that the administrators of government derived their powers from the consent of the governed. From it came the logical corollary that representation, to deserve the name, must be direct and in proportion to population and that all adult free males deserved the right to vote. Parliament still based its authority on its character as a microcosm of the realm. Its members, significantly not called representatives, theoretically derived their powers by virtue of membership in the body rather than from election by a constituency. It was not until 1832 and perhaps 1867 that the House of Commons could be called a representative body. This transformation took place more quickly and easily in the lower house of the American legislatures because once the principle was admitted, measures to implement it were not difficult to effect.

The bills of rights, although sometimes violated by the provisions of the constitutions they introduced, nevertheless set a standard of political liberty which governments could ignore at their peril. The constitutions themselves set definite limits to the sphere of political authority and specified the legitimate means of its exercise. Although only dimly recognized at the time, constitutions came to mean that those who made, administered, and interpreted law did so under authority derived from law.

The almost universal condemnation of plural officeholding and the placing of patronage in the hands of the people's representatives helped change the conception of public office from vested interest to public service. For many more years in England, places would be considered profitable enterprises which could be bought and sold, but in America a much higher standard of civil service came into being in a relatively few years which was not entirely lost with the acceptance of the spoils system during the Jackson administrations.

Finally, the short terms of office stipulated by the constitutions made representatives ever conscious of responsibility to their constituencies, limited though these might be. Today we would consider the one-year term for representatives too short for efficient management of government, yet in 1776 this provision seemed amply justified. The terms of assemblymen in colonial times were indefinite, lasting from a few weeks during periods of conflict with the governors to many years when relations were amicable. Representatives who were not compelled to account for their stewardship at stated intervals tended to ignore their constituencies. Short, definite terms of office helped remedy this situation.

If the Whigs perpetuated much that was undemocratic in their constitutions and if they sometimes acted in their own interest rather than that of the people at large, they nevertheless established the principle that the first duty of free government was to protect the rights of its citizens. It now fell to the Revolutionary democrats to assert, and maintain where they could, the principle that all men should be equal in political rights and that the sole authority for the creation of law to implement these rights was the will of the majority.

SIX

Protest and Rebellion in North Carolina,

1765-1771

THE previous chapters of this book have described the transitions from colonies to commonwealths in which the conservative leadership of the Revolution was able to maintain its political predominance by framing constitutions which contained checks on arbitrary government, political equality, and majority rule. The chapters which follow will be devoted to a description of the rise of democratic parties and the formulation of democratic ideas in the areas where these factors were of enough importance to have a serious effect on the course of politics and the writing of constitutions.

As previously noted, the democratic movements of the Revolution had their inception in the protest against aristocratic domination of government first heard in scattered instances during the late colonial period. The most articulate, comprehensive, and violent of these protests was the Regulator agitation in North Carolina. It is not surprising that social conflict should appear in the Carolinas, for there the inconsistencies between natural conditions and political institutions which marked the colonial period were amplified to an unusual degree. In all of the southern colonies there was some dissatisfaction because of the lack of representative local government, the enrichment of the wealthy and the impoverishment of the poor brought about by slavery, and the increasing sectional conflict between yoeman farmers of the piedmont and gentlemen planters of the tidewater. But in the Carolinas the contrast between rich and poor was greater, the sectional division sharper, and the government less suited to the needs and desires of the people. As a result, the history of the provinces during the colonial period was a record of almost continual unrest and occasional violence.

Until 1745 North Carolina was very sparsely settled, but after that time a steady influx of immigrants—many from Pennsylvania—made it the fourth most populous state by 1776. Nearly the entire increase was in the recently formed central and frontier counties, which by the time of the Revolution contained two-thirds of the population.[1] The tidewater counties either remained static or had a much smaller growth. Of the estimated 100,000 population in 1760, 40 per

1. Population figures for this period are unreliable, but from the best estimates the colony grew from 24,000 taxables in 1754 to 51,000 in 1769. In 1776 it had nearly 300,000 inhabitants. Evarts B. Greene and Virginia D. Harrington, *American Population before the Federal Census of 1790* (New York, 1932), 159-169. A writer in the South Carolina and American General *Gazette* noted, "There is scarce any history either ancient or modern which affords an account of such a rapid and sudden increase in inhabitants in a back frontier county as that of North Carolina. To justify the truth of this observation we need only to assure you that 20 years ago there were not 20 taxable people within the limits of the county of Orange, in which there are now 4,000 taxables. The increase of inhabitants, and the flourishing state of the other adjoining back counties are no less surprising and astonishing." March 11, 1768. On immigration see Wayland F. Dunaway, "Pennsylvania as an Early Distributing Center of Population," *Pennsylvania Magazine of History and Biography,* LV (1931), 134-169; William D. Cooke (ed.), *The Revolutionary History of North Carolina in Three Lectures* (Raleigh, 1853), 50; John S. Bassett, *The Regulators of North Carolina, 1765-1771* (Washington, 1895), American Historical Association *Report,* 1894, 144-145.

cent was Scotch or Scotch-Irish. Of the remainder, 45 per cent was English and 15 per cent German.[2] Whites outnumbered Negroes more than five to one in the piedmont, and although the whites were a minority in the tidewater area, the vast majority of the population were not slaveholders.[3]

The Germans tended to form centripetal peasant communities and kept themselves apart from the political life of the province. The same was generally true of the Highlanders, who had arrived direct from Britain under the benevolent patronage of the government.[4] During the Revolution, however, many of these Scots became aggressive and determined Loyalists.

Contemporary observers have left unflattering descriptions of the ignorance, indolence, and filth of the yeoman farmers of the Carolinas but at the same time have testified to their rugged individuality and disdain for the social distinctions held in such high esteem by the upper classes. William Byrd wrote that the common people "are rarely guilty of flattering or making any court to their governors, but treat them with all the excess of freedom and familiarity," and the Scottish "lady of quality," Miss Janet Schaw, sniffed at "the disgusting equality" she found in North Carolina.[5]

2. Archibald Henderson, *North Carolina, The Old North State and the New*, 2 Vols. (Chicago, 1941), I, 161.

3. In 1776 Orange County had 3,300 white and 600 Negro taxables. Greene and Harrington, *American Population before 1790*, 166.

4. See A. R. Newsome (ed.), "Records of Emigrants from England and Scotland to North Carolina, 1774-1775," *North Carolina Historical Review*, XI (1934), 39-54, 129-143; Robert O. DeMond, *The Loyalists in North Carolina during the Revolution* (Durham, 1940), 50-51.

5. William K. Boyd (ed.), *William Byrd's Histories of the Dividing Line betwixt Virginia and North Carolina* (Raleigh, 1929), 96. For further comments see pp. 55, 66, 92, 304. Evangeline W. and Charles M. Andrews (eds.), *The Journal of a Lady of Quality*, 2nd ed. (New Haven, 1934), 153. See also Josiah Quincy, Jr., *Memoir of Josiah Quincy, Jr.* (Boston, 1874), 94.

A population of this type might be expected in time to demand a share in the government of the colony, but the process was hastened by the unrepresentative character of colonial political institutions and the heartless corruption of many of the officials who controlled them. Royal government, instituted in 1729 after the authority of the proprietors had completely broken down, brought a semblance of order to North Carolina, but it also increased the tensions between rulers and ruled which had marked the proprietary period. During the next forty years, while yeoman farmers by the thousands settled in the piedmont counties of Orange, Rowan, Guilford, Anson, and Mecklenburg, tidewater aristocrats also carved out plantations in the region and some of them, with the help of an aggressive group of lawyers attracted by high profits, inaugurated a systematic exploitation of their poorer neighbors.

The overrepresentation of the eastern counties in the Assembly helped to fasten tighter the aristocratic control of the colony. By a right originating in the Proprietary period, the five small sparsely-populated counties of the Albemarle region—Chowan, Currituck, Pasquotank, Perquimans, and Tyrrell—sent five representatives apiece to the Assembly while the piedmont counties were allotted only two apiece.[6] In the following years the already glaring discrimination

---

The fullest and best balanced description of the Carolina back country is in Carl Bridenbaugh, *Myths and Realities: Societies of the Colonial South* (Baton Rouge, 1952), 119-197.

6. In 1754 the Privy Council refused to allow the Assembly to limit the number of representatives from the tidewater counties to two apiece. Lawrence F. London, "The Representation Controversy in Colonial North Carolina," *The North Carolina Historical Review*, XI (1934), 268. Governor Tryon in 1767 sent an admirable short description of the North Carolina government to the Privy Council: William L. Saunders (ed.), *The Colonial Records of North Carolina*, 10 Vols. (Raleigh, 1886-1890), VII, 472-491. For representation see p. 473.

against the West increased because the Assembly erected new counties in the piedmont only reluctantly, and then with such extensive boundaries that their population was much greater than that of the tidewater counties. For the privileged tidewater area in 1766 the ratio of representatives to white taxables ranged between 1:100 and 1:150 in some counties; in Orange County it was about 1:1600.[7]

But the ill effects of an unfair system of representation might have been mitigated if the farmers had utilized their power at the polls. Because of the ease of acquiring land many of them could meet the fifty acre qualification for voting.[8] Throughout the colonial period the royal government, anxious to have the province settled, had granted fifty acres as headright to every head of a family desiring it for only the cost of a survey and attendant legal fees. The widespread distribution of property may explain why no demand was made for the abolition of property qualifications until the very eve of the Revolution. Actually, it was more important for the settlers to use intelligently the voting right they possessed than to have it expanded. The trip to the polls on court day was long and arduous, and once one arrived the problem of staying sober was equally difficult. The sheriffs who conducted the elections were sometimes accused of fraud and intimidation.[9] Voting was *viva voce,* of course.

Unfair representation and occasionally rigged elections might have been borne, however, were it not for the heartless corruption common among many of the officials of local government. In the South there was no equivalent of the

7. Estimates made from figures in Greene and Harrington, *American Population,* 165-166.

8. Albert E. McKinley, *The Suffrage Franchise in the Thirteen English Colonies in America* (Philadelphia, 1905), The University of Pennsylvania, *Publications,* Series in History, II, 111.

9. Julian P. Boyd, "The Sheriff in Colonial North Carolina," *The North Carolina Historical Review,* V (1928), 173, 176-170.

New England town meeting through which the people could manage local affairs. All authority lay in the hands of the officials connected with the county courts—magistrates, clerks, registers of deeds, sheriffs, and constables. Most of them were nominated by the governor on the recommendation of the county assemblymen and the incumbent officeholders. Through this colonial equivalent of senatorial courtesy the courthouse group was able to control all nominations and pass lucrative offices about among themselves. Hence the designation "ring." [10]

The cost of public services was inordinately high because officials, regarding their offices as investment and paid by fee, tended to overcharge for their services. In nearly every colony there were complaints against such extortion and assemblies attempted to rectify the situation by establishing legal fees and providing penalties for nonobservance. But in North Carolina, at least, legislation of this type appears to have been disregarded.

Exorbitant fees were by no means the only official malpractices. Sheriffs usually defrauded the government in the collection of taxes. Although royal governors complained loudly of this, legislation to bring offenders to book was ineffective, for the connections between courthouse rings and Assembly prevented enforcement. When Tryon succeeded in 1769 in having a thorough accounting made of the colony's finances, a delinquency on the part of the sheriffs was found which amounted to £64,000, £3,000 more than the total taxes collected in the period 1748-1770. It was estimated that sheriffs embezzled more than one half of the annual rev-

---

10. For descriptions of local government in North Carolina see William C. Guess, *County Government in Colonial North Carolina* (Chapel Hill, 1911), James Sprunt Historical *Publications,* XI, No. 1; J. P. Boyd, "The Sheriff in North Carolina," *North Carolina Historical Review,* V, 151-181; Tryon's report, *Colonial Records,* VII, 479-483, 487-489.

enue.[11] Even more flagrant was their defrauding of the poor taxpayer. Sometimes they prevented publication of the tax rate and collected more than the legal amount. If a taxable could not pay—and this was often the case because of the scarcity of money—it was charged that they made distraints of much greater value than the amount of the tax, and, acting in collusion with other members of the courthouse ring, so rigged the vendue sales that insiders bought land and goods at a fraction of their value.[12] If the taxpayer belatedly raised enough money from neighbors to pay his tax and tried to overtake the sheriff on the road in order to rescue his distrained goods, it was asserted that the officer sometimes took by-ways in order to throw the former owner off the track so that he might then sell the goods at a distant town. Any balance from a vendue sale was naturally supposed to be returned to the taxpayer. Herman Husband, usually considered a Regulator leader, declared he never heard of a refund.[13]

If the sheriff acted as executive officer of the county, justices of the peace sitting as the county court were the local legislature and judiciary.[14] Apparently as a group their professional ethics were no higher than those of the sheriffs. Complaints of overcharging were often lodged against them. One method of exacting more than the law allowed appar-

11. Boyd, "The Sheriff in North Carolina," *North Carolina Historical Review*, V, 167-168.

12. George Sims, *Address to the People of Granville County*, in William K. Boyd (ed.), *Some Eighteenth Century Tracts Concerning North Carolina* (Raleigh, 1927), 188.

13. Herman Husband, *An Impartial Relation of the First Rise and Cause of the Recent Differences in Public Affairs etc.* (1770), in *ibid.*, 262.

14. Guess, *County Government*, James Sprunt Historical *Publications*, XI, 31; Tryon estimated in 1767 that there were 516 justices in the colony. These men, mostly planters and lawyers, constituted the governing class. All important county officeholders and the assemblymen were almost invariably chosen from among their number. *Colonial Records*, VII, 481.

ently used by several types of officeholders was to divide one service for which a fee could be charged into several distinct operations, each carrying a separate fee. Thus Edmund Fanning, Register of Deeds in Orange County, testified in 1768 that he took four fees for registering a conveyance—a single operation according to the letter of the law.[15] Overcharging by lawyers was part of the network of graft which covered every branch of the court's activities. In many cases they occupied official positions and so were able to fill their pockets with both hands.

Because of the greed of lawyers and officials, those who brought their causes before the bench of justice often came as lambs to be shorn. Herman Husband calculated that a litigant in a case for five pounds, after winning on appeal to the Superior Court, would recover fifteen shillings.[16] A writer in the Virginia *Gazette* declared that the cost of six cases for amounts totalling ten pounds was sixty pounds.[17] There is another instance on record where the cost of a court action was fourteen times the amount involved.[18] George Sims, whose *Address to the People of Granville County* was the tocsin of the Regulation, gives a sad description of the farmer within the grip of the law. He presents as a hypothetical case a man who has had execution levied on him by a merchant for a five pound debt secured by a judgment note.[19] Personal effects to the amount of the judgment are

---

15. Bassett, *Regulators of North Carolina*, 181.

16. Husband, *Impartial Relation, North Carolina Tracts*, 291.

17. The Virginia *Gazette*, Sept. 5, 1771.

18. Guess, *County Government*, James Sprunt Historical *Publications*, XI, 34.

19. A judgment note empowers a lawyer to confess judgment for the amount of the debt. Thus the creditor, to recover, need not sue on the debt but merely have a justice of the peace issue execution. Obviously, this puts the debtor at the creditor's mercy. From Sims's discussion it seems that the practice was usual in North Carolina. See Judgment Note, *Bouvier's Law Dictionary*.

seized, but the poor man's troubles are not over. For entering the judgment on the court docket and issuing the execution—"the work of one long minute"—the justice of the peace demands forty-one shillings and five pence. Unable to pay the fee, the unfortunate debtor is confronted with the alternative of a distraint or twenty-seven days work on the justice's plantation. But even after he has worked out his debt to the justice, the poor man's account is not settled. "Stay, neighbor," says Sims, "you must not go home. You are not half done yet. There is the damned lawyer's mouth to stop.... You empowered him to confess that you owed five pounds, and you must pay him thirty shillings for that or else go to work nineteen days for that pickpocket...; and when that is done you must work as many days for the sheriff for his trouble [in levying execution and selling the debtor's goods], and then you can go home to see your living wrecked and tore to pieces to satisfy your merchant." [20]

The settler's plight was even more hopeless when he became involved in a criminal indictment. Defense lawyers, taking full advantage of the predicament of the accused, raised their fees in accordance with the gravity of the charge. Husband declared that when he was arrested in 1768 for participation in a Regulator riot his lawyers made him sign over to them "all the money I had and bonds and notes for £150 more." [21]

For sheer effrontery the corruption in North Carolina resembles the graft uncovered by the muckrakers of the late nineteenth and early twentieth centuries. It lacks the connection with organized crime which has characterized corrupt government in recent times, but in extensiveness and in its implication of leading political figures, it equals the activities of more modern political machines. The activities

20. Sims, *Address*, in *North Carolina Tracts*, 189-190.
21. Husband, *Impartial Relation*, in *ibid.*, 286.

of the courthouse rings perhaps deserve more censure than those of ward bosses, however, for most corrupt politicians today at least give some thought to the interests of their constituents. It cannot be argued that the sheriffs, magistrates, clerks, and registers of North Carolina were merely exercising prescriptive privileges and for that reason must not be judged by contemporary standards of honesty. Prescriptive dishonesty is dishonesty notwithstanding. They were breaking the law and they knew it. While most prevalent in the piedmont region, corruption probably extended over the whole of the province to a lesser degree. A friend of Samuel Johnston's, the leading conservative of the Revolutionary period, wrote just after the Regulator war that the desire for militant reform had begun to make its appearance in the tidewater country years before. "I should not have been surprised," he said, "if I had heard that your battle of Alamance (the conclusion of the war) had been fought on the banks of the Pasquotank river instead of the Alamance or Haw river." [22] But the extortion in the piedmont region was harder to bear because it was impossible to avoid. New settlers were compelled to go to law to quiet titles and adjust differences with their neighbors. Litigants who won usually paid dearly and losers might see the result of years of work disappear before their eyes. Because of the scarcity of money great numbers of farmers fell into debt, and petty peculation then became a serious drain on their resources. Anyone who refused to go through the processes of the law regarding land titles risked ejectment with total loss of improvements. Considering the gravity of the grievances in North Carolina it is a wonder that the Regulator war did not break out sooner and become more violent than it did.

22. Alexander Emsley to Samuel Johnston, July 27, 1771, Samuel Johnston Papers, North Carolina Department of History and Archives.

The first rumblings of discontent came from the piedmont settlers of the Granville District, who not only had to suffer the depradations of corrupt court officials but were compelled to bear with a corrupt land office as well. In 1759 a band of vigilantes kidnapped one of the agents who had systematically pillaged newcomers to the region by charging outrageous prices for land entries and by occasionally granting pieces of land to more than one person. The agent promised restitution but once freed had his kidnappers thrown in jail. This ill-advised action caused a major riot. A mob released the prisoners and feeling ran so high that the government dropped all prosecutions. Although the Assembly bitterly denounced "the torrent of [the rioters'] licentious extravagances," the Granville District remained turbulent and restless until the outbreak of the Revolution.[23]

The first articulate protest to the corruption in North Carolina government was apparently the pamphlet by the simple farmer, George Sims, *An Address to the People of Granville County,* written in 1765. The *Address* was no invitation to revolt. Sims only asked that the government force the county officials to obey the law. Expressing great admiration for the British Constitution (possibly in an attempt

23. The District was a strip of territory south of the Virginia border stretching from the ocean on the east to the "South Sea" on the west. The property of the Earl of Granville—the only heir of the original eight proprietors who did not sell his share of the Carolinas to the crown in 1728—it included the best of the fertile piedmont region and embraced perhaps two-thirds of the population of North Carolina. Although the royal government exercised civil jurisdiction in the area, land was sold by Granville's agents. Their frauds absorbed so much of the revenue from the tract that the Earl closed the land office from 1763 to 1773. He reopened it in the latter year with Governor Martin as agent. The District contained many squatters who were given title to their farms by the Provincial Congress after the outbreak of the Revolution. E. Merton Coulter, *The Granville District,* James Sprunt Historical *Publications,* XIII (1913), No. 2, pp. 38, 46-47, 52-55.

to avoid charges of political radicalism), he advocated that the farmers draft a petition to the Governor asking that the courts be closed until grievances were redressed. But violence should be avoided at all costs. "First let us be careful to keep sober that we may do nothing rashly. Secondly, let us do nothing against the known and established laws of our land that we may not appear as a faction endeavoring to subvert the laws and overturn our system of government. Let us behave with circumspection to the Worshipful Court inasmuch as they represent his Majesty's person, we ought to reverence their authority both sacred and inviolable, except they interpose, and then, Gentlemen, the toughest will hold out the longest." [24]

The only immediate effect of the *Address* was a suit for libel instituted against Sims by the officials of Granville County. In 1766, however, opposition to the rings broke out simultaneously in such widely separated counties as Brunswick, Cumberland, and Granville when settlers in those localities refused to pay taxes.[25] At Hillsborough during the September session of the Orange County Court some of the settlers asked the officials in a public address to attend a conference devoted to a discussion of grievances. The authors cleverly played on the similarity between their grievances and the Stamp Act and pointed out that the sturdy opposition of the Whig leaders to Parliament did not prove that they were incorruptible or justify the activities of the court house rings. "That great good may come of this great designed evil, the Stamp Law, while the Sons of Liberty withstood the Lords in Parliament in behalf of true liberty, let not officers under them carry on unjust oppression in our own province... take this as a maxim, that while men are

24. Sims, *Address*, in *North Carolina Tracts*, pp. 185-186, 190-191.
25. Herman Husband, *A Fan for Fanning, and a Touch-Stone to Tryon* (1771), in *ibid.*, 348.

men, though we should see all those Sons of Liberty who have just redeemed us from tyranny set in offices and vested with power, they would soon corrupt again and oppress if they were not called upon to give an account of their stewardship." [26]

The officials were apparently caught off balance by this modest show of spirit and agreed to meet the people at a gathering to be held in October. But in the intervening period they recovered their aplomb and decided to ignore the whole matter. Husband believed they were dissuaded by Edmund Fanning, a Justice of the Peace and the Register of Deeds of Orange County who came to be a symbol of the settlers' grievances. Fanning's character exhibits such marked contradictions that it is impossible to tell whether he was the cause of the farmers' sufferings or the victim of circumstances. Born in Long Island, he graduated from Yale in 1757, studied law in New York, and came to Orange to practice in 1761. He soon grew wealthy, built a fine house in Hillsborough, and became an intimate friend of Governor Tryon. A ditty composed among the Regulators describes his rise to fame and fortune:

> When Fanning first to Orange came,
> He looked both pale and wan
> An old patched coat upon his back,
> An old mare he rode on.
>
> Both man and mare wa'nt worth five pounds
> As I've been often told,
> But by his civil robberies,
> He's laced his coat with gold.

26. The address is printed in *Colonial Records*, VII, 249-250; *Impartial Relation*, in *North Carolina Tracts*, pp. 257-258; *A Fan for Fanning*, in *ibid.*, 351-353.

Actually, Fanning was not impoverished when he came to Orange and apparently was never guilty of gross fraud or extortion. Put on trial in 1769 at the insistence of the settlers, he was acquitted after nothing more than misconstruction of the fee law could be proved against him. The settlers were not reconciled to the verdict, however, and severely beat him when they broke up the court in 1770. Nevertheless Fanning seemed to be remarkably free from malice, for even after this painful experience he introduced legislation into the Assembly to rectify the Regulators' grievances. He accompanied Tryon to New York in the next year and during the Revolution became an outstanding Loyalist. Successively Lieutenant Governor of Nova Scotia and Governor of Prince Edward Island after the war, he died in London in 1818 a full general in the British army.[27]

When the Orange Assembly delegates and the court officials failed to appear at the meeting requested by the settlers in 1766, those who had gathered to discuss grievances drew up a paper asking for a regular annual gathering at which the court officials would submit to an examination of their accounts and the Assembly delegates receive instructions.[28] The farmers were trying, in a limited sphere, to inaugurate responsible government. They had little chance of success when it came to calling court officials to account, for these were responsible to the Governor, but in claiming the right to control the county delegates they rested their case on the representative character of colonial assemblies so proudly

27. For biographical material on Fanning see Stephen B. Weeks, *Biographical History of North Carolina; D.A.B.;* Arthur P. Hudson, "Songs of the Regulators," *William and Mary Quarterly,* 3rd Ser., IV (1947), 470-485. Some of his correspondence is printed in *Colonial Records,* Vols. VII and VIII, and there are a few interesting MSS letters in the Hayes Collection, North Carolina Department of History and Archives.

28. Husband, *Impartial Relation,* in *North Carolina Tracts,* p. 260; Husband, *A Fan for Fanning,* in *ibid.,* 355.

asserted by the members themselves. The instruction of delegates had been practiced for many years in New England and Pennsylvania, yet it had never been common in the South. Hence the authors presented their request with diffidence, noting that instruction "was a thing somewhat new in this county, though practiced in older governments." Like the Sims' *Address,* this paper is remarkable for its generally humble tone. It reasons with the representatives and couches nothing in the form of a demand.

The officials and the delegates might well have agreed to these reasonable requests, for the settlers were asking for no more than the Whigs were demanding from Britain—responsible government and relief from arbitrary taxation. But, in Fanning's words, the court house group in Orange "refused to be arraigned at the bar of [the people's] shallow understanding." Apparently no meetings were held and the campaign for responsible government came to an end.

The movement was suddenly revived in 1768, however, when the Sheriff of Orange announced that as a result of a recent act of the Assembly he would not travel the county as usual to collect taxes but would receive them at five specified places. Taxables who would not make the journey to pay would be charged two shillings, eight pence for a personal collection.[29] On top of this came a rumor, subsequently verified, that the Assembly had appropriated £15,000 for a new governors' palace. As a result groups of Orange County settlers, taking the name from the Whig organizations, formed "Associations" "for regulating public grievances and abuses of power." In the heat of resentment some of the "Regulators" sent a paper to the court officials announcing their refusal to pay taxes until an accounting was reached. The paper asserted what the pronouncement of 1766 had

29. Husband, *Impartial Relation,* in *North Carolina Tracts,* p. 262; Husband, *A Fan for Fanning,* in *ibid.,* 359-360.

hinted, "... the nature of an officer is a servant to the public and we are determined to have the officers of this county under better and honester regulation than they have been for some time past." [30] Yet the settlers' interpretation of the rights of citizens regarding taxes was considerably more moderate than that of the Whigs. The farmers did not fulminate against taxation without representation but merely observed that "the king requires no money from his subjects but what they are made sensible what use it's for." They concluded by again requesting the assemblymen for a meeting.

The more conservative Regulators drew up a milder protest. Both groups, however, testified to their peaceful intentions. Indeed, the whole object of the Regulators was to force the court officials to obey the law. Nullification and violence were resorted to only when all other means of redressing grievances failed.

The officers made no attempt at conciliation. Deep in embezzlement, they could not submit to an accounting of their funds. Fanning, after an altercation with some settlers over the distraint of a mare, wrote to the governor a grim and exaggerated description of the strength of the Regulators and asserted that their intentions were seditious.[31] Tryon replied by issuing a proclamation calling on them to disperse.[32]

Now sure of the governor's support, Fanning took the drastic step of seizing Herman Husband and William Butler, reputedly the two outstanding leaders of the Regulator movement. Although Husband's name has always been linked to the War of the Regulation, he was apparently not a member of the Association. The Regulators themselves declared he was not one of their number and on one occasion he was called upon to arbitrate differences between them and the

30. *Colonial Records,* VII, 700.
31. *Ibid.,* 713-716.
32. *Ibid.,* 721.

officers of Rowan County. Nevertheless, he became so deeply involved in the agitation that in the end he suffered more than many of the actual leaders. Deeply religious, mystical, and eternally in conflict with his environment, he was an incurable radical. Unfortunately, however, he lacked a strong will and courage and so became indecisive and pusillanimous when faced with the demands of leadership.

Born in 1724 on a small farm in Maryland, Husband experienced a soul-searing conversion under the stimulus of the Great Awakening.[33] Reflecting the compelling imagery of Jonathan Edwards, he wrote that "the Flames of Hell, represented with Flames of Sulphur and Brimstone, seemed nothing in comparison of the Wrath of ... an Angry God." [34] In order to placate Providence he joined the Presbyterian church, but later, convinced that it did not teach the whole truth, became a Quaker. About 1750 he moved to North Carolina. Whether because of, or in spite of his ascetic habits —which were apparently in marked contrast to those of the inhabitants generally—he developed a flourishing plantation near Hillsborough and eventually possessed about 8000 acres.[35] Although disowned by the Quakers—a no doubt inevitable misfortune—he was universally respected because of his honesty, sobriety, and industry.[36]

Husband and Butler were arrested at their homes, and were brought to Hillsborough and threatened with summary execution unless they promised to sever all connections with the Regulators. Under the pressure Husband broke down

33. Husband has left a revealing account of his religious experiences in his pamphlet, *Some Remarks on Religion* (1761), reprinted in *North Carolina Tracts*, 201-246.
34. *Ibid.*, 221.
35. *Ibid.*, 195.
36. See sketch by J. G. de R. Hamilton in *D.A.B.* A more detailed but less discerning treatment of Husband is in Mary E. Lazenby, *Herman Husband* (Washington, 1940).

and promised to cease criticising the officers. Fanning then released him on bail, and Husband prepared to flee the country, for his defection had placed him in such bad odor with the more radical Regulators that he feared for his life. After a period of agonizing indecision, however, he returned to stand trial in the fall of '68 and was acquitted [37]—probably because the government had meanwhile quelled the disturbances which had led to his arrest and was anxious to allay hostility by leniency with offenders.

While Husband was screwing up his courage for his forthcoming trial, the Regulators in Orange County petitioned the governor and council for redress of their grievances.[38] In reply Tryon condemned their activities and called on them to drop their titles of Regulators and Associators and submit to government. He promised, however, that they might prosecute the officers in the courts after peace had been restored.[39] This was by no means a satisfactory response. Tryon's only inducement for the Regulators' return to obedience was to offer a means of redressing grievances which had already been proved fruitless. Of what use to prosecute corrupt officers in courts which were themselves corrupt? Hence the Regulator agitation kept spreading.

Foreseeing open revolt, Tryon then called up a militia force of over 1,000 men which he stationed at Hillsborough.[40] Mainly a gentlemen's affair, this array was officered by six lieutenant generals, two major generals, three adjutant generals, two majors of brigades, seven colonels, five lieutenant colonels, four majors, and thirty-one captains. Most of the Council and about 25 per cent of the House

37. Husband, *Impartial Relation,* in *North Carolina Tracts,* 291.
38. *Colonial Records,* VII, 760-761.
39. *Ibid.,* 793.
40. Bassett, *Regulators of North Carolina,* 176-177.

held commissions.[41] When the September term of court opened, during which Husband was to be tried, a large number of settlers marched on Hillsborough apparently to prevent the court from sitting; but after viewing the governor's reception committee they disclaimed all intentions of insurrection, handed over their leaders for trial, promised to pay taxes, and dispersed. The court officials, evidently wishing to return to the *status quo ante* without arousing antagonism, either released the leaders or gave them light sentences. Although the governor held to his word and allowed the farmers to bring suit against the officers, most of the suits ended in failure, or, as in the case of Fanning, in a nominal fine.[42]

For a time it appeared that the governor's prompt action had stifled the protests of the piedmont. The sheriff of Orange assured Tryon that farmers were again paying their taxes or suffering distraints with submission.[43] The governor himself informed the home government of the happy ending to the unpleasantness and declared with evident satisfaction, "It is with pleasure I can assure his Majesty not a person of the character of a gentleman appeared among the insurgents."[44]

The Regulator movement was not a complete failure, however, for attempts were made in the Assembly to rectify some outstanding abuses. Fanning, paradoxically, sponsored a bill to lower court costs and stay executions of judgment in suits for small debts. Measures to inaugurate triennial assemblies, regulate elections, and relieve insolvent debtors were brought in, and Fanning, again in the unexpected role of reformer, presented a plan to reduce the Provincial debt

41. *Ibid.*, 177-178.
42. *Ibid.*, 181-182.
43. *Colonial Records*, VII, 864.
44. *Ibid.*, 886.

and "relieve the present burden of taxation upon the poor." [45] All of these bills were killed either in the House or Council, however. Only one important reform measure became law—an act regulating the sale of distrained goods designed to prevent the frauds of which Sims had complained in his *Address to the People of Granville County*.[46]

On the whole, the tone of the Assembly was unfriendly to the Regulators. It presented an address of lavish praise to Tryon for his part in suppressing the "insurrection." Earlier it had given him additional powers over the militia, raised the fees of justices, and had compelled plaintiffs at the beginning of a case to put up a bond to cover court costs in case they lost their suit—a provision which made it even harder for the poor to sue the rich.[47] Nothing was done to prevent the taking of exorbitant fees, and attempts to make accession to courts easier by dividing Mecklenburg, Orange, and Rowan counties failed, possibly because this would have increased the representation of the back country.

But the Regulator spirit was far from dead in spite of the fiasco of September, 1768. In 1769, two petitions were presented to the government which showed a considerable advance in political thinking. One from Anson County carrying 261 signatures asked for ballot voting, taxation in proportion to wealth, the collection of taxes in commodities, and the printing of money with land as security. The document further requested that all debt cases involving amounts between forty shillings and ten pounds be tried by one justice and a jury with lawyers barred from the courtroom, and that the governor and Council cease making large land grants to individuals who held them for speculation.[48] "Us

45. *Ibid.*, 961.
46. Walter Clark (ed.), *The State Records of North Carolina*, Vols. 11-26 (Winston, Goldsboro, Charlotte, 1895-1905), XXV, 514-515.
47. *Ibid.*, XXIII, 762, 766.
48. *Colonial Records*, VIII, 75-80.

inhabitants of Orange and Rowan counties" wanted the governor to propose legislation which would prevent lawyers and clerks from holding seats in the House of Commons, put all officers on salary and do away with fees, and make inspection notes on imperishable commodities in warehouses legal tender. The inhabitants also desired regular publication of the laws, division of the large western counties, and the registering of votes on the Assembly journal "so that we may have an opportunity to distinguish our friends from our foes." The petitioners, like those of Anson County, were particularly insistent that the wealthy planters bear more of the tax burden. "For all to pay equal," they wrote, "is with submission, very grievous and oppressive." [49] Polls were the sole basis of taxation in North Carolina and the fact that slaves were also taxable did not alter to any great extent the regressive characteristics of the tax system. Noting that all attempts to bring the extorting officers to book had failed, "partly from their own superior Cunning and partly from our invincible Ignorance," the petitioners asked Tryon to vacate all commissions of present county clerks and install "Gentlemen of probity and Integrity" in their places. [50]

It is evident that the settlers whose only recourse a year before had been to throw themselves on the governor's mercy had matured considerably in political outlook. The proposals to register divisions in the House of Commons, publish the laws and journals, divide the western counties, and inaugurate secret voting were all much-needed reforms adopted in later years. The petitioners' requests for progressive taxation and legal tender secured by non-perishable commodities became elements in the agrarian programs of the nineteenth century culminating in the Populist movement.

49. *Ibid.*, 83. Petition, pp. 81-84.
50. *Ibid.*, 82.

This new grasp of political and economic realities on the part of the piedmont farmers bore fruit in the elections of 1769. The middle and frontier counties returned almost an entire new slate of delegates. Husband replaced Fanning as a representative of Orange and others of the old guard of whom the Regulators had complained were either defeated or failed of nomination.[51] Tryon soon dissolved the House because of its resolutions on the Townshend Acts, but most of the new members retained their seats in the elections which followed. James Iredell, a Whig who later became a Federalist and a justice of the Supreme Court, declared in 1770 that a majority of the House were "of regulating principles" and were determined upon "a levelling plan." [52] The legislative record of the House gives some justification for this comment. Attorneys' and clerks' fees were again fixed by law and penalties imposed for non-observance,[53] the chief justice was put on salary,[54] the act regulating executions was renewed,[55] and an act to ease court costs in litigation over small debts was passed.[56] The Assembly failed to take the necessary measures for enforcement, however. All penalties were civil and could only be

51. List of representatives elected in 1766, *Colonial Records*, VII, 342; those elected in 1769, *ibid.*, VIII, 106-107. Among those dropped were Samuel Benton of Granville, of whom Sims had complained, Samuel Spencer of Anson, and John Frohawk of Rowan, both of whom the Regulators detested. The votes on the Orange election were, according to Husband: Fanning, 314; Prior, 455; Husband, 642. Archibald Henderson (ed.), "Herman Husband's Continuation of the Impartial Relation," *North Carolina Historical Review*, XVIII (1941), 65. Although defeated in Orange, Fanning was returned from Hillsborough. The Regulators charged that the town had been given a representative by the governor solely to provide Fanning with an Assembly seat.

52. *Colonial Records*, VIII, 270.

53. *State Records*, XXIII, 789, 814-818.

54. *Ibid.*, 818-819.

55. *Ibid.*, 833-835.

56. *Ibid.*, 846-849.

imposed following a suit brought by an injured party. No effective redress of the Regulators' grievances was possible until the government took the responsibility of prosecuting violations of its legislation as criminal acts. The humble farmers of the piedmont naturally hesitated to bring suits in unfriendly courts against officials much better equipped for legal battles than themselves. Therefore it is not surprising that complaints of extortion continued to mount in spite of the remedial legislation of the "Regulator" Assembly. A petition from Orange County declared that clerks were still demanding exorbitant fees and that sheriffs were collecting more in taxes than the legal rate required.[57] Although the writers again testified to their peaceful intentions, nevertheless, "If we cannot obtain ... some security in our properties more than bare humor of officers, we can see plainly that we shall not be able to live under such oppressions and to what extremities this must drive us you can as well judge of as we can ourselves...." [58]

Extremities were closer than possibly either the officers or many of the Regulators realized. When the Orange County Court met in September, 1770, the Regulators invaded the town, pulled the judges from the bench, tried the cases on the docket themselves, and left a summary and blasphemous account of their administration of justice in the court record.[59] News of the riot reached New Bern about the same time as a report that Regulators of Bute and Johnston counties were marching on the capitol to prevent Fanning from taking his seat in the House. Alarm aroused by the possibility of open rebellion apparently led the majority of the members to abandon their "regulating principles." First

57. *Colonial Records,* VIII, 231-234.
58. *Ibid.,* 234.
59. For a detailed description of the Hillsborough riot see Bassett, *Regulators of North Carolina,* 190-192.

the delegates expelled Herman Husband for publishing a letter written by the Regulator James Hunter accusing some of the leading men of the province of corruption.[60] Secondly the members passed the Johnston Act—named for the future leader of the conservative Whigs—which made it a felony punishable by death for persons in a riotous crowd of ten or more to refuse to disperse on the order of a sheriff or justice of the peace. Anyone indicted under the act who failed to surrender himself for trial would be outlawed and could be shot on sight. The act was *ex post facto* in that some of its provisions applied to offenses occurring since March, 1770. The object was to punish the perpetrators of the Hillsborough riots.[61]

The Regulators received the Johnston Act as the crowning example of the perfidy of the officers. "The Assembly have gone and made a riotous act," some of them were quoted as saying, "and the people are more enraged than ever. It was the best thing that could be done for the county for now we shall be forced to kill all the clerks and lawyers. . . . If they had not made the Act we might have suffered some of them to live. A Riotous Act! There never

60. Hunter implicated two figures of great importance in the future history of the state, Abner Nash and William Hooper. Nash was to serve a term as governor in 1780-1781, and Hooper represented the state in Congress during part of the Revolutionary period. Like Johnston he was an outstanding opponent of democracy. Hunter also asserted that the Regulators would pay no more taxes "until we have some assurance they will be applied toward the support of government." He stressed the fact that the country needed no new laws but only the enforcement of the old ones. Originally printed in the North Carolina *Gazette,* the letter appeared in the Pennsylvania *Journal,* July 11, 1771. A photostatic copy of this latter printing will be found in Regulator Papers, Southern History Collection, University of North Carolina. After his expulsion, Husband was imprisoned for a short time at the instigation of Governor Tryon. Following his release he returned to his plantation in Orange County and, if present at Alamance, fled the field before the conclusion of the battle.

61. *Colonial Records,* VIII, 481-486.

was any such act in the laws of England or any other country but France. They brought it from France and they'll bring the Inquisition next." [62] Even the Privy Council agreed that the law was in part at least, unjustifiable. It informed Josiah Martin, Tryon's successor, that the outlawry clause was "irreconcilable with the principles of the constitution, full of danger in its operation and unfit for any part of the British Empire." [63]

The disturbances provided an opportunity for Governor Tryon to stamp out the Regulation by force of arms. When, at his instigation, hand-picked grand juries brought in sixty-two indictments against Regulator leaders in Orange, he arranged a military expedition with the ostensible purpose of seizing the culprits. Two columns, one from the East and one from the West, were to converge on the rebellious county. Gentlemen flocked to the colors. The roster of officers included representatives of almost every important family in the province—men who became the prominent Whig leaders in the Revolution. "With the exception [of the Governor and Fanning]," says the biographer of Tryon, "nearly every officer of note in the army... went heart and soul into the struggle for freedom during the Revolution; and, were the names of this galaxy of patriots omitted from the annals of the fight for independence, little material would be left for the historian of that epoch in North Carolina." [64] Many of these notables had been detested by the Regulators—particularly Abner Nash and Alexander Martin, both of whom were to become governors of the state; John Walker, a future aide-de-camp to Washington; and Francis Nash, a brigadier general during the Revolution who fell at the battle of

62. *Ibid.*, 519-520. The Regulators were supposed to have declared that they paid no regard to the laws of the last session. *Ibid.*, 538.

63. *Ibid.*, 516.

64. Marshall D. Haywood, *Governor William Tryon, and his Administration in the Province of North Carolina, 1765-1771* (Raleigh, 1903), 166.

Germantown. Other unpopular figures who supported Tryon were William Hooper, a future delegate to the Continental Congress, and Richard Henderson, a judge of the Orange County Court during the riot of 1770 and future promoter of the Transylvania Company.

Although the aristocracy breathed fire, there seems to have been little heart for battle among the rank and file. Rednap Howell, a Regulator leader and the possible author of much of the doggerel verse of the movement, wrote that at New Bern the militia broke ranks and declined to serve, and that only seven recruits could be secured in Dobbs County.[65] Most of the Wake County regiment refused to march against the Regulators. Only by threats and cajolery did Tryon succeed here in getting fifty "volunteers." [66] The most effective spur to recruiting was a bounty of forty shillings and good pay during service. By this means, according to an observer friendly to the Regulators, Tryon enlisted an army "of the meaner sort." [67]

To repel Tryon's expected attack a leaderless mob, many of its members without arms, gathered in Orange County. A newspaper writer declared that most of the men were "without principle because they had nothing to lose." But there were others, he said, "who had both property and principles, but with regard to government, were republicans. Such people ever look with jealous eye on public officers and are enemies from principle to that subordination so essential to the being of a well-regulated state. A man gen-

65. South Carolina and American General *Gazette,* April 10, 1771. An observer from Bute wrote that although 800 or 900 men turned out for muster, "there was not any would list, but broke their ranks without leave of their commanders and proclaimed for the Regulators." *Colonial Records,* VIII, 552.

66. *State Records,* XIX, 838-839.

67. *Colonial Records,* VIII, 636.

teelly dressed gave them the greatest offense." [68] The writer probably exaggerated the number of political radicals among the Regulators. Few if any of the piedmont settlers had ever indicated dissatisfaction with royal government. But he was more correct in recognizing the elements of class warfare. The yeoman farmers rose against the aristocracy not only as inhabitants of the piedmont but also as common men against gentlemen. As previously indicated, their grievances, although most evident in the western counties, were present to a lesser degree all over the province, and so also the antagonism aroused by these grievances. In the final alignment of forces, the Regulators who fought were apparently all from the piedmont counties, but Tryon's army contained nearly all the gentlemen of prominence in the province.

Tryon succeeded in raising a little over 1,000 men and a second force of about 300 under General Waddell was gathered in the western counties. [69] Some contemporary newspaper accounts pictured the governor as knight in shining armour. "God be thanked they have found a *Tryon*," declared a writer in the New York *Gazette*. He saw the Regulation as a curtain raiser for social revolution throughout the colonies. [70] A gentleman who took part in the campaign wrote that morale was high in the government forces, and that everyone was determined to "quell this dangerous insurrection and return to their allegiance a body of men who, under the color of redressing nominal grievances, have nothing more in view than overturning the civil government of this province." [71]

68. South Carolina *Gazette*, Sept. 12, 1771.

69. Bassett, *Regulators of North Carolina*, 201.

70. *Colonial Records*, X, 1025. A similar comment appeared in the Virginia *Gazette*, May 23, 1771.

71. *Ibid.*, Another writer saw the hand of God in the Battle of Alamance. He declared that the Lord caused the Regulators' rifle balls to fly over the heads of the governor's troops. *Ibid.*, July 4, 1771.

Tryon met the perpetrators of this "dangerous insurrection" on the field of Alamance, twenty miles from Hillsborough. General Waddell was not able to make his appearance as planned because of disaffection among his men and the loss of his baggage train. A description of the battle, possibly unreliable in detail but interesting in view of Tryon's difficulties in recruiting, gives the impression that it was a somewhat ludicrous affair because of a general reluctance of both sides to fight. "The two armies marched toward each other with the most profound silence, and such was the indisposition of either side ... that the ranks passed each other and were then compelled by a short retreat to regain their respective positons. At the distance of 25 yards apart the contending parties stood and occupied the solemn hour before battle with a verbal quarrel, each party uttering the most violent imprecations and bandying the most abusive epithets. The Regulators shook their clenched hands at the governor and Mr. Fanning and walked up to the artillery with open bosoms, defying them to fire. They were now face to face, each man engaged in a loud and clamorous quarrel with the nearest enemy on the grievances of the people and the virtues of Fanning. It was in vain that the governor roared out the word of command, directing the men to fire. Each loyal soldier was too busily occupied either in an argument or a fist fight to heed the ... decree." [72] Tryon, possibly fearing that his men would not fight, supposedly rode up and down the line shouting, in the best tradition of eighteenth-century military etiquette, "Fire on them or on me." This perhaps provided an interesting alternative for some of the men in his own ranks. Whether in obedience to his command or not, somewhere a gun went

72. Joseph S. Jones, *A Defense of the Revolutionary History of the State of North Carolina from the Aspersions of Mr. Jefferson* (Boston and Raleigh, 1834), 53.

off, and the battle was joined. The Regulators soon took to
their heels. The Regulators lost nine killed and numerous wounded. Tryon suffered nine killed and sixty-one
wounded.[73]

After the battle the government adopted a policy of summary punishment for known agitators and forgiveness of
their followers. Six leading Regulators were hanged after
court martial, and one was executed on the field of battle
without trial. The others were eventually released. Husband,
who had ridden off the field before or during the battle, fled
to Maryland. Little or nothing is known about his activities
from this time until 1794 when he characteristically became
implicated in the Whisky Rebellion. Condemned to death
for his part in it, he was later among those pardoned by
Washington. He died soon after, a rebel to the last.

Thus ended the War of the Regulation. On the surface it
appeared to be a complete victory for the colonial ruling
class. The settlers had failed to gain responsible government
and their plans for an agrarian program were stillborn. Yet
the war was to have important results in the Revolutionary
period. The repressed but profound bitterness for the ruling
aristocracy emerged in a strong Loyalist movement on one
hand and in a demand for democratic government on the
other. There can be little doubt that some of the king's ir-
regulars who followed the notorious partisan leader, David
Fanning (no kin to Edmund), were avenging the Battle
of Alamance. And from those settlers of the piedmont who
supported the patriot cause sprang a demand for democratic government when the time came to write a state
constitution in 1776. Against the united opposition of royal
governor and provincial aristocracy they had no chance at
all of securing a permanent redress of their grievances, but
when these two allies came to blows over the enforcement of

73. Bassett, *Regulators of North Carolina*, 204.

British imperial legislation, the opportunity suddenly arose of obtaining not only responsible government but political equality as well.[74]

74. Carl Bridenbaugh argues that the Regulators' grievances were exaggerated and were to some degree pretexts to avoid payment of taxes and submission to the normal restraints of government. I cannot agree. The sharp note of injury and the uniformity of complaints in the voluminous Regulator documents from all over the piedmont cannot be passed off lightly. No doubt the Regulators shared with the rest of mankind an aversion to taxes, but in this instance it must be remembered that a refusal to pay them was the only way they could hope to force a redress of their grievances. They had no political control over local officials and the courts were in the hands of their enemies. Nor were the Regulators' objectives somewhat obscure, as Bridenbaugh asserts. First they wanted local officials to obey the law, and second they wanted certain political and legal reforms which would give a measure of responsible local government. For Bridenbaugh's views see his *Myths and Realities: Societies of the Colonial South* (Baton Rouge, 1952), 160-162. For an estimate more favorable to the Regulators see Hugh T. Lefler and Albert R. Newsome, *North Carolina: the History of a Southern State* (Chapel Hill, 1954), 24-40.

SEVEN

Democratic Forces in the Revolutionary Movement
of North Carolina

THE War of the Regulation caused considerable newspaper comment, the northern papers usually supporting the Regulators and the southern papers the gentlemen of Tryon's army. To most northern minds the issue was apparently the maintenance of the liberties of the small farmer against the encroachments of the wealthy slaveholding planters.[1]

1. Thus "Leonidas," writing in the Massachusetts *Spy*, accused Tryon of fomenting hostilities by his "avowed connivance at the enormous villanies of the banditti of robbers, judges, sheriffs, and pettifoggers." Reprinted in the Virginia *Gazette*, July 25, 1771. A writer in the Boston *Gazette* described the campaign as characterized by "murdering temper" (*Colonial Records*, X, 1024), and shortly thereafter a Massachusetts printer —Daniel Kneeland of Boston—started to publish *A Fan for Fanning* in serial form. *North Carolina Tracts*, 337-338.

When the "Leonidas" article reached New Bern, a public meeting demanded that the issue of the *Spy* containing it be burned by the common hangman. The article was described as "replete with the basest misrepresentations, the most palpable falsities, abusive epithets, and scandalous invectives." The gentlemen extolled Tryon in terms resembling an address to a conquering Caesar. Apparently the printer of the *Spy* was also hung in effigy. *Colonial Records*, X, 1019-1021; South Carolina and American General *Gazette*, Aug. 12, 1771. "Phocion," in the Virginia *Gazette* also attacked the "Leonidas" article. Dubbing those who questioned the in-

The best contemporary evaluation of the Regulation appeared in the Pennsylvania *Gazette*. This is understandable because of the close relations between Pennsylvania and the North Carolina back country. Enumerating the grievances of the Regulators, the writer concluded, "They must appear to have been an illiterate, injured multitude, struggling against all the weight, influence, and artifice of their oppressors; without any one advantage except what they derived from the justness of their cause." He also suggested a parallel between the struggle of Regulators with courthouse officials and the conflict between the Whigs and Parliament —an important comparison which had been overlooked by all other observers. "How far subjects have a right to complain of public oppression and insist on having grievances redressed is at this day well understood," he wrote. "The design of government is acknowledged to be the good of the people.... We have many instances in which bad rulers have availed themselves of such establishments as seemed to insure Happiness to the people .... to perpetuate impositions and cruelties which would not have been borne but for a confidence in the laws and an attachment to the form." [2]

Outside of the North the Regulators received unexpected sympathy and understanding from Governor Tryon's successor in office, Josiah Martin. Although lacking tact, imagination, and political acumen, Martin was nevertheless sincere and upright and did not pant after personal glory

---

tegrity of the officers as "renegados," he denied that there were any real grievances behind the Regulator movement and explained the uprising as "natural to a people whose circumstances are mean and whose condition is poor." Virginia *Gazette*, Aug. 7, 1771. Another writer in the South Carolina and American General *Gazette* admitted that complaints were justified but insisted that the ultimate aim of the Regulators was rebellion. Sept. 12, 1771.

2. Reprinted in the South Carolina *Gazette*, Sept. 6, 1771.

as did Tryon. His comments to Lord Hillsborough on a trip through the back country made after his arrival in 1771 are worth quoting in full:

My progress through this country, My Lord, hath opened my eyes exceedingly to the commotions and discontents that have lately prevailed in it. I now see most clearly that they have been provoked by insolence, and cruel advantages have been taken of the people's ignorance by mercenary, tricking attorneys, clerks, and other little officers who have practiced on them every sort of rapine and extortion. By which having brought upon themselves their just resentment, they engaged government in their defense by artful misrepresentations that the vengeance the wretched people in folly and madness aimed at their heads was directed against the constitution. By this strategem they threw an odium upon the injured people.... Thus, My Lord, as far as I am able to discern the resentment of government was craftily worked up against the oppressed, and the protection which the oppressors treacherously acquired where the injured and ignorant people expected to find it drove them to acts of desperation ... which ... induced bloodshed, and I verily believe necessarily.[3]

This was a rather acute analysis of the Regulator troubles and shows some similarity to the comments of Colden and Gage on the "Great Rebellion of 1766" in New York. But Martin was being overcharitable in assuming that Tryon had been duped into the military campaign ending with Alamance. The governor had from the outset given full support to the Assembly and the courthouse rings even though fully informed of the cause of the agitation by the Regulators themselves. Although Tryon and the Assembly had

3. *Colonial Records,* IX, 330. Dartmouth, the successor to Hillsborough as Secretary of State, agreed with Martin. "I must confess to you," he replied, "that I see but too much reason to believe that those deluded people would not have been induced to involve themselves in the guilt of Rebellion without provocation." *Ibid.,* 362.

clashed over British imperial legislation and although antagonisms had flared to such a pitch in 1766 that a Whig mob had actually held him under house arrest,[4] nevertheless all quarrels were forgotten in the face of the threat from the Regulators. By his leadership of the campaign of 1771 Tryon became—in the eyes of the House of Commons and the Council at least—the most popular royal governor ever to hold office in North Carolina.

Former Regulators were as much impressed with Martin's sympathy as he by their grievances. Tough old James Hunter wrote to William Butler, who had fled with Husband to Maryland, "Martin has given us every satisfaction that could be expected of him." He told how the governor had promised to urge the Assembly to pass an act of oblivion, and how he had posted at every courthouse the defalcations of past sheriffs, "a thing we never expected to the great grief and shame of our gentry.... I think our officers hate him as bad as we did Tryon, only they don't speak so free." [5]

Martin was here presented with a golden opportunity to buttress the waning power of royal government in North Carolina. He might have cemented a friendship with the back-country settlers to counterbalance the growing Whig power in the Assembly in the same way that medieval kings kept a powerful and refractory nobility in check by a working alliance with the bourgeoisie. But Martin was not the kind of a man to make independent decisions. Lacking imagination and initiative, he felt bound more closely by his instructions than other royal governors, and even with his sudden sympathy for the settlers he would have found it almost impossible to turn against his own class. In 1774, with

4. R. D. W. Connor, *History of North Carolina: The Colonial and Revolutionary Periods*, Vol. I (Chicago and New York, 1919), 324.
5. Hunter to Butler, Nov. 6, 1772. Regulator Papers, Southern History Collection, University of North Carolina.

hostilities in the making, he awoke to the possibilities of arming the Regulators, but by then it was too late.

During the period between the Battle of Alamance and the outbreak of the Revolution the Assembly made some ineffective efforts to mollify the back country. Perhaps, as relations with Britain grew more bitter, the members awoke to the danger of a working agreement between the governor and the piedmont farmers. Maurice Moore and Abner Nash, possibly hoping to counterbalance the effect of Martin's tour of the back country, held a conference with Hunter in 1772. But the old Regulator made it pretty evident he had neither forgotten nor forgiven. "I think they are more afraid than ever," he commented to Butler.[6] The Assembly continued to pass reform legislation,[7] but enforcement was apparently as lax as had been the case with the measures effected before the Battle of Alamance. Only eight or nine of the county clerks obeyed an order by Martin to forward him a copy of the fee tables they had been directed to post in their offices.[8] An accounting of the sheriff's defalcations in 1773 showed that they owed the province the staggering sum of £52,455.[9] The inhabitants of Orange County complained that the law regulating attachments was continually abused.[10] An act of

6. *Ibid.*
7. The duties and responsibilities of court clerks were defined and fees again fixed. In case a clerk demanded and received an illegal fee, the court should "in a summary way take the matter under consideration" and fine the clerk, if found guilty, up to £5 for each offense. Two convictions amounted to a misdemeanor, and expulsion from office was then compulsory. *State Records*, XXIII, 898-899. An act was passed releasing insolvent debtors after twenty days' imprisonment on the condition that they deliver up all their assets. *Ibid.*, 900-904. All debt cases for amounts under £5 were to be tried before one justice, and execution of judgment in cases for amounts above 40 shillings could be stayed for two months. *Ibid.*, 934.
8. *Colonial Records*, IX, 279.
9. *Ibid.*, 575.
10. *Ibid.*, 701-702.

oblivion in favor of former Regulators still subject to penalties for their part in the uprising was voted down by the Assembly, but at the same time an act of indemnification was passed which protected those who took part in Tryon's campaign from civil suits.[11]

After the collapse of royal government in 1775, the Whigs intensified their efforts to capture the support of former Regulators and of foreign groups such as the Highlanders and Germans. Large numbers of the back-country settlers were understandably apathetic or hostile to the Whig cause, and this was a disquieting situation when the Whigs were also making enemies across the seas. In the spring of 1775 addresses of loyalty carrying about 500 signatures were sent to Martin by groups in Guilford, Rowan, Surry and Anson counties. As "an unhappy people, lying under the reflection of the late unhappy insurrection," they all condemned in the strongest terms possible the activities of the Whigs.[12] Nineteen inhabitants of Dobbs begged the governor "to open our eyes aright that we may not be deceived by every voice of cunning, crafty men...."[13] Samuel Johnston, the colony's leading Whig, reported during the summer that all the Regulators were supposed to be against the Whig cause and that Hunter was planning to lead a force against the Pro-

11. When this Act was disallowed by the Privy Council, an Orange County Committee wrote in its instructions of 1773 to the Assembly delegates, "We rejoice, Gentlemen, in this instance of His Majesty's fatherly attention; and we are sorry that in framing the law our Assembly had so little attention to the distresses of their innocent fellow subjects..." *Ibid.*, 705.

12. *Ibid.*, 1160-1164.

13. *Ibid.*, 1127. Martin forwarded copies of three addresses to Dartmouth suggesting an act of oblivion by royal proclamation. *Ibid.*, 1157. He reported that he was confident he could command the services of all the western counties in an emergency. As late as January, 1776, he believed that between two and three thousand Regulators would join the king's standard. *Ibid.*, X, 406.

vincial Congress which met at Hillsborough in August.[14] In order to counter disaffection the Congress appointed three committees, the first "to confer with such of the Inhabitants of the Province who entertain any religious or political scruples with respect to associating in the common Cause"; [15] the second to seek support from the Highlanders; and the third to draw up a vindication of the Whig position "in an easy familiar style and manner obvious to the very meanest Capacity." [16] Because of criticism that eastern members were dominating the Congress, several important committee positions were given to westerners, and John Penn of Granville was appointed to the Continental Congress in place of Richard Caswell, a tidewater planter.[17]

A meeting apparently took place between a committee of the North Carolina body and former Regulators sometime in the fall of 1775. Johnston, who was probably present, reported encouraging results. When the Regulators complained that they had been imposed upon by Tryon, he used the opening to justify Whig resistance to Britain. Following

14. Johnston to Hewes, June 27, 1775, Hayes Collection, North Carolina Department of History and Archives; Johnston to Iredell, Aug. 14, 1775, Charles E. Johnson Collection.

15. *Colonial Records*, X, 169.

16. *Ibid.*, 174. This document has apparently not been preserved.

17. Congress also passed a resolution of pardon for those engaged in the Regulation and gave the franchise to settlers on the Granville tract. Unable to secure title to their lands because of the closing of the Earl's land office, the farmers there were not freeholders. For a summary of Congress's attempts to win over the back country see Philip Davidson, *The Southern Backcountry on the Eve of the Revolution*, in Avery O. Craven (ed.), *Essays in Honor of William E. Dodd* (Chicago, 1935), 8-10. The western counties had objected to the appointment of William Hooper as a representative to the Continental Congress and to unequal representation. "It is not in character to dispute the power of Parliament when we say we are not represented, and yet quickly submit to so unequal a representation in a body formed by ourselves," wrote the merchant Andrew Miller to Thomas Burke. *Colonial Records*, IX, 1063.

the conference he reported to his brother-in-law, Iredell, that he had hopes of making the Regulators "members of society in good standing."[18]

One method of gaining support for the Whig cause in the back country was to engage the clergy as propagandists. During the Regulation the clergy of both the Church of England and the dissenting sects had been staunch supporters of the government. This was the natural course for the Church of England; the dissenting ministers—who might be expected to sympathize with their humble parishioners—were apparently won over by a promise from Tryon to found a college in Mecklenburg and to give them the power to perform marriages.[19] Thus the four Presbyterian ministers of North Carolina had addressed a memorial to the governor in 1768 "to express our abhorrence of the present turbulent and disorderly spirit that shows itself in some parts of this province" and another to their parishioners calling for submission to political authority.[20] To demonstrate that the Deity was on the side of the government they quoted Rom. 13:1-2, the strongest scriptural support for absolutism: "Let every soul be subject to the Higher Powers, for there is no Power but of God; the Powers that be are ordained of God. Whosoever therefore resisteth the power, resisteth the Ordinance of God, and they that resist shall receive to themselves damnation."[21] While the troops were in Hillsborough in 1768 they were treated to discourses by the Rev. Henry Patillo, Presbyterian, and Dr. George Micklejohn, Church of England; all apparently in this refrain. Micklejohn's sermon,

18. Johnston to Iredell, ——, 1775, Hayes Collection. The letter is so badly mutilated that further details are undecipherable.

19. "This is generally charged by all writers on the subject and the facts make the charge a probable one." Bassett, *Regulators of North Carolina*, 194n.

20. *Colonial Records*, VII, 813-814, 814-816.

21. *Ibid.*, 815-816.

printed as a pamphlet by order of the Assembly, was a peremptory demand for unquestioning obedience, and, as might be expected, Rom. 13:1-2 was the text.[22]

But in the first years of the Revolution the views of the dissenting clergy changed. The Privy Council had disallowed the bill designed to give them the power to perform marriages, Mecklenburg was still without its college and there were rumors that the lax vestry laws which enabled dissenters to avoid supporting the establishment would be changed. When Joseph Hewes, one of the North Carolina delegates to the Continental Congress, requested the Lutheran, German Reformed, and Presbyterian ministers in Philadelphia to send endorsement of the Whig cause to the brethren of their denominations in North Carolina, the Presbyterians responded quickly. Rom. 13:1-2 was conspicuously absent from their long pastoral letter. Instead, they called for a sturdy defense of colonial rights, by the sword if necessary.[23]

The clergy of the various denominations were able to find scriptural authority for their several courses during the Revolution. Anglicans, who looked to England for their preferment, with few exceptions stayed loyal to the king and rested their case on Paul's Epistle to the Romans. In Massachusetts, Baptists tended to view the Whigs with suspicion because of a conviction that the established Congregationalism of the colony constituted a greater danger to freedom than the distant threat of an established Anglicanism.[24] But the other dissenting groups saw the hand of God in the Revolution, and, like John Knox confronting Mary of Scotland, trans-

22. The sermon is reprinted in *North Carolina Tracts,* 400-412.
23. The pastoral letter is printed in *Colonial Records,* X, 222-228.
24. See below p. 140. The attitudes of the sects in Massachusetts are discussed in Lee N. Newcomer, "Yankee Rebels of Inland Massachusetts," *William and Mary Quarterly,* 3rd Ser., IX (1952), 161-162.

formed an obligation of obedience into an obligation to revolt. Giving a new reading to Rom. 13:1-2, they declared that only the "just" commands of those in authority need be obeyed. "Unjust" orders should be resisted. They were convinced that God would never enjoin his children to submit passively to evil; to do so would mean ignoring the command to work for the accomplishment of the Kingdom. Hence, carrying their logic one step further, they arrived at the conclusion that resistance to tyrants became obedience to God. Yet the unlettered North Carolina yeomen, remembering the injunction to submit preached in 1768, might well consider that they were damned if they resisted Great Britain and damned if they did not.

Two hundred copies of the address to North Carolina Presbyterians were distributed in the back country, but apparently to little effect.[25] Although at Hewes' request, the Continental Congress then sent two ministers to explain the new dispensation regarding resistance to the "Powers that Be," the majority of the Regulators still preferred the interpretation of Rom. 13:1-2 demonstrated by Tryon at Alamance.

The Moravians, naturally, stayed neutral throughout the war, but most of the Highlanders from the outset were Loyalists. Because of their previous military experience, they became Martin's chief hope for suppressing the revolt. Aided by some of the former Regulators, Highland chieftains formed a fairly impressive army which met a Whig force at Moore's Creek, February 26, 1776. The Loyalists were badly defeated and their supplies captured,[26] but their movement continued. It developed into a particularly vicious type of

25. Davidson, *The Southern Backcountry on the Eve of Revolution,* Craven, ed., *Essays,* 10-11.

26. For a detailed description of the battle see Connor, *History of North Carolina,* I, 385-387.

guerilla warfare which kept North Carolina in chaos throughout the Revolution.

The question of why some Regulators and many Highlanders turned Loyalist has been answered in various ways. In the case of both it has been suggested that they were reluctant to renounce oaths they had taken to support the government—the Highlanders on coming into the country and the Regulators after Alamance. Although there is considerable authority for this view,[27] possibly the Regulators and Highlanders pled the oath to hide deeper and more compelling motives. Many of the former would have been against the Whig leaders in any case, for their hatred of the gentry continued after Alamance. The few extant letters of James Hunter show resentment still seething. The biographer of Tryon shows considerable understanding of the Regulators' motives when he says, "It was largely to pay off old scores that the Regulators became Tories." [28] John Adams wrote in 1780 that Alamance "established in the minds of the Regulators such a hatred toward the rest of their fellow citizens that in 1775, when war broke out, they would not join them." [29] Oaths of allegiance in eighteenth-century America do not appear to have been held in

27. Robert O. DeMond, *The Loyalists in North Carolina During the Revolution* (Durham, 1940), 51; E. W. Caruthers, *A Sketch of the Life and Character of the Rev. David Caldwell, D.D.* (Greensboro, 1842), 169-172. Martin himself believed this to be the case. *Colonial Records,* IX, 1228. Col. Samuel Spencer of Anson, attempting to swing former Regulators to the Whig cause, stressed the fact that they were relieved of obligation under their oath because the King had broken his part of the social compact. *Ibid.,* X, 125. The Hillsborough Congress of 1775 made it plain that the Regulators could not be punished for refusing to join the royal forces, *Ibid.,* 169.

28. Marshall D. Haywood, *Governor William Tryon* (Raleigh, 1903), 185. The best discussion of the motivation of the Regulators is in *ibid.,* 184-190.

29. Charles F. Adams (ed.), *The Works of John Adams,* 10 Vols. (Boston, 1850-1856), VII, 284.

particular reverence. Revolutionary officers who held commissions from the king did not consider service in the Continental Army a blot on their honor, because, according to the compact theory of government, allegiance to government was a bilateral obligation. Oaths involving the personal code, on the other hand, were unilateral. Today the situation often seems reversed. Thus the Regulators would have had two justifications for renouncing their oaths of loyalty to Britain: first, because these were exacted under duress; second, because the king had broken his part of the social compact. Although the back-country farmers did not have the intellectual resources of Whig politicians or clergymen, nevertheless they must have realized that these avenues of escape from their obligation were open if they wished to take them.

The Highlanders also may have used the oath as a pretext to avoid giving support to the Whigs.[30] Having received favors from the British government which were in marked contrast to the treatment given the Scotch-Irish settlers from the north, gratitude and interest tied the Highlanders to the mother country. Brigadier General M'Donald made it plain to the Whig commander at Moore's Creek that his people were fighting for the king in order to repay a debt: "I cannot conceive" he said, "that the Scotch emigrants...can be under greater obligations to this country than to the King, under whose gracious and merciful government they alone could have been enabled to visit this western regions." [31] Rumors had been spread among the Scots that the Whigs would confiscate their land titles in the event the Revolution were successful. Even if these reports proved false, the Highlanders might be sure that their days of preferential treatment were over if independence materialized.

30. The loyalism of the Highlanders has been ascribed to a habit of obedience as well as the oath. DeMond, *Loyalists*, 51.

31. *State Records*, XI, 278-279.

During most of 1775 and 1776 North Carolina was governed by a congress, council, and committee system much like those of the other colonies.[32] The most effective revolutionary jurisdiction was exercised by the county committees, which, although elective, were usually dominated by the aristocracy.[33] These bodies arrested, tried, and often whipped Loyalists, and seized debtors suspected of intention to abscond (although revolutionists, the ruling Whigs were still creditors). "The advancement of the great American cause, and not justice, was the motto of the county committees,"[34] declared a nearly contemporary observer. "This conflicting jurisdiction, however, did not uproot the foundations of civil society as predicted by Governor Martin, for the notable Esquires of the court were generally the leading members of the county committees. The original Whig party of North Carolina comprised the wealth, the virtue, and the intelligence of the Province; and from this source alone moved the Revolution."[35]

From 1765 to 1776 the aristocracy in North Carolina had steadily increased in power and prestige. At the Battle of Alamance it had vindicated its authority against yeoman farmers who protested against the corruption in local government; at Moore's Creek it checked a Loyalist counter-revolution. But these victories were only temporary. Beginning in the spring of '76 the ruling Whigs were faced with

---

32. See Bessie L. Whitaker, *The Provincial Council and Committees of Safety in North Carolina* (Chapel Hill, 1908), James Sprunt Historical *Monograph,* VIII; Enoch W. Sikes, *The Transition of North Carolina from Colony to Commonwealth* (Baltimore, 1898), Johns Hopkins *Studies,* XVI, 522-527.

33. Joseph S. Jones, *A Defense of the Revolutionary History of the State of North Carolina from the Aspersions of Mr. Jefferson* (Boston and Raleigh, 1834), 203.

34. *Ibid.,* 205.

35. *Ibid.,* 202, 205.

new challenges. Loyalism grew to such an extent that it threatened to throw the province into civil war and the protest of the piedmont farmers developed into a demand for democratic government. Until the outbreak of the Revolution the opposition of the farmers was not primarily to institutions but to those individuals who exercised power through them. When the Regulators denounced the gentry it was never because the latter possessed special status or that they ruled because of it, but rather because they used their position to exploit the unprivileged. Few if any critics appear to have had serious objections to the political framework under which they lived.

But this attitude was to change when the question of independence arose. The ruling aristocracy, by its failure effectively to redress the grievances of the farmers within the framework of aristocratic government, obliged them to seek their objectives by a reform of government itself. The victims of exploitation had fruitlessly urged the aristocrats to purge themselves of corruption; by 1776 the feeling grew that the only way to achieve honesty in politics was to keep gentlemen out of office. The necessity to draft a new constitution provided the final impetus which changed a movement for redress of grievances into a demand for democratic government.

EIGHT

The North Carolina Constitution of 1776

THE instructions of Orange County to its Assembly delegates in 1773 are perhaps the first evidence that democratic ideas were beginning to filter into the back country. The mere fact that instructions were given at all is of course important. As a Regulator paper had stated in 1766, they were "a thing somewhat new to this county, though practiced in older governments." Who drew them up and how they were presented to the representatives is unknown, but probably they were drafted by a small group and were ratified by acclamation on court day. The farmers of Orange County were thoroughly convinced that their delegates should be the agents of their will: "Gentlemen, we have chosen you our Representatives at the next General Assembly and when we did so we expected and do still expect that you will speak our Sense in every case when we shall expressly declare it, or when you can by any other means discover it.... This is our notion of the Duty of Representatives, and the Rights of Electors." [1]

The provisional government which Mecklenburg established in 1775 was an attempt to implement the concept of

1. *Colonial Records,* IX, 699-700.

responsible government by appropriate institutions. For some reason there seems to have been no Regulator movement in the county comparable to that of Guilford, Orange, Rowan, or Anson. Possibly frontier conditions prevented the rise of a local aristocracy able to match the exploitation of the courthouse officials in the piedmont. Far removed from the seat of government, the settlers probably enjoyed considerable autonomy and therefore welcomed the prospect of independence because it would enable them to give legal sanction to their preferences in political institutions. It is possible that the desire for western lands also impelled them toward radicalism. Certainly this played a part in turning the farmers of eastern Connecticut, Frederick County, Maryland, and the valley of Virginia against the British government. But whatever the motives of the Mecklenburg settlers in severing the tie with Great Britain, they regarded independence as the means of establishing an equalitarian democratic government.

Thus the county resolves of May 31, 1775, which suspended British sovereignty (not to be confused with the spurious "Mecklenburg Declaration of Independence" of May 20), placed all authority formerly exercised by the county court in the hands of eighteen "selectmen" elected on a basis of manhood suffrage.[2] This preliminary move was followed by a comprehensive demand for democratic reform of provincial government in the instructions to the county representatives at the Hillsborough Congress of August, 1775. This document called for freemen suffrage, abolition of property qualifications for members of the Assembly, and representation in accordance with population.[3] The county insisted on a legislature dependent on the people in much the same terms as did the author of *The People the Best Governors:*

2. *Ibid.,* 1283.
3. *Colonial Records,* X, 239.

"You are instructed to vote that Legislation be not a divided right, and that no man or body of men be invested with a negative on the voice of the people duly collected...." Plural officeholding should be prohibited, practising lawyers excluded from the legislature,[4] and clerks and sheriffs popularly elected. In general, "All officers who are to exercise their authority in any of the [districts of the state should] be recommended to the trust only by the freemen of said division." The articles dealing with religion foreshadowed what was to become the settled program of democratic groups in the colonies. All connection between church and state was to be severed and all denominations placed on equal footing, but at the same time Protestant Christianity was to be established as the official religion, "the religion of the State to the utter exclusion forever of all and every other (falsely so called) Religion, whether Pagan or Papal...." No privileges were to be extended to Catholics. "You are to oppose the toleration of the popish idolatrous worship."

It is significant that in the Revolutionary period the toleration of non-Protestant belief was not a principle of the democrats but rather of the more liberal Whig leaders.[5] The hatreds bred by the religious wars of seventeenth-century Europe still lived in the hearts of back-country farmers, fostered by localism and the enthusiasm of the Great Awakening. Most democrats were certain that all Catholics would take orders from Rome in political matters and therefore could not be trusted with public office. They felt that a

4. "You are instructed to vote that no Chief Justice, Secretary of State, no Auditor General, no Surveyor General, no practicing lawyer, no clerk of any court of record, no sheriff and no person holding a military office in the State shall be a representative of the people in Congress or Convention. If this should not be confirmed, contend for it." *Ibid.*, 240.

5. The author of *The People the Best Governors*, for example, advocated a religious test for officeholding. Frederick Chase, *History of Dartmouth College* (Cambridge, 1891), 661.

refusal to acknowledge the plain and simple truths of the Protestant faith could arise only from sheer perversity or a desire to extend the sway of the Pope. The upper classes generally did not share the obsessions of the farmers who had received the gospel according to Tennent, Whitefield, and Jonathan Edwards. Eighteenth-century liberalism had largely dispelled any hatred the Whig leaders may have felt for Catholicism as a faith. Their quarrel was with the clerical state which compelled conformity in religious matters.

As in South Carolina and Maryland, the ardor of many North Carolina Whigs began to cool by the middle of 1775. Looking back nostalgically to the halcyon days before 1763, they reiterated their faith in the British constitution and prayed for an accommodation short of war. The Provincial Congress, meeting at Hillsborough, unanimously adopted a resolution to this effect written by Hooper which also explained to the British that committees and congresses were only temporary expedients and did not indicate an objection to monarchy. "As soon as the cause of our Fears and Apprehensions are removed," the resolution declared, "with joy will we return these powers to their regular channels; and such Institutions formed from mere necessity shall end with that necessity that created them." [6] Maurice Moore, in a clandestine letter to Governor Martin of January 9, 1776, surmised that the province as a whole wanted to return to its allegiance.[7] Johnston in April felt that a complete break from Britain would be extremely unwise unless foreign alliances were secured beforehand.[8] James Iredell probably spoke for many Whigs when he wrote in June: "The unhappy subject...independency...has led to the brink of

6. *Colonial Records*, X, 202.
7. *Ibid.*, 396.
8. Johnston to Hewes, April 4, 1776. Hayes Collection, North Carolina Department of History and Archives.

destruction. Some are enflamed enough to *wish* for independence and all are reduced to so unhappy a condition as to dread at least that they shall be compelled in their own defense to embrace it." [9]

It is fairly plain that fear of civil strife and doubt about the chances of success in a war with Britain were primary factors in shaping the outlook of these North Carolina Whigs. Yet by the spring of 1776 most of them realized that the course of events precluded any alternative except independence or submission, and submission was unthinkable. Armed conflict had broken out between Loyalists and Whigs in the back country. North Carolina, like Massachusetts, was at war. Britain had not backed down in the face of opposition as she had done before. Both antagonists were deeply committed to irreconcilable objectives. Hence the Provincial Congress, meeting at Halifax in April, empowered its delegates in the Continental Congress to vote for independence and prepared to frame a constitution. Although the vote regarding independence was unanimous, the attempt to write a constitution provoked a long and bitter struggle.

The historian Joseph Seawell Jones, who apparently had access to contemporary materials not available today, declared that there was a violent and "dominant" democratic element in the Congress arrayed against "the advocates of a splendid government." [10] Its influence was apparently so great that the committee to draft a constitution, which included many of the colonial leaders, resolved after several days of deliberation "to establish a purely democratic form

9. Griffith J. McRee, *Life and Correspondence of James Iredell*, 2 Vols. (New York, 1857), I, 321-322. A one volume reprint edition is available (New York, 1949).

10. Joseph S. Jones, *A Defense of the Revolutionary History of the State of North Carolina from the Aspersions of Mr. Jefferson* (Boston and Raleigh, 1834), 135.

of government."[11] After an altercation over bicameralism and suffrage,[12] a compromise plan was worked out which called for a two-house legislature with both houses elected by the people. The suffrage would be wide, but the principle of restriction would be retained. Householders would be qualified to elect the lower house and freeholders the upper. A popularly elected president and council would exercise executive functions.[13] Apparently the democratic group also succeeded in inserting a provision for the election of county court judges.[14] Conservatives, violently opposed to an elective judiciary, wanted a balanced government similar to that proposed by Adams and Jefferson with an upper house and council nominated by the lower house and an independent judiciary. The problem, as Johnston saw it, was "how to establish a check on the representatives of the people," or in other words, how to impose restraints on the elected branches of the government.[15]

Apparently the faction striving for a democratic government was strong enough to cause Johnston serious concern. "From what I can at present collect of their [the committee's] plan," he wrote to Iredell, "it will be impossible for me to take any part in the execution of it. Numbers have started in the race of popularity, and condescend to the usual means of success."[16] But the success of the democratic group was short-lived. The committee apparently could not draft a complete instrument but merely reported a series of resolu-

11. *Ibid.*, 278. Jones makes the statement as a quotation. Since there is no such resolution on the journal, it must have been made by the drafting committee.

12. Frank Nash, *The North Carolina Constitution of 1776 and its Makers,* James Sprunt Historical *Publications,* XI (1912), No. 2, pp. 13-14.

13. McRee, *Iredell,* I, 278.

14. Jones, *Defense of North Carolina,* 134-135.

15. McRee, *Iredell,* I, 276.

16. *Ibid.*

tions to the House, April 27,[17] which never came to a vote. On April 30 the attempt to write a constitution was dropped for the time being—probably indicating a complete deadlock —and a new committee was appointed to draft a temporary plan to be in effect until the end of the next Congress.

Johnston's reputation suffered because of his opposition to the proposals of the democratic faction.[18] Although President of the Congress he was denied a seat on the drafting committee for the temporary form of government and on the new Council of Safety. The inveterate opposition of the radicals continued even after adjournment, wrote Jones, "and many, even of the most respectable of the Whigs, professed to doubt the sincerity of his attachment to the American cause ... the private letters of that day exhibit a well-concerted scheme of intrigue to ruin his character as a patriot and statesman." [19]

Circumstances suggest that the democratic faction, defeated in the Congress, attempted an indirect appeal to the people. A short time before the end of the session a resolution was passed urging the voters to "pay the greatest attention" to the coming elections of October for the Congress which would draft and put into effect fundamental law.[20] "The idea was constantly put forth," says Jones, "that the Conservatives were intent upon the erection of a system of

17. On April 27, the House went into committee of the whole to consider the resolutions proposed for a constitution. *Colonial Records*, X, 545. The first attempt to form a constitution in North Carolina is summarized in Fletcher M. Green, *Constitutional Development in the South Atlantic States, 1776-1860: A Study in the Evolution of Democracy* (Chapel Hill, 1930), 47-50.

18. Johnston had written to Iredell with apparent satisfaction on May 2, "Affairs have taken a turn within a few days past. All ideas of forming a permanent constitution at this time are laid aside." McRee, *Iredell*, I, 279.

19. Jones, *Defense of North Carolina*, 282.

20. *Colonial Records*, X, 696. Green, *Constitutional Development in the South Atlantic States*, 66.

government adverse to the liberty of the people, and that they were in reality the advocates of monarchy." [21] The resolution may also indicate a dim realization that a special mandate was needed for the formation of fundamental law.

From all accounts the North Carolina elections of October, 1776, were among the most hotly contested in the state's history. Riots were a common occurrence, particularly in the piedmont. According to R. D. W. Connor, historian of the state, "Abner Nash in New Bern and Thomas Jones in Chowan, both conservatives, won seats only by narrow margins from constituencies in which they had rarely had serious opposition. In New Hanover so strong was the opposition to William Hooper that, to assure his having a seat in the convention, Cornelius Harnett relinquished his hold on the borough of Wilmington in Hooper's favor, himself standing for election in Brunswick county." [22] Samuel Spencer, a determined foe of the Regulators, was defeated in Anson. The climax of the campaign was the fight in Chowan County against Johnston. Although President of two of the four Revolutionary Congresses, he was resoundingly defeated and burned in effigy by his opponents. Willie Jones, of Halifax, one of the wealthiest men in the province but reputed to have democratic leanings, was elected.

The elections spurred Iredell, who had campaigned for his brother-in-law, Johnston, to write a revealing little squib entitled *Creed of a Rioter*. Although an exaggerated and bitter satire of democratic aspirations, it nevertheless reveals indirectly some of the main issues of the election. Primarily it shows the extent to which political alignments were based on class. "I am the sworn enemy to all gentlemen," the *Rioter* declares. "I believe none in that station of life can possibly possess either honor or virtue.... I impute

21. Jones, *Defense of North Carolina,* 283.
22. Connor, *History of North Carolina,* I, 411-412.

to *gentlemen* all our present difficulties.... I am of the opinion that our affairs would prosper much better if gentlemen who read and consider too deeply for us were totally banished from our public business." The *Rioter* labels all who are not of his political persuasion Tories, and boasts that he has no respect for private property. Finally he distrusts the gentry because of their latitudinarianism on religion. "I am none of those overwise and *irreligious* men." [23] Stripped of its hyperbole, the *Creed* would bear comparison with some of the Regulator papers.

Yet after the sound and fury had died, it is doubtful whether the democratic faction had strengthened its position in the Congress. Although there were many new names on the roster of delegates, and although the West had sent only men known for their opposition to the aristocracy, yet the colonial leaders of long standing had their usual ascendency. Moreover, events had put the conservatives in a much stronger position than they had enjoyed at the April meeting.

In the first place, Maryland, Virginia, South Carolina, Delaware, and New Jersey had adopted constitutions on the Adams model. Secondly, William Hooper, a delegate to the Continental Congress during 1776, had condemned democratic government in a series of letters to the North Carolina body. "I am well assured," he wrote, "that the British constitution in its purity (for what is at present stiled the British constitution is an apostate), was a system that approached as near to perfection as any could within the compass of human abilities." [24] It afforded an opportunity for the "selected few whom superior talents or better opportunities for improvement had raised into a second class" to exercise their leadership without danger of a degeneration into tyranny.

23. McRee, *Iredell*, I, 335-336.
24. *Colonial Records*, X, 866.

He echoed Adams in his abhorrence of unicameralism. "A single branch of legislation is a many-headed monster which without any check must soon defeat the very purposes for which it was created, and its members become a tyranny dreadful in proportion to the numbers which compose it." [25] Eventually it would make its own political existence perpetual. The democratic Constitution of Pennsylvania, with its one-house legislature, was for Hooper the apotheosis of all that was evil in government. It had been adopted by the Pennsylvania Convention in the fall of 1776 and its reception by Whig leaders seemed to give some promise of repudiation by the people.[26]

In addition to the state constitutions already ratified and Hooper's polemic against unicameralism, the conservatives in the November Congress had another piece of heavy artillery in their armament—*Thoughts on Government*. It will be recalled that Adams had originally written the pamphlet for Hooper and Penn. It apparently did not exert much influence on the April Congress, possibly because it did not

25. *Ibid.*, 867. Green, *Constitutional Development in the South Atlantic States*, 68.

26. See below, pp. 271-282. The Philadelphia conservatives, who styled themselves Anti-Constitutionalists and later Republicans, called a series of meetings to protest against the new instrument. For a while it looked as if they could muster enough strength to call another convention or at least prevent a government from functioning under the Constitution. But by spring of 1777 the pressure of the western part of the state in favor of the Constitution had made itself felt, and a government was formed. Hooper overestimated the extent of Republican sentiment. He wrote to Hewes, October 27, "The monster the people called a government has expired with the political existence of those who created it, and Cannon and Matlack, with some other factious demagogues, have slunk back into their pristine obscurity." Hayes Collection, North Carolina Department of History and Archives. By November 1 he realized that the Constitution was not as dead as he had thought. In discouragement and alarm he wrote again to Hewes, "If Matlack's system prevails, farewell to this country." *Ibid.*

arrive until the session was nearly over, but by November it had been printed and was so highly esteemed that it was written into the executive letter book. Sikes, in his *Transition of North Carolina from Colony to Commonwealth,* believes it was of great importance in shaping the final draft of the constitution.[27]

The democratic program in the convention was summed up in the instructions of Mecklenburg and Orange counties to their representatives. These two documents, taken together, are among the most complete and articulate statements of democratic aspirations to come out of North Carolina during the Revolutionary period.[28] The Mecklenburg instructions were written by Waightstill Avery and John M. Alexander, two figures who had played an important part in the drafting of the Mecklenburg papers of 1775. Those of Orange are in the handwriting of Thomas Burke.[29]

Burke was a remarkable man, and his life in many ways typifies the course of some Revolutionary democrats. Born in Ireland, he received a good education and came to the colonies to make his fortune. After studying medicine and law, he settled down to practice both in Orange County. In the Provincial Congress of April, 1776, he was a member of the committee which drafted the temporary form of government and apparently a leader of the democratic faction.[30]

27. Enoch W. Sikes, *The Transition of North Carolina from Colony to Commonwealth* (Baltimore, 1898), Johns Hopkins *Studies* in History and Political Science, XVI, 557-560.

28. Orange and Mecklenburg were presumably the only two counties which instructed representatives. No instructions from other counties have been found.

29. *Colonial Records,* X, 870a, 870f.

30. Hooper wrote to Hewes, April 17, "Abner Nash and Burke are framing a Constitution for this colony to preserve it from total anarchy. They differ very materially in their ideas from Mr. Johnson, Penn, and

Appointed a delegate to the Continental Congress, he enunciated the doctrine of state sovereignty during the debate over Dickinson's draft of the Articles of Confederation. Yet by 1780 Burke's fondness for democracy and decentralization began to abate, probably because of the civil war in North Carolina and because Congress could not provide adequate military support against Cornwallis's invasion. In 1781 he served a term as governor but left office severely criticized for breaking his parole to the commander of the British army in Charleston after capture by Loyalist guerillas. He died a few years later, bitter because of what he believed to be shabby treatment by the state. Thoroughly disillusioned by popular government, he wrote during his brief retirement some of the severest indictments of democracy which have come down to us from the Revolutionary period.[31]

The Orange and Mecklenburg instructions at the outset show a clear realization of the distinction between constituent and legislative power. "Political power is of two kinds," they declare in identical language, "one principal and superior, the other derived and inferior.... The principal supreme power is possessed only by the people at large... the derived and inferior power by the servants which they employ.... Whatever persons are delegated, chosen, employed and intrusted by the people are their servants and can possess only derived inferior power.... The rules by which the inferior power is to be exercised are to be constituted by the principal supreme power, and can be altered, suspended and abrogated by the same and no other...."[32] The instruc-

---

myself." Hayes Collection, North Carolina Department of History and Archives.

31. For a detailed biographical sketch, see Elisha P. Douglass, "Thomas Burke, Disillusioned Democrat," *North Carolina Historical Review*, XXVI (1949), 150-186.

32. *Colonial Records*, X, 870b, 870f, 870g.

tions did not call for a constitutional convention, which might be expected as the logical result of any distinction between fundamental law and statute law, but they did demand that the finished instrument be sent to the counties for popular ratification before being put in force.[33]

The instructions proceed on the assumption that only a democratic form of government can satisfy the requirements of the theory they assert. Thus Mecklenburg ordered its representatives to "endeavor to establish a free government under the authority of the people of the State of North Carolina and that the Government be a simple Democracy or as near it as possible.... In fixing the fundamental principles of Government you shall oppose everything that leans to aristocracy or power in the hands of the rich and chief men exercised to the oppression of the poor." [34] Both counties demanded approximately the same institutional framework. Orange wanted a two-house legislature with both branches responsible to the people and an elective executive.[35] Mecklenburg wanted clerk and sheriffs to be chosen by the voters of each county. Also Mecklenburg favored a unicameral legislature,[36] was silent on the executive. Both sets of instructions call for a separation of powers, meaning—in this instance—the abolition of plural officeholding and the division of functions but not the establishment of governmental organs independent of the electorate. As expressed in the document from Orange, "No person shall be capable of acting in the exercise of any more than one of these branches at the same time lest they should fail of being proper checks on each other and by

33. *Ibid.*, 870d, 870g.
34. *Ibid.*, 870a.
35. *Ibid.*, 870h.
36. On the margin of the Mecklenburg instructions was a notation that the people in public meeting had voted against a bicameral legislature. *Ibid.*, 870a.

their united influence become dangerous to any individual who might oppose the ambitious designs of persons who might be employed in such power." [37]

In religious matters both sets of instructions call for the separation of church and state and a religious test for office designed to exclude Catholics. Mecklenburg referred to the Catholics by name; Orange denied the privilege of office-holding to any who "acknowledge supremacy eccelesiastical or civil in any foreign power or spiritual infallibility or authority to grant the Divine Pardon to any person who may violate moral duties or commit crimes injurious to the community." [38]

Scattered through the instructions are some of the demands for reform legislation reiterated over the past ten years. Appeals were made for taxation in proportion to wealth, salaried justices of the county courts, the establishment of a college in the West, changes in attachment laws and the lowering of court fees, and elections by ballot.[39]

The Orange instructions alone refer to suffrage requirements, and neither set mentions property qualifications for officeholding. As far as Mecklenburg is concerned, manhood suffrage was probably implicit in the demand for a democratic government. In Orange, however, the drafters made a concession to Whig theory in principle if not in fact by limiting suffrage for the lower house to householders and for the upper house to freeholders.[40] These provisions probably disqualified few potential voters; the only free men denied the franchise for the lower house would be adult sons living under the paternal roof and the freehold qualification for

37. *Ibid.*, 870h.
38. *Ibid.*, 870g. This would presumably apply to Recusants as well as Papists.
39. *Ibid.*, 870a-870h.
40. *Ibid.*, 870h.

the upper house was not difficult to meet. Land was easy to acquire and most of the squatters in Orange, Granville, and Guilford counties automatically became freeholders in 1774 when the Provincial Congress recognized possession of land as title in an attempt to settle the confused situation resulting from the closing of Lord Granville's land office.

When the Congress met November 12 the attempt to form a constitution went much more smoothly than in April. The democratic faction seems to have been weaker in spite of an apparent unity of sentiment in Mecklenburg and Orange. The conservatives probably held the balance of power on the drafting committee,[41] for the instrument reported to the house on December 6 was closer to the views of Johnston and Hooper than to those of the piedmont and frontier counties. Johnston himself, who was in Halifax at the time on business, gave it grudging endorsement. "As well as I can judge from a cursory view of it," he wrote to Iredell, "it may do as well as that adopted by any other colony." [42] But the document incorporated at least one of the demands of the democrats—the popular election of county court judges.

The draft was debated and amended periodically from December 9 until December 18, when it was finally passed.[43] Although cast in the Whig form, the Constitution was considerably more democratic than any other already adopted except that of Pennsylvania. Probably this characteristic resulted from the efforts of a minority which Johnston described as "a set of men without reading, experience, or principle," and which moved him to remark, "Everyone who has the least pretensions to be a gentleman is suspected

41. *Ibid.*, 918-919. Several more western members were later added, however.

42. McRee, *Iredell*, I, 337.

43. *Colonial Records*, X, 962-963, 974.

and born down *per ignobile vulgus.*" [44] Both houses of the legislature were to be directly elected, although the upper by a somewhat smaller constituency than the lower. The suffrage qualifications were relatively low. Tax-paying freemen could vote for members of the lower house and fifty-acre freeholders for members of the Senate (Arts. 7, 8.).[45] Since taxation was by poll, all males over twenty-one except sons living under their paternal roof, apprentices, slaves, and indentured servants were enfranchised.

Several articles of the Constitution can be traced to demands for reform originating during the Regulator disturbances. For example, "no Persons who heretofore have been or hereafter may be receivers of public monies, shall have a seat in either house of General Assembly, or be eligible to any office in this state, until such person shall have fully accounted for and paid into the treasury all sums for which they may be directly accountable and liable" (Art. 25). Treasurers would not be eligible for future public office until they had settled their accounts at the end of their terms (Art. 26). The governor, judges of the Supreme Court and

44. McRee, *Iredell,* I, 336-337, 338. The authorship of the Constitution has been the subject of considerable discussion. McRee attributes the instrument to Thomas Jones, a lawyer of Chowan and a friend of Johnston. McRee, *Iredell,* I, 337. Joseph S. Jones notes that Johnston refers in one of his letters to "Jones' constitution." *Defense of North Carolina,* 287. In another place, Joseph S. Jones states that Willie Jones collaborated in the work. *Ibid.,* 139. Richard Caswell, President of the Congress, and Thomas Burke may have had a hand in it. Blackwell P. Robinson, "Willie Jones of Halifax," *North Carolina Historical Review,* XVIII (1941), 24; Nash, *The North Carolina Constitution of 1776,* James Sprunt Historical *Publications,* XI, no. 2, p. 21. Burke was returned in a special election as a member for Orange after the Congress had upheld charges of irregularities in the original election. Before he took his seat, however, he was present in Hillsborough and in constant contact with the drafting committee.

45. The Constitution is printed in Francis N. Thorpe, *Federal and State Constitutions,* 7 Vols. (Washington, 1909), V, 2787-2794.

Admiralty Court, and the attorney-general were put on salary, thus partially relieving litigants of burdensome court fees. The separation of powers in the democratic sense was partially secured by the disqualification of these judges and the chief administrative officers from seats in the legislature or Council of State (Arts. 29, 30). The demands of democratic groups regarding religion were adopted in their entirety. The Anglican Church was disestablished, support of religion was to be voluntary, all denominations were put on equal footing, and Catholics were barred from public office.[46] A provision abolishing imprisonment for debt was written into the Constitution (Art. 39). The state recognized a responsibility to establish public schools and "one or more universities" (Art. 41), and the legislature was enjoined to "regulate intails in such a manner as to prevent perpetuities" (Art. 43).

Although the suffrage was widened by the Constitution, an unfair representation was solidified into fundamental law. Each county, regardless of population, was allotted two representatives and one senator, and borough towns were given one representative apiece (Arts. 2, 3). Although this was an improvement over the colonial system in that the tidewater counties were deprived of the tremendous advantage of five representatives each, nevertheless, the populous piedmont was still relatively outweighed in the legislature. Representation in proportion to population was not even recognized in principle, as it was in the more aristocratic

46. Any person who "shall deny the being of God, or the truth of the Protestant religion... or hold religious principles incompatible with the freedom and safety of the state" was disqualified (Arts. 34, 32). The provision against Catholics was uniformly disregarded, however, for several prominent Catholics held office before the Constitution was altered in 1835 to disqualify only those who denied the truth of the Christian religion. W. K. Boyd, *History of North Carolina: The Federal Period* (Chicago, 1919), 146, 163-164.

constitutions of New York and Massachusetts. Apparently it was the indifference of the piedmont to the issue rather than any opposition from tidewater conservatives which was responsible for the failure to reform the existing system. During the Revolutionary period, western sections of Virginia and Maryland, as well as North Carolina, tacitly acquiesced to the discrimination against them. Jefferson's demand for proportionate representation was not echoed in the Valley of Virginia,[47] nor did the inhabitants of Frederick County, Maryland, apparently object to equal representation of all counties in the Assembly. Beginning about 1790, however, reform of the representation became a burning issue in all of the southern states.[48]

One important democratic demand was ignored entirely. The Constitution was not submitted to popular ratification but was put in force by the Congress which drafted it. This procedure in theory, if not in practice, largely rendered nugatory the distinction between primary and derived power emphasized by the Orange and Mecklenburg instructions. Perhaps as a token concession, however, the Congress sent one copy of the Constitution to each county.[49]

Property qualifications for officeholding to some extent countered the advantage the people had gained in the low suffrage requirements. Members of the lower house were required to own 100 acres of land, senators 300, and the governor a freehold worth £1000 (Arts. 5, 6, 15). Probably these stipulations, in the case of legislators, restricted candidates to the upper ranks of the yeoman farmers; in the case of the governor, to the planter class. Although judges of the

47. Freeman H. Hart, *The Valley of Virginia in the American Revolution* (Chapel Hill, 1942), 64.
48. Green, *Constitutional Development in the South Atlantic States,* chs. 4 and 5.
49. *Colonial Records,* X, 974.

Supreme Court were salaried, administration of justice in the counties was still supported by the fee system.

The prohibition against plural officeholding among the highest officials did nothing to break the connection between courthouse rings and Assembly. Justices of the peace were still appointed by the governor on recommendation of the respective county delegates (Art. 33) and they were specifically exempted from any general prohibition against plural officeholding (Art. 35). No decision was made as to the method of appointing sheriffs, coroners, and constables, so in the absence of any new provision, they would be chosen again by the governor or by the county court as in the colonial period. Thus the Constitution failed in large measure to inaugurate responsible local government; the courthouse rings remained intact, if shorn of some of their opportunities for graft.

Democrats probably considered the Bill of Rights a victory which materially added to their qualified gains because its twenty-five articles accorded a specific recognition of the supremacy of the people as stated in the instructions of Orange and Mecklenburg counties. Actually, however, the document did little to advance the cause of democracy. The bills of rights in the first state constitutions were valuable as the basis for restricting the sphere of governmental authority and as expressions of liberal political philosophy, but they did nothing to make government more responsive to the people. The attainment of democracy required political equality and majority rule; theoretical restrictions on governmental authority and assertions of popular sovereignty, while salutary, could not accomplish the objective alone. As long as the constitutions restricted political privileges and maintained classified citizenship, the popular sovereignty emblazoned on the fundamental law of the new states was a symbol rather than an operative principle. At the time they were written, the effect of the bills was to emphasize the liberal ideals of the Revolutionary constitutions.

Thus democracy in North Carolina did not advance as far as might be expected considering the accumulated grievances of the piedmont farmers resulting in the Regulator War, the strength of the democratic faction in the spring of 1776, and the development of democratic ideas illustrated by the Orange and Mecklenburg instructions. The most important reason perhaps was the lack of leadership among those opposed to the Whig ruling class. The labored expression and sometimes primitive political conceptions of the Regulator papers, and the helplessness of the yeoman farmers in the grip of the courts bear eloquent testimony to what some Regulators called "our invincible ignorance." A man from the lower orders with the qualities of leadership was ambitious to become a gentleman; hence he utilized any success or wealth he achieved to pass into the ruling class and adopt its credo. There was no one who would say, as Eugene Debs was to do later, "I do not wish to rise from the lower classes, but with them." Men like Burke or Nash, who had shown democratic sympathies in April, 1776, were apparently content with the qualifications of their ideas injected into the Constitution. Thus there were few, if any leaders in responsible positions who would press for literal acceptance of democratic demands as outlined in the various papers from Orange and Mecklenburg counties.

Also, the yeoman farmer, recognizing his limitations, tended to accept the ruling class as a more or less inevitable condition of life. To men who could not read—and a majority of the farmers were illiterate or semiliterate—a property qualification for office was academic. Even if elected, they would be incapable of participating in a representative body. Hence of necessity they were compelled to turn to the rich and powerful in order to secure effective government. Moreover the yeoman farmers had a natural identity of economic interests with the rich planters. Both groups shared a conviction of the sacredness of private property and both were interested in the considerations which dominate a farmer's world—high prices for crops, cheap land, cheap money, and low tariffs. For these reasons the yeoman farmers were more inclined to entrust their political destinies to the planters than they would have if there had been serious economic conflict. Finally, the Constitution as adopted gave the farmers a considerably more equitable and representative government than they had known under the crown. The Whig aristocrats had repudiated arbitrary government and had reiterated their devotion to the rights of equal importance to all classes. Under the circumstances, therefore, the aristocrats by inclination, interest, and training promised to be adequate trustees of the public welfare.

NINE

Revolution and Internal Conflict in

Massachusetts, 1774-1776

THE Revolution produced in Massachusetts a democratic movement more articulate and sustained, but ultimately no more successful than the one in North Carolina. Yet the advocates of political equality and majority rule in the Bay State made a signal contribution to democracy by showing its intimate connection with the compact theory of government and by making the philosophic doctrines of the Revolutionary leaders the justification for internal reform as well as for separation from Britain. The Whig leaders had contended in their struggle with Britain that compact and consent were the only justifiable bases for the formation and administration of government; the Massachusetts democrats were to demonstrate that only democratic political procedures and relationships could realize these concepts in practice.

As in North Carolina, class and sectional tensions had occasionally appeared in Massachusetts during the eighteenth century. Back-country farmers protested often against high legal and court fees, and occasionally against the engrossment of vast tracts of land on the frontier by speculating town proprietors.[1] Plural officeholding excited much more resentment than it did in the South. Most of the provincial councillors sat on the benches of the higher courts and the town delegates were often judges of the lower courts and justices of the peace.[2] But objections to the practice were based to some extent on political considerations; although the Whig leaders denounced the plural officeholding of Hutchinson and his clique, a bill to prevent members of the legislature from sitting on the bench of the Superior Court was defeated by the House of Representatives in 1762.[3]

The attempt in 1740 to found a land bank empowered to issue notes secured by mortgages and other evidences of indebtedness provoked a sharp struggle between debtor and creditor classes. The merchants of the seaboard towns, fearing the danger of runaway inflation, bitterly opposed the scheme and banded together for a last-ditch fight against "the needy part of the province," "the Mobility," "the Idle and Extravagant."[4] Prompt action by Governor Belcher forestalled an attempt by back-country farmers to march on Boston and join local advocates of the bank scheme in forcing "the griping and merciless usurers" to accept the bank's paper. When Parliament declared the bank scheme illegal, "its belated action in clamping the lid on colonial radicalism

1. The standard monograph on the town proprietors is, Roy H. Akagi, *The Town Proprietors of the New England Colonies* (Philadelphia, 1924).

2. The career of Hutchinson provides an illustration of the extent to which plural officeholding was carried. In 1762 he was at once Lieutenant Governor of the province, Commander of the Castle, member of the Council, Judge of Probate for Suffolk County, and Chief Justice of the Superior Court. He had no formal legal training. Ellen E. Brennan, *Plural Officeholding in Massachusetts, 1760-1780* (Chapel Hill, 1945), 32.

3. *Ibid.*, 50.

4. John C. Miller, "Religion, Finance, and Democracy," *New England Quarterly*, VI (1933), 31. See also the discussion of the Land Bank in J. T. Adams, *Revolutionary New England, 1691-1776* (Boston, 1923), pp. 155-160.

saved Massachusetts from passing under the control of the common people, but it did not extinguish democracy or ill-feeling between rich and poor." [5] John Adams stated in 1774 that "the act to destroy the Land Bank scheme raised a greater ferment in this province than the Stamp Act did." [6] The Great Awakening, in full tide at the time of the Land Bank episode, also played a part in provoking internal conflict. When revivalist preachers like Gilbert Tennent and James Davenport declared many clergymen of note to be "unregenerate," sneered at education, and denied the ability of the established churches to save souls, conservatives among the clergy struck back by making strenuous efforts to silence or drive out the revivalists. This policy aroused antagonism on the part of humble and enthusiastic believers. [7]

A more important result of the Great Awakening was the impetus it gave to the demands for religious freedom. Under the Charter of 1691 all town inhabitants, regardless of religious belief, were taxed for the support of the Congregational Church. This raised so much opposition from dissenters that the General Court, beginning in 1728, passed a series of exemption acts which allowed them to pay their religious taxes toward the support of their own churches. But this indulgence did not satisfy the communicants of unofficial faiths. Only Baptists, Anglicans, and Quakers were accorded recognition, and claimants could only obtain exemptions by proving that they were members in good standing of an established church. [8] Many communities nullified the

5. Miller, "Religion, Finance, and Democracy," *New England Quarterly*, VI, 41.
6. Charles F. Adams (ed.), *The Works of John Adams*, 10 Vols. (Boston, 1850-1856), IV, 49.
7. Miller, "Religion, Finance, and Democracy," *New England Quarterly*, VI, 37-54.
8. For summaries of this legislation see Alvah Hovey, *A Memoir of the Life and Times of Isaac Backus* (Boston, 1859), 167-172; Isaac Backus,

exemption laws, and dissenters there who refused to pay the rate for church support suffered distraints and considerable mistreatment. In all cases they were compelled to spend much time and money in the courts in order to legalize their status. Because of religious conflict, therefore, the separation of church and state became a much more important issue in Massachusetts than in North Carolina, where the Anglican church was too weak to secure enforcement of the laws for its support.

The Baptists found an articulate and resourceful leader in Isaac Backus, pastor of the Baptist church in Middleboro. A product of the Great Awakening, he was born and brought up in Norwich, Connecticut, where his mother had been periodically imprisoned for failure to pay the rates for support of the established church. Becoming first a Separate Congregationalist and then a Baptist,[9] he settled at Middleboro and started a campaign to abolish taxation for religious purposes. Backus probably spoke for many dissenters when he wrote in a pamphlet of 1773, "Those who now speak great swelling words about *Liberty* are themselves servants of corruption." [10] Like the Regulators, he accused the Whig leaders of maintaining at home the very abuse for which they denounced Parliament: "You tell us you are taxed where you are not represented. Is it not really so with us? You do not deny the right of the British parliament to impose taxes within her own realm; only complain that she extends her

---

A History of New England with Particular Reference to the Denomination of Christians Called Baptists, 2nd ed., 2 Vols. (Newton, 1871), II, 140-142; Anson P. Stokes, *Church and State in the United States,* 3 Vols. (New York, 1950), I, 418-423.

9. Hovey, *Backus,* 60. This was a familiar progression because Separates usually were not recognized as a separate sect and so could not claim exemption.

10. Isaac Backus, *An Appeal to the Public for Religious Liberty* (Boston, 1773), 3.

taxing power beyond her proper limits; and have we not
as good a right to say you do the same thing? And wherein
you judge others you condemn yourselves? Can three thousand miles possibly fix such limits to the taxing power as
the difference between civil and sacred matters has already
done?" [11]

The religious conflict led many Baptists to oppose independence because separation from Britain would remove
the last check on the Congregational church.[12] But none
of them appear to have become active Tories, probably because the small towns in which Baptist churches were
located were also centers of Whig sentiment. Most Baptists
probably shared Backus's attitude of suspicion and reproach
and perhaps like him hoped to obtain guarantees of religious
freedom in return for a nominal support of the Revolutionary movement. In a letter to Sam Adams of January, 1774,
Backus reiterated his demand for complete abolition of
religious taxation and ended on an ominous note by expressing the hope "that so large a number of as peaceable people
and as hearty friends to their country as any in the land, may
not be forced to carry their complaints before those who
would be glad to hear that the Legislature of Massachusetts
deny to their fellow servants that liberty which they so
earnestly insist upon for themselves. A word to the wise is
sufficient." [13]

When the First Continental Congress met, Backus prevailed upon other Baptist leaders in New England to send
him to Philadelphia to plead the cause of religious liberty

11. *Ibid.*, 54.

12. Backus, in his *History*, quotes with approval a passage of a letter
from a friend: "Formerly there was a check on the licentiousness of
power in America by an appeal to the crown; but where shall the perse-
cuted Americans appeal now? They can only appeal to their oppressors
and accusers." Backus, *History*, II, vii.

13. Hovey, *Backus*, 197.

before the assembled delegates. He was cordially received in the city of brotherly love by his coreligionists and had conferences with Israel and James Pemberton, outstanding Quaker leaders. They persuaded him not to appear before Congress but to confer with the Massachusetts representatives—the two Adamses, Thomas Cushing, and Robert T. Paine—at a private meeting. Possibly the Pembertons suggested this move because they did not want in any way to recognize the Congress, but more likely they wanted an opportunity to humiliate the leaders of the radical faction by calling into question the sincerity of their devotion to the cause of freedom. Thus when Adams and his friends arrived for what they expected would be a small and friendly conference, they were surprised to find a large and hostile gathering of Philadelphia Quakers and moderates who subjected them to some rather sharp criticism of the Massachusetts ecclesiastical establishment.[14] Adams confessed he was somewhat "warm" at what he regarded as an underhanded trick on the part of that "artful Jesuit," Israel Pemberton. The delegates minimized the Massachusetts establishment as a "very slender one" and promised to do what they could to make the obtaining of exemptions easier, but they would not relinquish the principle of state support for religion.

As will be described later, the Baptists kept up their agitation throughout the Revolutionary period. The districts where they were numerous generally became strongly democratic.

Internal conflicts in Massachusetts, while occasionally bitter, did not grow to the proportions reached in the South partly because of the representative local government. Town

14. Both Adams and Backus have left full accounts of this meeting. See Adams, *Works*, II, 398-400; Hovey, *Backus*, 204-213. There is a shorter account in Backus's *History*, II, 201-202.

meetings of all adult, free males performed the legislative functions carried out by the southern county courts such as levying local taxes and holding officials to account. Executive duties were performed by selectmen responsible to the meetings. Town representatives in the General Court were delegates in the truest sense. Although chosen by a restricted electorate (the forty-shilling freeholders), they were instructed by and were responsible to the full town meeting. Local government in Massachusetts, by providing a forum for debate, machinery for rectifying local grievances, and a means of expressing the will of the people in the provincial legislature, therefore made possible the peaceful and legal settlement of disputes which could only be solved by violence in North Carolina.

The larger issues of Parliamentary taxation, royal instructions to governors, and "improper" use of the prerogative power probably also tended to mitigate local controversies. The appeals of the Baptists for religious freedom were drowned out by the thunderous warnings of the clergy against an impending American episcopate and the spread of Catholicism via the Quebec Act. The Revolutionary ferment diverted attention from the "griping usurers" of Boston to the grasping ministry which would squeeze the last farthing from every man-jack in the province. The plural officeholding of Whig politicians was temporarily overlooked in the general denunciation of Hutchinson's attempt to monopolize political patronage. Grievances originating in Britain certainly loomed larger than those arising from sectional and class tensions.

But with the suppression of royal government, local issues assumed a new importance. An alarming lawlessness prevalent throughout the province—perhaps in some measure the result of discontent with internal conditions—led county conventions to urge the people "not to engage in any riots, routs, or licentious attacks on the property of any persons whatsoever" (presumably Tories as well as Whigs).[15] The militia companies, often officered in the lower ranks by men outside the ruling class, were increasingly hard to control. As in Maryland, the defenders of their country sometimes showed scant regard for traditional social distinctions and apparently felt that their sacrifices gave them a claim to a higher regard than they had been accorded in the past. Dr. Joseph Warren, later to become the martyr of Bunker Hill, wrote in November, 1774, "It will require a very masterly policy to keep this province, for any considerable time longer, in its present state." [16] By May of 1775 he was much more insistent. "I see more and more the necessity of establishing civil government here, and such a government as shall be sufficient to control the military forces." He declared to Sam Adams, "I assure you, *inter nos,* that unless some authority sufficient to restrain the irregularities of the army is established, we shall soon find ourselves involved in greater difficulties than you can imagine. The least hint from the most unprincipled fellow, who has perhaps been reproved for criminal behavior, is quite sufficient to expose the fairest character to insult and abuse among many.... My great wish, therefore, is that we may restrain everything which tends to weaken the principles of right and wrong, more especially with regard to property." [17] Warren and other Whig leaders felt that the Revolution might result in the exchange of British tyranny for military dictatorship. "As an army is now

15. Suffolk Resolves, in *Journals of Each Provincial Congress of Massachusetts* (Boston, 1838), 605. For similar statements of other county conventions, see *ibid.,* 627, 651, 653-654.

16. Richard Frothingham, *Life and Times of Joseph Warren* (Boston, 1865), 395.

17. *Ibid.,* 495.

necessary, it is obvious to everyone if they are without control, a military government will certainly take place." [18] Ephraim Doolittle echoed this fear when he warned that only civil government could thwart "ambitious men who are endeavoring to break our companies in pieces to get promotion." [19] Elbridge Gerry informed the Massachusetts delegation in Congress that "[the people] now feel rather too much their own importance...from the frequent delineation of their rights,...and it requires great skill to produce such subordination as is necessary. This takes place principally in the army." [20]

Responding to the needs of the hour, the Provincial Congress in 1775 took steps to legitimatize its rule. In South Carolina and New Hampshire the necessity for sovereign powers was met by the establishment of "temporary" constitutions in late '75 and early '76, but in Massachusetts an even better expedient was at hand—"resumption" of the colonial Charter. The Whig leaders had consistently maintained that the Massachusetts Government Acts, which had altered the Charter in order to establish centralized British control, were illegal. From this premise it was logically possible to argue that since the Government Acts were null and void, the Charter must still be in force. On the other hand, the compact theory of government led to a quite opposite conclusion. Locke had made it very plain that when the social compact between rulers and ruled is broken by either party, the people revert to a state of nature and remain in this condition until the formation of a new compact. A few radicals, relying on the Lockean logic, asserted that the Government Acts, by destroying the compact with the crown symbolized by the Charter, entitled the people "to

18. *Ibid.*, 485.
19. *American Archives,* 4th Ser., II, 177.
20. *Ibid.*, 905.

take what form of government they pleased," [21] but the Provincial Congress preferred to consider the Charter still in force.[22] Such a position had two obvious advantages: it would keep the door open for reconciliation and would shift the onus of revolutionary intent to Gage and the Tories. By "resuming" the Charter the Whig leaders could have their cake and eat it too, for they would establish a government which would be at once sovereign, independent, and ostensibly constitutional.

Before taking such a step, however, the Provincial Congress felt the need for outside support. On May 12, 1775, the Massachusetts body asked the Continental Congress to recommend a form of government, after previously informing the colony's delegates in Philadelphia that a resumption of the Charter would answer the purpose. Although John Adams, characteristically independent, argued for a complete seizure of the sovereignty by means of a constitutional convention,[23] a majority in the Continental Congress advised on June 9 that a new government "as near as may be to the spirit and substance of the Charter" be established by the election of a House of Representatives empowered to choose a Council. In perhaps unconscious imitation of the tradition of 1688, Congress recommended that the governor and lieutenant governor be considered "absent" because of their unconstitutional rule. But the avenue to reconciliation was kept open by a provision that the new regime was to last only until "a governor of His Majesty's appointment will consent to govern the Colony according to its Charter." [24]

Apparently the need for a legitimate government in Massa-

21. Frothingham, *Warren*, 376.
22. *American Archives*, 4th Ser., I, 850.
23. Adams, *Works*, III, 16, 20.
24. The text of the resolution with the covering letter of Hancock, President of Congress, are in *American Archives*, 4th Ser., II, 955.

chusetts had become extremely critical while Congress discussed the matter. On June 11, two days after passage of the resolution quoted above but before its arrival in Massachusetts, the Provincial Congress unanimously resolved to send another letter to Philadelphia to stress the gravity of the situation. "There are in many parts of the colony," the letter declared, "alarming symptoms of the abatement of the sense in the minds of some people of the sacredness of private property, which is plainly assignable to the want of civil government; and your honors must be fully sensible that a community of goods and estates will soon be followed by the utter waste and destruction of the goods themselves." [25] The writers may have consciously exaggerated the dangers of the moment in order to prod the Continental Congress into quick action. But assuming their fears were genuine, did they mean to indicate that there was a serious movement afoot to divide large estates? Certainly the American Revolution had its "Levellers" as well as the English Revolution before it, but did it also have the equivalent of those primitive agrarian communists known as "Diggers"? There seems to be no evidence to substantiate such a supposition. Both rich and poor in the Revolutionary period acknowledged the sacredness of private property, to a large extent because of its widespread ownership. In the coming years democratic groups were to object to the rich exercising political power because of their wealth, but rarely, if ever, did even the most radical question the right of the wealthy to enjoy their possessions undisturbed. Nevertheless, the disregard of private rights resulting from the lack of adequate government probably led men of property to anticipate a deeper radicalism unless order was restored.

Shortly after the receipt of Congress's advice, the Provincial Congress, with great punctilio, "resumed" the Charter of

25. *Ibid.*, 959-960.

1691. New elections for the House were held, Councillors were nominated, and a majority of the Council was declared to be the executive power. Thus the problem of legitimacy appeared to be at least temporarily solved, and in a manner which could give considerable satisfaction to most Whig leaders. The support of Congress seemed fairly well assured, the responsibility for initiating hostilities was effectively shifted to the British, sovereign powers necessary to secure internal control of the colony could be legally exercised, and —perhaps most important—the traditional political forms and relationships of the province could be retained.

Although the General Court issued paper money, gave representation to every town, validated the resolves of the former Congresses, and commissioned courts,[26] it demonstrated its conservatism by refusing to tamper with the established church. When Isaac Backus presented a strongly worded petition for religious liberty,[27] some members, led by Gerry, wanted it rejected as impertinent and disrespectful. They were opposed by Joseph Hawley of Northampton, a lawyer who later became a strong advocate of democratic reform. In connection with the debate on the petition he was quoted to the effect "that the established religion of the colony was not worth a groat." A member was given liberty to draft a bill providing in some measure with Backus' demands, but apparently he never made a report.[28] The Council

26. *Ibid.*, III, 335, 350, 357-358.

27. Backus had presented an earlier petition previous to the resumption of the Charter which the Congress tossed back to him with the reminder that as a body it was "by no means vested with power of Civil Government whereby it can redress the grievances of any person whatsoever." *Ibid.*, I, 1004. The text of the petition is in Hovey, *Backus*, 215-221.

28. *American Archives*, 4th Ser., III, 1448, 1456, 1489. The circumstances surrounding the incident are fully described in a letter to Backus from a Baptist member of the House. See Hovey, *Backus*, 227-228.

also revealed a basic conservatism by asserting the supremacy of the Charter over natural rights. In a controversy with the Representatives over the appointment of militia officers the upper house asserted its firm attachment to "the natural rights of men," but "if there is any incompatibility between those rights and the Charter Constitution of the Colony, the Council can only lament their being bound to the observation of such a Constitution." [29] By placing final authority in man-made law rather than inherent rights the Council retreated considerably from former interpretations of the natural rights philosophy.

Both houses made it plain that they were determined to maintain the ancient virtues and a proper spirit of sub-ordination. In a proclamation of January, 1776, reviewing the course of the struggle, the General Court exhorted the people in terms reminiscent of the seventeenth century to look to their manners and morals: "That piety and virtue, which alone can secure the freedom of any people, be en-couraged, and vice and immorality suppressed, the Great and General Court have thought fit to issue this Proclama-tion, commanding and enjoining it upon the good people of this colony that they lead sober, religious, and peaceable lives, avoiding all blasphemies, contempt of the Holy Scrip-tures and of the *Lord's* Day, and all other crimes and mis-demeanors, all debauchery, profaneness, corruption, venality, all riotous and tumultuous proceedings and all immoralities whatsoever, and that they decently and reverently attend the publick worship of God." The Court acknowledged govern-ment by consent to be its guiding principle and declared with

29. *American Archives,* 4th Ser., III, 1514. For other papers bearing on this case, see pp. 1476, 1499, 1509, 1514, 1515. The Council wished to refer the dispute to the Continental Congress, but the Massachusetts dele-gation opposed the move. See *Warren-Adams Letters,* 2 Vols. (Boston, 1917, 1925), Massachusetts Historical Society, *Collections,* LXXII, LXXIII, I, 191-192; *American Archives,* 4th Ser., III, 1662-1663, 1705.

evident satisfaction that the people of Massachusetts could be congratulated on having a free government "more immediately in all its branches" under their influence and control. Everyone was enjoined to acknowledge the authority of the judicial courts, and those who refused were declared "deserving of exemplary punishment." [30]

Under the auspices of the Charter the Revolutionary leaders took over all the offices formerly occupied by Tories. In pursuance of this necessary course they apparently forgot their former antipathy for plural officeholding. Thomas Cushing, a Congressional delegate, became Chief Justice of the Suffolk County Court, a Justice of Probate, Justice of the Peace and Justice of the Quorum, and Special Justice of the Pleas and Justice throughout the Colony. Sam Adams held three posts in addition to his membership in the General Court, although not without qualms. John Adams, in addition to minor judicial positions, was Chief Justice of the Superior Court of Judicature from 1775 to 1777.[31] Since these men spent most of their time in Philadelphia, they were rarely able to assume their duties in Massachusetts. Although the Adamses never made any serious attempt to hold their plural offices and eventually resigned them, the Whig leaders as a whole showed no lack of eagerness to enjoy the fruits of political control.

With the resumption of the Charter it was apparent that the Whig rulers regarded the internal revolution as completed. Basically conservative, they considered that the essential freedoms for which they undertook the Revolution were secured by the abolition of the prerogative and the reestablishment of the traditional institutions of the colony. But the means by which government had been formed and the use to which the Whig leadership had put its powers

30. *Ibid.,* IV, 834.
31. Brennan, *Plural Officeholding,* 112-115.

antagonized many of the humbler people of the province—particularly in the West—who identified liberty with democratic reform. Although the Great and General Court might congratulate them on having a free government "more immediately in all its branches dependent on the people," many of the politically unprivileged felt that the tyranny still remained although the tyrants had been driven out. Thus on December 26, 1775, Berkshire county dispatched a remonstrance to the Court, written by the Rev. Thomas Allen, of Pittsfield, a close friend of Hawley's and like him an advocate of democratic reform.

Allen had travelled a circuit of the towns in the West denouncing the General Court and calling for the adoption of a constitution incorporating local autonomy and religious liberty.[32] "Since the suppression of government," he wrote in the Berkshire remonstrance, "we have lived in peace, love, safety, liberty, and happiness except the disorders and dissentions occasioned by the Tories. We find ourselves now in danger of returning to our former state, and in undergoing a yoke of oppression we are no longer able to bear." Sensing danger to freedom in the "nominating to office by those in power," he declared that all officials should be elected—governor, lieutenant governor, county magistrates, justices of the peace, and militia officers. He called for the establishment of a new constitution containing "no more of our ancient forms than is just and reasonable" and settled on "a broad basis of civil and religious liberty." [33]

Open conflict broke out when the Boston government attempted to establish a county court in Berkshire, disregarding a warning by Allen in the Remonstrance that any effort on the part of Eastern creditors to collect debts would lead

32. J. E. A. Smith, *History of Pittsfield* (Boston, 1869), 166-168, 177, 199, 333-343.
33. *Ibid.*, 343-345.

to trouble. The local Committee of Inspection, originally organized to enforce the Continental Association, prevented the court from sitting and Allen fanned resentment against the Charter government by describing it as "oppressive, defective, and rotten to the very core." He urged the people to contest its legitimacy, significantly basing his argument in part on "a pamphlet called Common Sense." [34] The relationship between debts and the hostility to the General Court was plainly revealed by "A Berkshire Man" writing in the Boston *Gazette:* "The state of our government is alarming because of...the tories who are everywhere crying for a new government to make men pay their debts. This was one objection we had to the old government, yet these unfeeling tories would fain bring us into the same state again. Strange that men don't understand the nature of liberty better." [35] The tendency to identify liberty with the repudiation of debts was apparently not limited to the West. John Adams spoke feelingly in his autobiography of the "horse jockey" who rejoiced that Massachusetts would never see another court. John Winthrop of Harvard, a pioneer American mathematician, physicist, and astronomer, noted that "the true ground of the opposition [of the people to the Charter government], at least with many, is an unwillingness to submit to law and pay their debts." [36]

During the spring and summer of 1776 considerable protest against plural officeholding appeared in the press. "The members of the Assembly have divided among themselves and their particular friends, all the civil and military offices in the colony," declared a writer in the *Spy,* and went on to

34. Allen's statements are contained in a report of the judges to the General Court. This report was considered of enough importance to be written into the Journal of the House—a very unusual procedure in Massachusetts. *American Archives,* 4th Ser., V, 1275-1276.

35. Boston *Gazette,* Sept. 16, 1776.

36. Massachusetts Historical Society *Collections,* 5th Ser., IV, 307.

note the distressing similarity between the nepotistic practices of the former Council and those of the present House of Representatives.[37] Another editorialist asked whether a government administered by false patriots and self-seeking officeholders could succeed.[38] "Watchman," calling attention to the increasing concentration of power in a few hands, declared, "We are but dupes to the weakness and wickedness of human nature if, while we fight and defend ourselves against a foreign slavery we suffer a domestic one to spring up in our own country."[39] The Boston town meeting, condemning plural officeholding, ordered its delegates in May, 1776, to press for a separation of powers in the Charter government.[40]

The religious establishment and the restricted suffrage also received criticism. "I should have thought," wrote an observer, "that the present exertions in the cause of liberty would have for a while prevented such glaring instances of religious tyranny as the establishment. But tell it not in England, publish it not in the streets of London. Are we contending for liberty that we may have it in our power to trample on the rights of others?"[41] A writer in the Boston *Gazette* noted the injustice of denying the vote to anyone who paid taxes and gave his full support to the war for freedom,[42] but it was William Gordon who apparently first saw the fundamental inconsistency of property qualifications in a political society supposedly based on equal rights.

Best known as the author of the first complete history of the Revolution, Gordon was also a prolific newspaper writer

37. Massachusetts *Spy*, May 18, 1776.
38. New England *Chronicle*, July 11, 1776.
39. *Ibid.*, June 20, August 29.
40. *Boston Town Records, 1770-1777* (Boston, 1887), 238.
41. Massachusetts *Spy*, May 24, 1776.
42. Boston *Gazette*, Sept. 23, 1776.

and an unsparing critic of the General Court. Born in England and educated there for the independent ministry, he emigrated to America and became pastor of the Congregational Society in Roxbury. Through a voluminous correspondence he acquired a wide circle of acquaintances among political leaders but was often regarded as something of a sycophant and gossip monger. John Adams thought him "vain, not accurate nor judicious, and fond of being thought a man of influence." Nevertheless, his newspaper writings show a considerable analytical ability, and he was among the first to couple the doctrine of government by consent to internal reform. Labelling property qualifications "the most hurtful remnant of the Feudal Constitution," he declared, "The rich will have enough advantage against the poor without political advantage. Mere riches are no qualification, why should the want of them be a disqualification?" He countered Adams' argument that only a certain amount of wealth could bring the independence necessary for honest voting by pointing out that the rich often gained their wealth by corrupt methods.[43] Gordon continued to advocate manhood suffrage and the abolition of property qualifications for office throughout the Revolutionary period.

The mounting criticism of the Charter government gradually crystallized into a movement for a new constitution. "Massachusettsensis" of Salem probably spoke for many when he suggested, "Examine with candour, my brethren, and you will find a great deal of contemptible, but superstitiously-worshipped rubbish, both in church and state, which has been swept down to us from heathenism and popery by the great net of time. It is now high time to examine the net, cull out the good fishes and cast the bad

43. *Independent Chronicle*, Sept. 5, 1776. For biographical details, see introduction to *The Letters of William Gordon*, Massachusetts Historical Society, *Proceedings*, 68 Vols. (Boston, 1791-1952), LXIII, 303-613.

away," [44] Outside of Massachusetts the adoption of constitutions was favored by nearly all Whig politicians in the spring of 1776 as a means of checking the drift toward anarchy, but since an adequate government was already established in the Bay State, conservatives there were naturally opposed to any further change. Yet the inconsistency between a "resumed" Charter and the dialectic of compact government made the legitimacy of the government questionable and provided a convenient avenue of attack for those radicals who demanded democratic reforms. Thus Thomas Allen, relying heavily on Locke in a second memorial to the General Court, justified the refusal of Berkshire to acknowledge the authority of the body on the ground that the Charter was void by act of the king and the government established under it pure usurpation. Giving constitutional status to a philosophical fiction he declared that the people were in a state of nature. Legitimate government could only be reconstructed by institutionalizing the processes of compact, which meant in this instance the drafting of a constitution by the existing legislature and ratification of the instrument by the people. Mere reform of the present government would be insufficient. "Even if commissions be recalled, if the fee table be reduced ever so low, and multitudes of other things be done to still the people—*all is to us nothing* while the foundation is unfixed, the corner stone of government unlaid." The people of Pittsfield had learned their Whig political philosophy well. "We have heard much of government being founded in compact," Allen chided the Court, "What compact has been formed as the foundation of government in this province?" [45]

The logic of compact made it plain, therefore, that no succession government could acquire legitimacy without

44. *American Archives*, 4th Ser., V, 1157.
45. Smith, *History of Pittsfield*, 352-354.

invoking the constituent power in the people. Indeed, strictly speaking, succession government was impossible, for after the dissolution of the compact there was no authority which could be carried over into the new regime. In placing the stamp of illegitimacy on any government not inaugurated by a specific act of the constituent power, Allen provided a theoretical basis for the objections to the succession regimes of Virginia and New York voiced respectively by Jefferson and the New York Committee of Mechanics. In Massachusetts the dissatisfaction of the West with the Charter government promoted a search for radical doctrines which would justify a repudiation of the document. As events were to prove, the conservative Whigs dominating the General Court, eager as they were to invoke the right of revolution, showed considerable reluctance to face the consequences inherent in the Lockean logic of compact.

Of course, the translation of a philosophical concept into a political institution required modifications. If Locke's logic were followed literally, a constitution would bind only those who agreed to be bound by it; no one could be forced to emerge from the state of nature. Since the formation of government would be impossible under these circumstances, it is not difficult to understand why the principle of majority rule was adopted for the ratification process. Yet the requirements of higher than simple majorities, an extended suffrage, and the suspension of normal voting units in reaching constitutional decisions may possibly indicate an attempt to retain a semblance of the original compact theory. Measures of this kind would give a higher value to individual consent and would emphasize the difference between constituent and legislative power.

In 1776 Allen had no objection to giving the *de facto* legislature the power to draft a constitution; apparently he regarded ratification a sufficient exercise of the constituent power. But in the coming years as radicals became more suspicious of the General Court they began to demand a constitutional convention for the formation of the political compact. Jefferson's ideas were apparently moving in the same direction and apparently also were propelled by a fear of self-interest on the part of legislatures. The significance of the trend of thinking on constitutional questions illustrated by Jefferson and the Massachusetts radicals lies in its indication of the close relation of compact theory and American constitutional practice. It is no exaggeration to say that American conceptions of the proper treatment of constitutional issues are a partial realization of the myths surrounding the formation of government in the state of nature.

Many Whig leaders viewed the agitation for a constitution with foreboding. "What other change is expected," asked Sam Adams after the resumption of the Charter. "Certainly the people do not already hanker after the onions and garlick?" [46] John Adams, explaining that it was his constant endeavor "to contrive some method for the colonies to glide insensibly from under the old government into peaceable and contented submission to new ones," warned Mercy Warren that in spite of his efforts, "there is Danger of Convulsions, but I hope, not Great Ones." [47] Unless the people exhibit "Decency, Respect, and Veneration for persons in authority of every Rank, We are all undone," he wrote to Mercy's husband, James.[48] Warren stated that he dreaded "the consequences of the levelling spirit, encouraged and drove to such lengths as it is." [49] James Otis, in a rare moment of sanity, observed, "When the pot boils, the scum will rise," and John Eliot, the celebrated divine, commented

46. *Warren-Adams Letters*, I, 195.
47. *Ibid.*, 222.
48. *Ibid.*, 234.
49. *Ibid.*, 219.

on the epigram, "If he had his senses as acute as ever, he could not have made a better speech or mixed so much sentiment with so few words." [50] "There is such a spirit of innovation gone forth as I am afraid will throw us into confusion," complained John Winthrop. "It seems as if everything [is] to be altered. Scarce a newspaper but teems with new projects." [51]

A few prominent members of the Massachusetts clergy shared the alarm of the ruling Whigs. Although many pastors opposed the General Court and preached radical political doctrines,[52] others, chiefly in the seaboard towns, hastened to buttress the established order by extolling the virtues of obedience. "Put them in mind to be subject to principalities and powers, to obey magistrates, to be ready for every good work," intoned Samuel West of Dartmouth in the annual election sermon delivered before the General Court in 1776.[53] Lapsing into the language of the Tories, he called on his hearers to obey magistrates "because they are the ministers of God for the good of the people" and declared that a person who opposed good government was "a monster in nature, and an enemy to his own species." [54] Samuel Langdon, President of Harvard, lashed out at dissidents within the state with rhetoric formerly reserved for the British government. "Submission to the tyranny of hundreds of imperious masters firmly embodied against us, and united in the same cruel design of disposing of our lives and subsistence at their pleasure, and making their own will our

50. Massachusetts Historical Society *Collections,* 6th Ser., IV, 104, 109.
51. *Ibid.,* 5th Ser., IV, 308.
52. The attitudes of the radical clergymen on constitutional matters have been examined by Alice M. Baldwin, *The New England Clergy and the American Revolution* (Durham, 1928), 134-153.
53. John W. Thornton, *The Pulpit of American Revolution: or, The Political Sermons of the Period of 1776* (Boston, 1860), 267.
54. *Ibid.,* 276.

law in all cases whatsoever, is the vilest slavery, and worse than death." [55] Like many Whigs, he felt that democracy was a worse tyranny than despotism. Few of the Congregational clergy in this period saw any inconsistency between a state-supported church and religious freedom. As we will see later, they considered government sponsorship of religion necessary as a protection for morality.[56]

By 1776 the demand for a new constitution first heard in Berkshire County was repeated in the House, probably because an act reapportioning representation in accordance with population had resulted in the election of many new members formerly outside the Whig ruling class.[57] James Sullivan, a young lawyer from the northern frontier who was destined to serve twice as governor and become a leader of the Democratic-Republican party, testified to the rebellious tendency of the House when he complained that "the solemnity of a senate has left us" in a great surge of "the levelling spirit." [58] A committee was appointed June 4 to prepare a draft of a constitution,[59] but it failed to bring in

55. *Ibid.*, 250.

56. For expressions of opinion in this matter by Samuel West and Phillips Payson, see *ibid.*, 298, 340.

57. An act passed in August, 1775, declaratory of a right existing under the Charter, gave every town the right to send at least one representative. *American Archives,* 4th Ser., III, 335. A second act of May, 1776, allotted 3 representatives to all towns with 220 freeholders, 4 to towns with 320 freeholders, and so on in the same scale. *Acts and Resolves of the Province of Massachusetts Bay,* 21 Vols. (Boston, 1869-1922), V, 502-503. Joseph Hawley declared after the election of May, 1776, that over half the members of the House were new. *American Archives,* 4th Ser., VI, 1015. A writer in the Boston *Gazette* noted with disdain that among the new arrivals was "a tavern keeper from the East coast, a raw, inexperienced man." June 3, 1776.

58. Thomas C. Amory, *Life of James Sullivan, with Selections from his Writings,* 2 Vols. (Boston, 1859), I, 77.

59. *A Journal of the Honorable House of Representatives, 1776* (Boston, 1776), 13.

a report, possibly because it contained among its members James Warren and Timothy Pickering, two conservatives who consistently resisted constitutional changes. After the Declaration of Independence stripped the government of its fictional legitimacy, however, no argument could be advanced against a new constitution. Obviously the Charter of 1691 was void, and the government in operation under it not only lacked specific authorization, but was tainted by the royal connection. An insistence on the validity of the Charter might well be considered treasonable. Thus a writer in the *Chronicle,* admitting that the General Court no longer had a legal right to legislate, advised the public to "connive at their proceedings" until legitimate government could be established.[60] As Oscar Handlin puts it, "The fund of revolutionary theory, universally accepted, supplied an insurmountable obstacle: here was no consent of the governed, only a relic of the tyranny Massachusetts was fighting."[61]

Hence it was now inevitable that the people of Massachusetts would pass judgment on their traditional political institutions and relationships. As yet few supporters of the Revolutionary movement had opposed their leaders or had questioned the authority of the Provincial Congress and the fictitious *de jure* government under the "resumed" Charter. But the apparent determination of the ruling clique to limit any internal revolution to a change of administration and

---

60. New England *Chronicle,* Aug. 29, 1776.

61. Oscar and Mary F. Handlin, *Commonwealth; a Study of the Role of Government in the American Economy: Massachusetts, 1774-1861* (New York, 1947), 6-7. The authors point out that after 1776 new radical and conservative factions formed from the former radical party of the Adamses, Hancock, and the Warrens, and that there was no relation between the radical-moderate alignment before independence and the radical-conservative alignment after it. See their "Radicals and Conservatives in Massachusetts after Independence," *New England Quarterly,* XVII (1944), 343-355.

their eagerness to accumulate the offices formerly occupied by Tories had aroused the resentment of the West, as the memorials from Berkshire county indicated. Moreover, the dissenting sects, always lukewarm toward Whig agitation, continued to regard the new regime with suspicion. In the coming years opposition to the original Revolutionary leadership was to grow in intensity and crystallize into a multitude of specific plans for reform. From dissatisfied groups throughout the state were to come demands that Whig doctrines be translated into political institutions. Many of the yeoman farmers of the back country were to interpret popular sovereignty as the right of the people to establish their government by constitutional convention and thereby specifically determine the conditions under which political authority could be exercised. Some dissatisfied groups were to demand the separation of church and state and the extension of the voting right to all adult males, and others were to insist that property possessed no special right of representation in a legislative house. Many conceived the separation of powers as the abolition of plural officeholding and not the separation of the people from absolute power.

All of these developments were to become somewhat disquieting to the Whig leaders who had so lavishly used the vocabulary of freedom before 1776. It had apparently not occurred to them that anyone besides Tories could question their right to represent the whole people in all cases whatsoever, or that their own doctrine might be used as a platform for reform of the very government through which they exercised power. For them the traditional checks and balances of Anglo-American political science were in no way inconsistent with the ideals of the Declaration of Independence; indeed, they considered restrictions on the people to be just as necessary for the preservation of freedom as restrictions on a potential despot. From their study of history they knew that all too frequently revolutions had resulted merely in the exchange of one kind of tyranny for another. The Greeks had overthrown the tyrants only to enthrone the mob of the ecclesia; the Romans had exchanged a republic for military dictatorship and ultimately the worst of personal despotisms; the English had decapitated a Stuart only to put the Long Parliament in his place, and finally—with relief—return the Stuart's son to the throne.

Therefore it is understandable that conservatives, with these and like precedents in mind, resisted any attempt to change the traditional institutions of the state which had proved their value in practice. But they fought against increasingly heavy odds. Without the British as convenient targets for opprobrium, internal tensions could not be released by such stimulating activities as dumping tea into Boston harbor and driving royal hirelings from the bench. Like the leaders of many Revolutionary parties the Whigs of 1776 were to find out that what were ends to them were only means to many of the rank and file; they were to find out that liberty, to great numbers of the people of Massachusetts, meant more than independence from Great Britain.

TEN

The Search for a Principle of Authority:
The General Court

ALTHOUGH sentiment in favor of a constitution increased in the House during the summer of 1776, the Council was opposed to the idea, apparently because some members were afraid that a unicameral legislature would be established under the new instrument, thus dispensing with an upper house entirely.[1] Therefore the representatives, compelled to initiate proceedings without the concurrence of the upper chamber as would have been required by the Charter, recommended to the adult males of the state on September 17 that they gather in town meetings and vote on the question of granting the General Court permission to draft and enact a constitution. Since the two Houses were to meet together for the purpose, the Council would be deprived of a veto over the finished instrument. Apparently realizing the revolutionary character of the proposal, the representatives did not enter it on the Journal but dispatched it directly to the towns.[2] Although the two Houses were to exercise legisla-

1. "Watchman," in New England *Chronicle*, Aug. 29, 1776.
2. The resolution was worded "that it be recommended to the Male inhabitants of each town in this state, being free and twenty-one years of age upwards, that they assemble as soon as they can in Town Meet-

tive as well as constituent powers and "enact" the constitution without popular ratification, the proposal nevertheless shows a considerable advance in democratic procedures by inviting all free adult males to vote on whether constituent powers should be granted. Henceforward in Massachusetts a double standard in the right of suffrage was adopted. Although the franchise was limited in regular elections, conservatives as well as radicals apparently agreed that on constitutional issues every free adult male should have the right to vote. As previously suggested, this extension of the franchise where the constituent power of the people was involved may have resulted from implications in the compact theory of government.

The replies of the towns to this and future questions on constitutional issues comprise the most important single source for any study of democratic ideas among the common people during the Revolutionary period. Some of the returns record only votes but most summarize the majority opinion on the issues which provoked extended discussion. A few of the documents are twenty to thirty pages in length and amount to elaborate disquisitions on political theory.[3]

The response to the House resolution of September 17 was overwhelmingly favorable. Although only one-third of

---

ing...and at their meeting they consider and determine whether they will give their consent that the present House of Representatives,... together with the Council, if they consent in one body with the House, and by equal voice, agree and enact...a Constitution." There are several copies of the handbills carrying the resolution in the MS Massachusetts Archives, Vol. 156.

3. Samuel E. Morison is the only historian who has made an extensive use of this material. See his excellent article, "The Struggle over the Adoption of the Constitution of Massachusetts, 1780," *Massachusetts Historical Society Proceedings*, 68 Vols. (Boston, 1791-1952), Vol. L, pp. 353-410. The material is so copious and so significant that there is room for still further research. Morison restricted himself to returns bearing on the Constitution of 1780.

the towns replied, three-fourths of this number were in favor of granting constituent powers to the General Court.[4] Most seemed to accept the view of York that "the General Assembly ... are from long usage under the former administration the supreme legislative power in this state and to whose acts all individuals in the state ought to be held and pay due obedience."[5] Yet the dissents are the more significant because they show a growing awareness of the distinction between constituent and legislative powers and indicate considerable suspicion of the motives of the incumbent legislators. Thus nine towns, of which Boston was one, denied that a legislative body was competent to form a constitution and demanded a special convention for the purpose. As Concord put it, "The same body that forms a Constitution have of consequence a power to alter it, and a Constitution alterable by the legislature is no security at all to the individual."[6] Boston felt that a constitution must be drafted with the people themselves "consulting, acting, and assisting."[7] Marlboro based its objections on the fact that the limited suffrage for the House disqualified it from acting in the name of the whole people.[8] Somewhat surprisingly, only Attleboro objected specifically to the lack of provision for popular ratification.[9]

4. According to one tabulation 97 towns replied, 74 in favor of granting constituent power to the Court and 23 opposed. Morison, "The Vote of Massachusetts on Summoning a Constitutional Convention, 1776-1916," Massachusetts Historical Society *Proceedings,* Vol. L, 242. By my own tabulation, 106 towns replied, 84 in favor and 22 against the granting of constituent power.

5. Massachusetts Archives, 156, p. 187.

6. *Ibid.,* 182.

7. *Boston Town Records, 1770-1777,* 248.

8. Massachusetts Archives, 156, p. 181.

9. *Ibid.,* 171. Topsfield and Lexington indicated that they would have no objection to the House drafting a new constitution if new elections were called and members duly instructed. *Ibid.,* 183, 178.

Several towns feared that the members of the Court would use constituent powers to secure all posts of profit for themselves. Thus Norton considered the request of the House "pregnant with power," [10] and Lexington foresaw the creation of oligarchy. Middleboro declared it would resist plural officeholding "to the utmost of our capacities." [11] As early as May, 1776, Boston had instructed its representatives to secure laws "as shall make it incompatible for the same Person to hold a Seat in the Legislative and Executive Departments of Government at one and the same time." [12] Although no stipulation to this effect appeared in the town's objections to the House resolve, the fear that the Court would sanction plural officeholding probably was an important reason for the withholding of constituent powers.

Some of the towns based their refusal on the unequal representation in the House. In most of the colonies the apportionment of representatives had discriminated against the piedmont and frontier regions, but in Massachusetts the reverse was true. Under the Charter of 1691, every incorporated place was given one representative, every town of 120 or more voters two, and Boston four. The seaboard towns did not object to the injustice of the apportionment, which increased with time, because many of the small communities of the interior would not assume the expense of sending delegates. Hence in practice representation was not as disproportionate to population as the Charter would indicate. But in 1776, reform along this line became a burning issue because of the distress arising from the war.

The Boston Port Bill and the subsequent blockade of other coastal towns had cut off or reduced the income of artisans,

10. Massachusetts Archives, 156, p. 146.
11. Ibid., 147.
12. Boston Town Records, 1770-1777, 238.

seamen, laborers, and traders. When, added to this, commodity prices rose steeply, there was real suffering in mercantile communities.[13] The people accused the farmers of the interior of profiteering and clamored for price controls. When the West used its power in the House to block all such measures, the seaboard towns realized that nothing could be done until there was a reapportionment of the representation. An Essex County convention of April pointed out in a memorial to the General Court that the seaboard towns paid the lion's share of the provincial taxes, yet had only one-fifteenth the representation of the interior. This situation, the convention asserted, was very close to taxation without representation.[14] According to a newspaper report, the House received the convention's memorial a few days before the end of the session in May after most of the western representatives had gone home. On the strength of it the eastern delegation pushed through the bill establishing proportionate representation which shifted the balance of power to the mercantile East.[15]

When the seaboard towns then succeeded in imposing price controls, the bitterness of the interior knew no bounds. The agrarian towns now demanded a return to the colonial apportionment. They construed "equal" representation to mean the maintenance of the old sectional balance in the General Court. Warwick expressed this view in its answer to the query of the House relative to a constitution when it recommended that each town be granted at least one representative in the new government, and none more than four

13. Oscar and Mary Handlin, *Commonwealth*, 7-9.
14. The broadside calling the convention is printed in The Essex Institute Historical *Collections*, XXXVI (1900), 104. The memorial of the convention appears in *Acts and Resolves of the Province of Massachusetts Bay*, V, 542-543.
15. Massachusetts *Spy*, Jan. 16; Apr. 24, 1777. See above, p. 158.

or five "in order to preserve the ballances of power." [16] A
Worcester County convention, called in the spring of 1777,
recommended that the town deputies work for repeal of
the Act of 1776 because it "tends to fix an object of contention and opposition between the landed and mercantile
interests in the state." [17] The convention justified the old
system on the grounds that the smaller House under the former apportionment was less of an expense to the taxpayers.
Throughout the Revolution representation was a bitterly
contested issue.

The great majority of the towns in their reply to the House
resolution of September 17 gave no specific recommendations
for reforms to be incorporated in a new constitution. Probably most agreed with Berwick: "We most respectfully desire
that whatever form of government may by you be framed
may be the most Easy and plain to be understood by People
of all Denominations, whereby a line may be drawn that the
Rulers and the Ruled may know their duty, and that
Tyranny on one hand and Anarchy on the other, may be
avoided as much as possible." [18] But the returns from a few
towns showed a small, but significant body of opinion favoring alteration of existing conditions. Thus Warwick wanted
a unicameral legislature, the right of recall against representatives who violated instructions, and manhood suffrage.[19]
Ashfield, although willing to accept a constitution framed
by the Court, "voted that we will take the Law of God for
the foundation of the form of our Government." The village
Hampdens wanted "No Govrnor but the Govrnor of the
Univarse, and under him a States General to consult with

16. Massachusetts Archives, 156, p. 132. Topsfield, Marlboro, and Attleboro also objected to the apportionment of representation under the Act
of 1776.

17. Massachusetts *Spy*, Apr. 24, May 29, 1777.

18. Massachusetts Archives, 156, p. 163.

19. *Ibid.*, 132.

the rest of the *U. S.* for the good of the whole." This "States General" would be a one-house legislature, and its acts would be subject to popular referendum. The town also asked for the separation of church and state and locally elected judicial officials.[20] Middleboro, home of Isaac Backus, voted to give the Court constitutent powers but requested a moratorium on litigation in order "to quiet and lengthen the Peace and Harmony of the People." [21]

There appears to be no significant sectional distribution of the vote. Near Boston the towns objecting to the exercise of constituent powers by the Court were slightly more numerous than elsewhere, possibly because of the influence of the Boston leaders. Berkshire and Barnstable were the only counties without a dissent to the House's resolution. In the case of the former the Rev. Thomas Allen's influence was probably an important factor.

If the vote does not show that social revolution was imminent, it at least indicates the points of controversy in the succeeding years. Whether a legislative body was qualified to draft fundamental law, the apportionment of representation, the abolition of plural officeholding, and the introduction of democratic reforms which would make the government directly responsible to the people—these were questions which would arouse class and sectional antagonisms before legitimate government could be established.

Although the Court had received permission to draft and put into effect a constitution, no action toward that end was taken during the fall of '76 and spring of '77. Probably the objections of Boston and the few other large towns gave greater weight to the unfavorable responses than would be indicated by the results of the vote. Moreover the Council was nearly unanimous in opposing a constitution—an under-

20. *Ibid.,* 131.
21. *Ibid.,* 147.

standable position since its members risked the loss of a good many lucrative offices by a change of government.[22] According to Warren, even some town delegates were now "lukewarm" to a change of government.[23] Thus no action was taken until April 4, 1777, when the House proposed to the Council that in the coming elections of May the people be asked to empower their representatives to draft a constitution which would be referred back to the towns for ratification.[24] Probably the proposal represented a compromise between the demands of the radicals for the constitutional convention and the determination of the conservatives to resist any change whatsoever. The Council reacted as might have been expected. Although admitting that the present form of government might be altered "in some particulars," the members of the upper house were "filled with serious apprehensions" that an attempt to draft a constitution in wartime would lead to anarchy and levelism, and they pointed to Pennsylvania and her democratic constitution as an example.[25] The House rejoined by reminding the Council that in the present state of public opinion the only choice lay between a constitution drafted by the Court and one drafted by a convention chosen for the purpose. The representatives suggested that an intransigent attitude might result in a strengthened demand for a constitutional convention. "There are many reasons, obvious to your honors, why this matter should be determined in the mode pointed out rather than by a convention called for the purpose, and we conceive many of the evils feared by your honors will be

22. "The Council...are almost to a man against the new constitution, and are forced to come to it with the greatest reluctance," wrote Warren to Adams. *Warren-Adams Letters*, 2 Vols. (Boston, 1917, 1925), Massachusetts Historical Society, *Collections*, LXXII, LXXIII, I, 341.

23. *Ibid.*

24. Massachusetts Archives, 156, pp. 200-202.

25. *Ibid.*, 158, pp. 77-80.

avoided by this alternative." [26] The Council chose the lesser of the two evils and assented to the House proposal. The members of the upper body probably realized that a constitution drafted by the Court would, in all likelihood, be less radical than one drafted by a convention.

Thus on May 5, 1777, by a resolution of both houses, the Court "recommended" to the towns that they devolve both constituent and legislative powers on the representatives to be elected at the end of May. Together with the Council the delegates would draft an instrument which would become fundamental law if ratified by two-thirds of the manhood population. It is significant that although only qualified voters could elect delegates, all property qualifications were removed for the ratifying process.[27] The resolution thus shows a growing awareness of the implications of consent government and a steady advance toward modern constitutional procedure.

Apparently a majority of the towns instructed their representatives as recommended, for beginning June 17, House and Council met at intervals as a constitutional convention.[28] Yet not all of the towns approved of the General Court's procedure. The Boston town meeting instructed its delegates to act only in a legislative capacity and voted unanimously against giving the Court constituent powers: "We apprehend this matter [forming a constitution] will at a suitable time properly come before the people at large, to delegate a *Select Number for that Purpose, and that alone.*" The decision of the town meeting was plainly motivated by a fear that the Court would use its powers to monopolize profitable political

26. *Ibid.*, 83.

27. Resolve printed in *Acts and Resolves of the Province of Massachusetts Bay,* XIX, 932-933.

28. A separate journal kept by the convention is in Massachusetts Archives, 156.

offices. The Boston delegates were instructed to condemn "the lately too prevalent custom of accumulating Offices in One Persone; we could wish to establish it as a certain Rule that no One Persone whatever be intrusted with more than *One* office at a time (and for the discharge of it let there be honorable allowance)." [29] Little Topsfield refused the request for constituent powers because "so many valuable men that are and will be in the army cannot deliberate on Such a Momentous Affair." [30] A check through town histories and printed town records reveals that many communities ignored the request entirely. Yet most of the towns which did reply replied favorably.[31]

Soon after the elections a committee containing the conservatives John Pickering, Thomas Cushing,[32] and James Warren was appointed to draft an instrument. But the members of the committee were apparently indifferent to their task almost to the point of hostility, for despite repeated urging from the convention they did not prepare a report until December 11, almost six months after their appointment.

The people at large, however, showed considerably more interest in a constitution than the members of the committee, as is evidenced by an increasing amount of newspaper comment on the issue. A few writers advocated an equalitarian democracy with a government elective in all its branches

29. *Boston Town Records, 1770-1777*, 284.

30. *Town Records of Topsfield* (Topsfield, 1920), II, 378.

31. See D. P. Corey, *History of Malden* (Malden, 1899), 773; *Plymouth Records* (Plymouth, 1903), III, 328; *Records of Weston, 1754-1803* (Boston, 1893), 239.

32. Cushing's Boston constituents had ordered him not to consent to the formation of a constitution by the Court, but the injunction did not prevent him from taking a seat on the drafting committee, nor did he find his multiple positions incompatible with his constituents' condemnation of plural officeholding.

and based on manhood suffrage. "My idea of government
is that it is easy, simple, and cheap," wrote "Clitus," a
democrat following in the tradition of Paine and the writer
of *The People the Best Governors.* "We debase ourselves in
reintroducing the worst parts of British rule. The plain
question is, are we fighting and lavishing our blood and
treasure to establish the freest and best government on earth,
or are we about to set up a formidable court interest? ...
The origin and essence of government is in the people.
Therefore *let us keep the staff in our own hands.*" "Clitus"
felt that the basic requirements of government could be
satisfied by a unicameral legislature unencumbered by a
governor and elected by all free adult males.[33] "Faithful
Friend," representing the conservative point of view, regarded such proposals as visionary and dangerous. "Man,
considered abstractly and individually, is perhaps the most
selfish, fierce and cruel animal in the whole creation of God,
nor can he be restrained from acting as such but by Government and laws," he wrote. "The stuff of power never was,
nor never can be, in the nature of things, in the people's
hands. As a people we have no power in our hands we can
safely exercise, but of choosing our guardians once a year.
... We are not fighting for this or that form of government,
but to be free from *arbitrary power* and the *Iron Rod of
Oppression* on one hand, and from *Popular Licentiousness
and anarchy and confusion on the other.* Dreadful alternatives!" [34] Although the language of "Faithful Friend" might
label him as an extreme conservative, his thought was not
much different from the prevailing Whig philosophy as
expressed by Adams and Warren. Both had testified to the

33. *Independent Chronicle,* July 10, 1777.
34. *Ibid.,* August 7, 1777. For other examples of the conservative point
of view see articles by "Philadelphus," *ibid.,* Apr. 17; and by Phileleu-
therus," *ibid.,* March 6, 20.

depravity of man and consequently had doubted whether free government could exist without stringent controls over the people. In posing the "dreadful alternatives" of oppression from abroad and anarchy at home, "Faithful Friend" reflected the determination of the Revolutionary leaders to keep clear of the Scylla of British power and the Charybdis of "popular licentiousness." The differences between "Faithful Friend" and "Clitus," like those between Paine and Adams, illustrate the ideological conflict inherent in the Revolution.

William Gordon, standing between the extremes of equalitarianism and conservative Whigism, suggested a compromise designed to achieve political equality without sacrificing the practicality of the conservative proposals. "A restricted suffrage is not fit for a free society," he declared. "It is not the estate, neither freehold nor personal, that makes the state, but the persons of the people." Yet he echoed Adams in his distrust of a unicameral legislature. "I am fully of the opinion," he declared, "that whenever the Supreme Legislature shall be vested in a single Assembly, ambitious men will have more than a little ground for building up their own particular greatness upon their country's ruin." [35] Although Gordon trusted the people, he still feared the demagogue—a figure who seldom entered into the calculations of the democrats. But he did not use the necessity of protection against unscrupulous leaders as an excuse for depriving the people of active control over their government. In combining manhood suffrage and a bicameral legislature, Gordon in part anticipated the political structure of modern American democracy.

The report which the drafting committee presented December 11, 1777, would, if adopted, have given Massachusetts a more democratic government than the state received

35. See articles in *ibid.*, March 20, 27, and April 3.

until well into the nineteenth century. The instrument provided for a bicameral legislature and a governor, but no property qualifications either for voting or officeholding were mentioned.[36] Towns with 100 voters were allotted one delegate, those with 250 voters two, those with 500 three, and onwards in the same ratio. Communities with less than 100 voters were required to join together to gain representation. This solution of the problem of apportionment obviously favored the larger towns.

Apparently the report caused considerable controversy among the members of the committee.[37] After it came before the General Court sitting in convention, conservatives succeeded in inserting the traditional safeguards of property. By the terms of the final draft adopted February 28, 1778, for transmission to the towns, all free, white, taxpaying males over twenty-one could vote for representatives but only those worth £60—a not inconsiderable sum—could exercise the suffrage for senators, governor, and lieutenant governor (Sect. V).[38] Representatives must be worth £200, senators £400, the lieutenant governor £500, and the governor £1000. In all cases, one-half of the property qualification had to be in real estate (Sect. III). Senators were selected from lists of names drawn up by the Court on the basis of preference primaries held in five senatorial districts (Sect. VIII-IX). The governor was directly elected, but his powers

36. On order of the Court 300 copies of the report were printed for members only, and they were instructed to keep the contents secret. After the printing the type was broken up in the presence of a special committee. A copy of the printed report is in Massachusetts Archives, 156, pp. 203-210.

37. In September Warren had declared that he was tired of the controversies over the constitution and feared that the instrument "would not be marked with the wisdom of the ages." *Warren-Adams Letters*, I, 368.

38. The rejected constitution of 1778 is printed in *Journal of the Convention, 1779-1780* (Boston, 1832), 255-264.

were very limited and he was specifically denied the veto. The provisions on representation were a compromise between the desires of the East and those of the West. The convention, after considerable debate, had voted to give at least one representative to every town regardless of population.[39] This decision meant that proportionate representation would be impossible. Since many towns had only twenty-five or thirty voters, the ratio of delegates to constituents would have to be set so high that a House of thousands would result. Thus a system involving an increasing mean number was adopted whereby the ratio of representation varied between approximately 1:25 and 1:250 for small towns to about 1:365 for Boston (Sect. VI). In return for this concession, the small towns were required to pay their own representatives. There were no provisions against plural officeholding except that delegates to the Continental Congress were forbidden to hold certain important administrative and judicial positions (Sect. XXVIII). Only Protestants were "allowed" free exercise of religion and were permitted to hold office (Sects. XXIX, XXXIV). The laws regarding state support of the Congregational church were unchanged, although they had been challenged in the convention.[40]

Outside of the representation clause there is little to distinguish this constitution from the others of the Revolutionary period. It was an instrument which protected the rights gained by the Revolution under a government dominated by the Whig aristocracy.

Throughout the spring of 1778 the towns discussed the

39. Massachusetts Archives, 156, p. 291. The vote was 93-66. The fact that this was the only division recorded in the Journal shows its importance.

40. A motion from the floor Feb. 26 that "no person shall be obliged to pay toward the support of any teacher except of his own persuasion or where they usually attend public worship" was voted down. *Ibid.*, 290.

constitution. The returns, although marred by execrable spelling, bad grammar, and almost illegible penmanship, show a surprising eagerness on the part of the people to come to grips with fundamental problems of government. No town was too small or humble to speak its mind. The village solons made it plain that just as all men are equal in the sight of God, so all men are equal in the creation of fundamental law.

The constitution was rejected by an overwhelming majority of 147 to 31. Again there does not appear to be any sectional significance to the vote. Since Boston and the larger towns were in the majority, and since the town votes were often unanimous or nearly so, the action of the people amounts to a remarkable condemnation of the General Court. The great variety of objections makes generalization difficult, but usually the larger towns, where the returns were written by men of superior education, emphasized the theoretical faults of the constitution and criticized the drafting procedure, while the small towns tended to attack the articles which centralized power in the General Court, removed the government from popular control, and denied political equality.

Thus Boston, rejecting the instrument by a vote of 968-0, reiterated the danger of allowing the Court to draft fundamental law: "A Convention for this, *and this alone,* whose Existence is known No Longer than the Constitution is forming, can have no Presuppositions in their own Favor while... the General Court..." may form a government "with peculiar reference to themselves." [41] The town meeting regarded the constitution as a charter of monopoly. William Gordon, with considerable penetration, described the drafting procedure as "a certain state legerdemain, akin to British

41. *Boston Town Records, 1778-1783,* 23.

legislative omnipotence." [42] Many members of the Court, he charged, were only "pretended sons of liberty" who "wished the establishment of no new constitution which would endanger their being left out of office." [43] A newspaper writer even foresaw another rebellion if means were not found to curb the power-grabbing of the legislators.[44]

The small towns showed less willingness to accept the traditional structure of government and the restriction of political rights. In addition to a constitutional convention and the abolition of plural officeholding, some of them demanded democratic reforms such as unicameralism, manhood suffrage, and elective judicial officers. Little Boothbay, for example, in a constitutional draft of its own, asserted that a governor and lieutenant governor were "needless in a free state" and opposed an upper house "because we cannot consent to the setting up of any branch of the legislature under the name of Senate or Council which shall be able to control the people's representatives." [45] The author of *The People the Best Governors* objected to an independent upper house for the same reason.[46]

The suffrage qualifications raised a storm of indignation in some of the towns. Thus New Salem pontificated, "We

42. *Continental Journal*, Apr. 2, 1778.

43. *Ibid.*, Apr. 16. Gordon's hostility had not been lessened by the fact that he had lost his position of chaplain to the Court because of his generally critical attitude. Incensed against the prevalence of plural officeholding, he suspected that members of the Court would like to "entail" their seats to their descendants. *Ibid.*, Apr. 23, 1778.

44. "A Bystander" pointed out that many of the members of the Court had never been authorized by their constituents to participate in the formation of a constitution. *Independent Chronicle*, Jan. 22, 1778. The Boston *Gazette*, May 25, 1778, contained a strong attack against the Council.

45. Massachusetts Archives, 156, p. 369. See also returns of New Salem, *ibid.*, 366, and Greenwich, *ibid.*, 327.

46. Frederick Chase, *History of Dartmouth College* (Cambridge, 1891), 662.

think that where the Great Author of Natur hath furnished a man to the satisfaction of the Electors...he ought to have a seat and voice in any society of men or to serve in any office whatsoever." [47] "There are qualifications of the person which ought rather to be deemed indispensable," said Boothbay. The farmers of Sutton remembered their Whig indoctrination. *"The law to bind all must be assented to by all"* they informed the Court,[48] and Greenwich labelled the suffrage a natural right.[49]

One of the most interesting aspects of the suffrage controversy was the occasional objection to the disfranchising of Negroes, mulattos, and Indians. Although there were probably not more than twenty-five blacks in the back country of Massachusetts, and although many a citizen had never laid eyes on one, a few towns were surprisingly eager to grant full political rights to the "inferior" races. Thus Georgetown declared it manifestly wrong that a man "born in Africa, India, or ancient America or even being much sunburnt deprived him of a vote...." [50] Sutton asserted the disfranchisement of Negroes "manifestly adds to the already accumulated load of guilt lying upon the land in supporting a slave." [51] The inconsistency between the institution of slavery and the natural rights philosophy was evident to many New Englanders.[52]

47. Massachusetts Archives, 156, p. 366.
48. *Ibid.*, 369. "The Great Secret of Government is governing all by all," declared Spencer. *Ibid.*, 160, p. 7. See also returns of Chesterfield, *ibid.*, 156, p. 343, and Williamstown, *ibid.*, 344.
49. *Ibid.*, 327.
50. *Ibid.*, 407.
51. *Ibid.*, 369.
52. William Gordon, in an article of October, 1776, had declared after quoting the preamble of the Declaration of Independence, "If these, Gentlemen, are our genuine sentiments, and we are not provoking the Deity by acting hypocritically to serve a turn, let us apply ourselves earnestly to the extirpation of slavery among ourselves." *Independent Chron-*

Various other radical proposals were advanced in the interest of democratic reform. Royalston and Southampton demanded the local election of all judicial officials.[53] "Who has the boldness to say that the people are not suitable to put powers in the hands of their own officers?" asked Westminster.[54] New Salem called for local autonomy in all judicial matters and asked for a constitutional limit on "Sallarys, Pencions, and fees." Sutton wanted a popular referendum on all legislation. The demand for provisions against plural officeholding came from scores of towns. Many felt the need of a bill of rights. Little Greenwich summed up well the objections of the democratic opponents of the constitution. "It would entirely divest the good people of this state of many of the privileges which God and nature has given them, and which have been so much contended for, and giving away that power to a few individuals which ought forever to remain with the people inviolate who consider themselves free and independent." [55]

The great majority of towns calling for democratic reforms were in the interior or western part of the state. It is significant that not a single demand of this nature came from Suffolk, Bristol, Middlesex, or Barnstable counties. This does not necessarily mean, however, that democracy was purely a doctrine of the toil-hardened farmers and village solons of the newly settled regions. There may have been a good deal of democratic sentiment among the lower classes in Salem, Ipswich, and Boston—indeed, mob activities in the early years of the Revolution suggest there was—but it did not

icle, Oct. 3, 1776. He labelled the disfranchising clause in the constitution "blacker than any negro" and evidence to the world that "they [the Court] mean their own rights only and not those of mankind." *Continental Journal*, Apr. 9, 1778.

53. Massachusetts Archives, 156, pp. 312, 321.
54. *Ibid.*, 160, p. 18.
55. *Ibid.*, 156, p. 327.

become articulate at this time. The merchant and lawyer class was usually able, through its control of town meetings, to direct the expression of public sentiment. The returns from the smaller communities of the interior, therefore, probably express much more accurately the views of the majority of the people because of the lack of a dominant class able to secure acceptance of its views.

If democrats denounced the constitution because it did not provide for political equality and majority rule, some conservatives, mostly in the larger eastern towns, opposed it because they thought it lacked adequate safeguards for accumulated wealth. The clearest statement of the conservative position is contained in *The Essex Result,* a memorial to the General Court adopted by an Essex County convention called to protest the discrimination against the East in the apportionment of representation.[56] Printed as a pamphlet which was widely circulated throughout the state, the memorial was written by young Theophilus Parsons, a self-styled "moderate" Whig who was destined to become an outstanding New England Federalist.[57] The most remarkable aspect of *The Essex Result* is the manner in which it appropriated the philosophy of natural rights for the protection of property. In Jeffersonian terms Parsons acknowledged that "All men are born equally free" and can only be bound by laws to which they have given their consent.[58] Like many

56. William Gordon computed that under the apportionment of the proposed constitution, 10 towns of 60 voters each would have exactly the same number of representatives as 5 towns of 519 voters apiece, a difference in ratio of 10:600 against 10:2,595. *Continental Journal,* Apr. 16, 1778. Plymouth noted in its return that the coastal towns would be at a disadvantage "whenever any commercial question is agitated in the General Assembly." Massachusetts Archives, 156, p. 426.

57. The pamphlet is printed in Theophilus Parsons, Jr., *Memoir of Theophilus Parsons* (Boston, 1859), 359-402.

58. *Ibid.,* 365-366.

democrats, he criticized the constitution because it contained
no bill of rights and made no provision for proportionate
representation and religious liberty. But while desiring reform in these matters his formula for a free government
was to divide political power between the propertied minority and the unpropertied majority in such a manner that
the holders of accumulated wealth would always have a veto
over legislation harmful to their interests. To bring about
what at first appears to be an equal distribution of power between the two groups, Parsons would give each a predomi-
nant voice in legislation which affected its interests: "If the
law affects only the persons of the members, the consent of a
majority of members is sufficient. If the law affects the property only, the consent of those who hold a majority of the
property is enough. If it affects (as it will very frequently, if
not always), both the person and the property, the consent of
a majority of the members, and of those members also who
hold a majority of the property, is necessary." [59] If the consent
of the holders of property is not obtained to a law affecting
them, "those who make the law in this case give and grant
what is not theirs. The law, in its principles, becomes a second
stamp act."

To give institutional form to the dualism represented by
the objects of legislation, he planned for the Senate to be the
exclusive representative of property and the House, of
persons. Members of the upper chamber would be substantial
property owners, elections would be indirect, and suffrage
qualifications high. Counties would be the units for representation and the apportionment of delegates made on the
basis of the taxes paid by each, thus securing the dominance
of the mercantile East. The lower house was to be a microcosm of the unpropertied majority. All freemen "of independence and discretion" would have the right to vote, no

59. *Ibid.*, 371.

property qualifications were to be required of members, and representation, based on the town unit, would be proportionate to population.

At first glance, Parsons' scheme of bicameralism might seem to strike a balance between the interests of property and persons. But actually the propertied minority would be dominant. While, according to his plan, the middling poor would be excluded from any influence in the Senate, the wealthy could bring their power to bear in the lower house both as voters and members. Also, proportionate representation would give greater weight to the eastern towns controlled by the upper classes than to the democratic communities of the interior. But most important, Parsons would require a property qualification of more than £1000 for the governor and would give him an absolute veto with the consent of his Council.[60] The wealthy chief executive might be considered no less a guardian of property than the Senate. With two of the three main departments of government prepared to oppose radical legislation, the will of a majority of persons could never be translated into law if it infringed upon the sanctity of accumulated wealth.

It is interesting to note how Parsons anticipated Calhoun's doctrine of the concurrent majority. The insistence by the southern statesman that no proposal involving the rights of the South should become law without the consent of the southern states parallels Parsons' dictum, "The holders of property must be in the majority in any question affecting property." Both men considered the principle of concurrent majority to be an equitable corollary of majority rule rather than a negation of it.[61] Their logic was based on an assump-

60. *Ibid.*, 384, 397.
61. "The legislative power must be so formed and exerted, that in prescribing any rule of action...the majority must consent," Parsons declared. *Ibid.*, 370.

tion that political society was not merely an aggregation of people, but a collection of interests as well. Any true majority, therefore, must include interests other than the will of a majority of persons.

Parsons' rationale for bicameralism is taken almost verbatim from *Thoughts on Government.*[62] But he and Adams had quite different conceptions of the purpose of the upper house. Adams, thinking in terms of a republican equivalent for king, nobles, and commons, wanted representation for the upper caste of society, not necessarily the propertied men. In his eyes, property qualifications were not exclusively designed to separate the friends from the foes of property, but served to indicate the men who were industrious, stable, and devoted to the best interests of the community. Adams was in the best sense a Puritan, interested in values and not accumulation. His admiration for the secularized puritan way of life of the eighteenth century was deep, and he conceived his first duty to be the maintenance of that tradition. The thing he most deplored about the changes that had taken place since 1776 was not the violence done to property but the new men of no background and—as he conceived it—selfish aims, who had been thrown to the top by the revolutionary ferment. His greatest fear was that they would knock the props from under the essentially stable colonial society in a wild rush to benefit from its destruction.

Although Adams had designed the lower house to be the representative of the people, he did not expect it to represent what were to him the dregs of society. The only people who mattered politically, or any other way, were the substantial people, and these could be recognized by the possession of some property. Certainly it would be highly dangerous to

62. Compare *Thoughts on Government* in Charles F. Adams (ed.), *The Works of John Adams,* 10 Vols. (Boston, 1850-1856), IV, 195-196, and *The Essex Result* in Parsons, *Memoir,* 376-379.

provide representation in government for those whose main aim would be to overthrow it or at least turn it to their own selfish ends. Thus there was no inconsistency, from his point of view, between a restricted suffrage for the lower house and his statement in *Thoughts on Government* that the house should "think, feel, reason, and act" like the people at large. Parsons, on the other hand, regarded the lower house rather as a safety valve for pent-up popular passions, which, if not provided means of escape, would explode and destroy property. More materialistic than Adams, he abandoned the attempt to make government the sponsor of moral values. In *The Essex Result* there is little or no nostalgia for the old order, no lamentation over the viciousness of the times, no idealization of balanced government, no trumpeting of doom or forecast of anarchy.[63] The conservatives of the Essex convention resigned themselves to the need for innovations and paid their devoirs to the liberal clichés of the day. In return for this concession they demanded absolute protection for property. Thus in effect they turned the natural rights philosophy into a property rights philosophy. The first theorists in America to enlist political liberalism in the service of special interests, they resemble the industrial capitalists of the nineteenth century who transformed the doctrines of *laissez faire* economics into a defense of monopolistic capitalism. *The Essex Result* foreshadows the Federalist compromise with the internal results of the Revolution.

In conclusion, the proposed constitution of 1778 was defeated by the united action of three distinct political groups in Massachusetts, each of whom had a different set of objec-

---

63. For examples of the old conservatism, see "Spectator," Boston *Gazette*, Feb. 10, 1777; "Mentor," *ibid.*, Apr. 20, 1778; "Benevolus," *Continental Journal*, May 27, 1779; "Faithful Friend," *Independent Chronicle*, July 27, Aug. 7, 1779.

tions in mind. First were those who would probably have accepted the instrument except for the fear that the members of the General Court would utilize it to perpetuate themselves in power. In the terms of the Boston return, they demanded that fundamental law be drafted by a convention which could not profit by its own handiwork and that the final instrument contain strict rules against plural office-holding. The second group, whose ideas are well expressed in *The Essex Result,* felt that the proposed constitution was defective because it did not guarantee the political dominance of the propertied minority. The third group—yeoman farmers from the interior towns—repudiated it because it did not introduce democracy.

Although vague and confused as to the practical methods of institutionalizing their ideal, these primitive democrats shared common assumptions regarding the status of citizens and the authority for government. In the first place, they felt that every adult male should have an equal right to participate in political life regardless of status based on possessions. Here they came into conflict with the overwhelming majority of the politically active class, who would carry equality no farther than equal legal rights and the abolition of hereditary privilege. The upper classes regarded property qualifications for participation in politics as almost an element of natural law, for the purpose of these qualifications was to protect that most important natural right—property itself. In the second place, the advocates of democracy assumed that all government should be a function of representation, and that the will of a majority of citizens, faithfully reflected in a legislature, should be the ultimate authority for political decision. The Whig leaders, on the other hand, regarded representation as a function of government. They believed that political authority should contain a large discretionary element. Not majority will, but justice, as interpreted by the propertied ruling class, should constitute the standard for political decision. In the third place, the democrats had a deep suspicion of centralized authority. They felt that the wider the area over which a single government extended its sway, the farther it retreated from the reach of the governed. Hence they tended to identify centralization with tyranny. The Whig leaders preferred a certain amount of centralization because it strengthened their control over the Revolutionary movement while contributing to the efficiency of the government.

The returns on the proposed constitution of 1778 had made it clear that the formation of a constitution required a special convention. But would the representatives of the people with constituent powers alone be actuated by different motives than the representatives of the people with legislative powers? Would a mere narrowing of authorization make delegates more responsive to the desires of the common people? Opposition to the General Court had temporarily obscured the large area of disagreement among its opponents. It was evident that democrats and conservatives, their ideas crystallized by the constitution of 1778, would clash even more bitterly during the next attempt to write fundamental law.

ELEVEN

The Search Concluded:
The Constitutional Convention

THE need for a strong and confident administration in Massachusetts had never been greater than during the years 1779 and 1780, the nadir of the Revolution. While British armies crisscrossed the South and Washington was immobilized on the Hudson, the disastrous Penobscot expedition, undertaken by the militia, had left a large part of Maine in the hands of the enemy and had saddled the state with a new load of debt. Eastern and western towns accused each other of profiteering as the currency plunged and prices spiralled.

Not the least of the problems facing the government was a threat of secession from the towns of Berkshire County. Swayed by the Lockean logic of Thomas Allen, the people there refused to recognize the Charter government and steadfastly maintained that they were still in a state of nature. The proposed constitution of 1778 and the attempts to reopen the courts aroused so much antagonism that a county convention warned the government—with considerable sarcasm—that there "are other States, which have Constitutions who Will, we doubt not, bad as we are, gladly receive Us." [1] Although the General Court sent a commission to ascertain the grievances of the intransigent farmers and gratuitously passed an act of oblivion—which was highly resented because it appeared to be a strategem whereby the Court could obtain acceptance of its jurisdiction—the towns reiterated their determination to withhold recognition. They made it plain that nothing less than a constitution drafted by a convention and accepted by popular referendum could give legitimacy to political authority. Until the ratification of the Constitution of 1780 the county was, for all intents and purposes, an independent republic even though it maintained representation in the General Court. No doubt many of the farmers were more interested in preventing the establishment of courts in which they could be sued for debt than in the intricacies of constitutional procedure. But regardless of their motives, their position appeared to have enough justification by the theory of consent government so that the Boston regime, beset by enemies from within and without, did not feel capable of forcing its jurisdiction on the county.[2]

On February 19, 1779, the General Court formally bowed to the demand for a convention by requesting the town selectmen throughout the state to put two questions to the qualified voters: "First, whether they choose at this time to have a Constitution or Form of Government made; Secondly, whether they will empower their representatives for the next year to vote for the calling of a State Convention, for the sole purpose of forming a new Constitution...." [3] The returns of the towns, in terms of popular vote, showed 6,612

1. *Acts and Resolves of the Province of Massachusetts Bay*, 21 Vols. (Boston, 1869-1922), V, 1028-1029; J. E. A. Smith, *History of Pittsfield* (Boston, 1869), 360-362.

2. Documents bearing on the controversy between the Berkshire towns and the General Court will be found in *Acts and Resolves of the Province of Massachusetts Bay*, V, 1029-1032, 932-933; Smith, *Pittsfield*, 362-365.

3. *Journal of the Convention, 1779-1780* (Boston, 1832), 189.

in favor of the two propositions, 2,639 opposed.[4] The strongest support for them, as might be supposed, came from the West. The vote in Berkshire was 972 to 3, but the voters of Essex, Barnstable, and the Maine counties opposed the propositions by a considerable majority.[5] The probable reason for the hostility of these eastern counties was the fear that the West would use the occasion to force a revision of the proportionate representation in effect since 1776. In Essex, where Parsons and his friends exerted influence, there might also have been a feeling that the people were not fit for the delicate task of drafting fundamental law.

After tabulation of the vote the Court directed the selectmen to call town meetings for the election of as many delegates to the Convention as the towns were entitled to send representatives. The suffrage was extended to free adult males and the Court further recommended that the Convention be empowered to put the constitution into effect if accepted by two-thirds of the voters.[6]

The body so elected met September 1, 1779, in Cambridge and chose as its president James Bowdoin, possibly the wealthiest man in the state. Although there were 293 members, the highest recorded vote on any question was 247.[7] A committee of thirty, appointed to draft an instrument, delegated the task to a subcommittee of three consisting of Bowdoin and "the brace of Adamses," John and Samuel.

John Adams approached the task with a conservatism that had hardened with the years. His experiences in the Continental Congress had not increased his faith in mankind nor

4. Samuel E. Morison, "The Vote of Massachusetts on Summoning a Constitutional Convention," Massachusetts Historical Society, *Proceedings,* 68 Vols. (Boston, 1791-1952), Vol. L, 246.

5. See Morison's tabulation of the vote. *Ibid.,* 248 ff.

6. *Journal of the Convention,* 5-6; Morison, "The Struggle over the Adoption of the Constitution of Massachusetts, 1780," *Proceedings,* 355.

7. Morison, "Constitution of Massachusetts," *Proceedings,* 356.

eased his pessimism regarding the permanence of free government. After the British connection had been severed, his enthusiasm for popular participation in constitution-making had diminished to such an extent that when informed by Warren of the plan to submit the constitution of 1778 to the people he had replied, "It is a Pity you should be obliged to lay it before them. It will divide and distract them." [8] Samuel Adams, no less conservative than his cousin, showed no desire to liberalize the provincial government after royal authority had been suppressed. Essentially in agreement with John Adams on political questions, he shared the Whig leaders' distrust for political parvenus and composed conventional jeremiads on the corruption of the times. Replying in 1777 to a letter of Warren's complaining of dissidents in Massachusetts who did not see eye to eye with the Court leaders, he declared, "I will say in the Apostolick language 'I would they were all cut off (banished at least) who trouble you.'" [9] The extent of Sam Adams' participation in the framing of the Constitution is in doubt, but he is reputed to have been the author of the Declaration of Rights.[10] John Adams also claimed this honor.[11] Little is known of Bowdoin's political opinions, but it is safe to say that they differed little from those of John Adams, particularly since Adams later recommended him for the governorship.[12]

8. *Warren-Adams Letters,* 2 Vols. (Boston, 1917, 1925), Massachusetts Historical Society, *Collections,* LXXII, LXXIII, I, 322.

9. *Ibid.,* 339.

10. Adams' part in the constitutional convention has been examined by Wells. See William V. Wells, *The Life and Public Services of Samuel Adams,* 3 Vols. (Boston, 1865), III, 80-86 (note).

11. See letter of John Adams to W. D. Williamson printed in Massachusetts Historical Society, *Proceedings,* 1873-1875, 301 (note).

12. In the early years of the Revolution, Bowdoin's radicalism regarding the imperial relationship was of the same color as the Adamses. See

Recognizing Adams' superior ability in matters of political science, the two other members of the subcommittee devolved upon him the task of composing the draft.[13] More comprehensive and detailed than most other constitutions of the period, the result of his labors provided for the rigid separation of the organs of government and conferred an absolute veto upon the governor. Possession of real property yielding an annual income of £3 or a £60 estate in personalty was required of all voters. The property qualifications for officeholders, although about the same in money value as those in the constitution of 1778, required that the entire amount be in real estate. All judges held their offices during good behavior and were appointed by the governor with the consent of his council. Restrictions on plural officeholding were limited to prohibiting judges from holding seats in the legislature. In addition to his absolute veto, the governor was given complete control of the military and was empowered to prorogue the General Court for as much as ninety days and adjourn it in case of disagreement between the two houses. Representation was proportionate to polls for the House and to tax receipts for the Senate. Towns with less than 150 taxpayers were required to join with other communities in order to obtain representation.

The Adams draft is one of the most conservative to come from the pen of any Revolutionary leader. To some extent the exigencies of the times and Adams' disillusionment may have been responsible for its undemocratic nature, but his desire to revive the institutions of royal government in republican form was also important. He felt that only a return to

---

Francis G. Walett, "James Bowdoin, Patriot Propagandist," *New England Quarterly*, XXIII (1950), 320-338.

13. The Adams draft is printed in *Journal of the Convention*, 191-215, and in Charles F. Adams (ed.), *The Works of John Adams*, 10 Vols. (Boston, 1850-1856), IV, 219-267.

traditional forms and the exclusion from the political process of all who might benefit from an alteration of the *status quo* could bring permanent stability and the maintenance of essential human rights. It is significant that Adams raised the suffrage requirement for all elections to the same level which Parsons had stipulated for the Senate in *The Essex Result*. Adams may have felt that once political power was placed in the hands of those who could use it intelligently, honestly, and disinterestedly, there was no reason why the same electorate should not choose the governor, senators, and representatives. His was a conservatism of values and relationships rather than a conservatism for upper-class interests as exhibited by Parsons. The protection of property was of course an important consideration for Adams, but only as a means of maintaining the type of society in which all rights would be protected.

From the beginning of the Constitutional Convention in the fall of 1779 until its dissolution in the late spring of 1780 the sessions were poorly attended, partly because of the hard winter—the worst since 1717. Only the Boston-Hartford road was open to travel in the central part of the state and in April the snow still covered the fence posts in some of the western towns.[14] During the fall sessions, after Adams had left for Europe, democrats made efforts to amend his draft and the Declaration of Rights. They attacked good-behavior tenure for judges, the two-house legislature, and state support of religion. This last provision particularly aroused their antagonism.

The rejected constitution of 1778, by ignoring the religious question, had made disestablishment of the Congregational church possible by legislation. But Article III of the new Declaration of Rights, by declaring that the legislature had

14. Morison, "Constitution of Massachusetts," *Proceedings,* 357.

the right to require the towns to tax for church support and by identifying such taxation with the maintenance of public morality, gave constitutional sanction to the establishment and raised a formidable obstacle to the separation of church and state.[15] Dissenters had not ceased their agitation for complete religious freedom after the rebuffs Backus had received from the General Court. In 1778 a series of writers in *The Independent Chronicle* called for a definition of the rights of conscience [16] and a satirist of some talent delivered a poetic blast against the church which reads in part:

> Religion should be well supported,
> With arms and constables escorted,

. . . .

15. The article reads in part: "As the happiness of a people, and the good order and preservation of civil government, essentially depend upon piety, religion, and morality; and as these cannot be generally diffused throughout a community but by the institution of public worship of God and of public instruction in piety, religion and morality: therefore, to promote the happiness, and to secure the good order and preservation of their government, the people of this Commonwealth have a right to invest their legislature with power to authorize and require, and the legislature shall from time to time authorize and require, the several towns, parishes, and precincts and other bodies politic, or religious societies, to make suitable provision, at their own expense, for the public worship of God, and for the support and maintenance of public Protestant teachers of piety, religion, and morality, in all cases where such provision shall not be made voluntarily.

"And the people of this Commonwealth also have a right to, and do invest their legislative with authority to enjoin upon all the subjects an attendance upon the instructions of the public teachers aforesaid, at stated times and seasons, if there be any upon whose instructions they can conscientiously and conveniently attend." *Journal of the Convention*, 223.

John Adams said later, "The article relative to religion was not drawn by me or by the sub-committee. I could not satisfy my own judgment with any article I thought would be acceptable, and further, I thought that some of the clergy or older and graver persons than myself would be more likely to hit the taste of the public." Massachusetts Historical Society *Proceedings*, 1873-1875, 301 (note).

16. See issues of Feb. 26, March 5, April 9, 1778.

Let heretics no more presume
To fault our creed or read our doom.

. . . .

Let prisons, halters, tests and axes
Support our Parsons' yearly taxes.
Shall every clownish fellow choose
What priest he'll hear, what prayer he'll use?
And justify such independence? [17]

Backus, in an effective pamphlet, *Government and Liberty Described, and Ecclesiastical Tyranny Exposed,* again charged that compulsory support of religion amounted to taxation without representation. To illustrate how far the Congregational leaders had departed from the liberalism they had professed when confronted by the threat of an American episcopate, he quoted from a sermon delivered by Charles Chauncy before the war: "We are, in principle, against all religious establishments. It does not appear to us that God has entrusted the state with a right to make religious establishments. We desire no other liberty than to be left unrestrained in the exercise of our principles, insofar as we are good members of society. All religions are equal by the Charter of Massachusetts." [18]

Conservatives and the clergy retorted to attacks with two arguments of some validity. In the first place, they insisted that the tax-supported Congregational church could not properly be called an establishment as long as dissenters could secure exemptions. Although perhaps theoretically valid, the point rested on a rather narrow definition of terms. Establishment or no establishment, the Congregational

17. *Ibid.,* Feb. 26, 1778.
18. Isaac Backus, *Government and Liberty Described, and Ecclesiastical Tyranny Exposed* (Boston, 1778), 4-5.

church nevertheless occupied a privileged position, and dissenters found the securing of exemptions to be a difficult and expensive process. The defenders of the church also replied to critics by asserting that state support of religion amounted to support of public morality and that taxation for religious purposes was as necessary as legislation against obscenity, fornication, and perverted sexual practices. As one writer put it, "All republics depend on religion. Should the state not preserve the basis of its own existence?" [19] "But we are attempting to support (it is said) the kingdom of Christ," wrote a committee of the Boston town meeting reporting on the Constitution of 1780. "What will be the consequence of [a refusal to do so]? The greatest disorders, if not a dissolution of society. May we not be permitted to assist civil society by an adoption, and a teaching of the best set of morals that were ever offered to the world? To object to these morals or even to the piety and religion we aim to inculcate, because they are drawn from the Gospel, must appear very singular to an assembly generally professing themselves Christians." [20] As another newspaper writer declared, "When men enter into a state of society, certain duties result from such a state which they owe to each other.... For this end it is necessary that the people should be informed of their duty.... All the government has done is to provide suitable instructors." [21]

Some conservatives foresaw anarchy and chaos if the state withdrew its sponsorship of religion. Thus Parson Phillips Payson declared in 1778, "Let the restraints of religion once be broken down, as they infallibly would be by leaving the subject of public worship to the humor of the multitude, and we might well defy all human wisdom and power to sup-

19. *Independent Chronicle,* Apr. 20, 1778.
20. *Boston Town Records, 1778-1783,* 134.
21. Boston *Gazette,* Jan. 18, 1779.

port and preserve order in government and state." [22] One member of the Convention probably spoke for those clergymen who feared for their livings if compelled to rely upon the uncertain bounty of their parishioners: "If there is no law to support religion, farewell meeting houses, farewell ministers, farewell all religion." [23] An explosion of indiscriminate rancor by "Irenaeus" in the *Continental Journal* March 9, 1780, showed the intensity of feeling over the issue. He labelled the opponents of Article III "a certain junto, composed of disguised Tories, profane and licentious deists, avaricious worldlings, disaffected sectaries, and furious blind bigots."

"Philanthropos," another newspaper editorialist, gave an effective answer to the advocates of state-sponsored religion which was echoed by scores of towns in their returns on the Constitution of 1780. Pointing out that religion and morality had thrived when independent of the state and wilted when under its control, he assured doubtful clergymen that the gospel of Christ was strong enough to stand without political support and that morality was an inherent trait in mankind. He felt that any religion which relied upon the patronage of the state for its existence was rotten at the core and deserved oblivion. Therefore he proposed a substitute for Article III:

All men have a natural and inalienable right to worship God according to their own conscience and understanding; and no man ought or of right can be compelled to attend any religious worship, or erect or support any place of worship, or maintain any ministry contrary to or against his own free will and consent. Nor can any man who acknowledges the being of God be justly deprived of any civil right as a citizen, on account of his religious sentiments, or peculiar mode of religious worship. And that no

22. Backus, *Government and Liberty Described*, 6-7.
23. *Independent Ledger*, April 17, 1780.

authority can or ought to be vested in, or assumed by, any power whatsoever, that shall in any case interfere with, or in any manner controul the right of conscience in the free exercise of religious worship.[24]

This statement in many ways reflects the spirit of Jefferson's Bill of Religious Freedom, but it is important to note that by implication it would allow the state to place disabilities upon atheists and might even be construed to allow a general assessment scheme like that proposed in Virginia. Jefferson, of course, would place religion completely outside the sphere of government.

While the religious question raised tempers all over the state, attempts were being made in the Convention to liberalize the Adams draft. On the whole these were unsuccessful, partly, no doubt, because of thin western representation. When the Convention resumed its deliberations January 27, 1780, after an adjournment, only 60 out of some 300 delegates were present, most of them from Suffolk, Essex, and Middlesex counties.[25] Half the counties had no representation at all. On February 12, after an extended debate, Adams' proposal to give the governor the power of judicial appointment was endorsed.[26] A few days later judges of common pleas were assured tenure during good behavior.[27] The Convention refused by a vote of 64-27 to eliminate the suffrage qualifications for the lower house,[28] but some alterations were adopted reflecting the views of the interior towns. The governor's veto was made suspensive, and part of his military patronage was removed.[29] After inconclusive discussions on the question of

24. *Independent Chronicle*, Apr. 6, 1780.
25. *Journal of the Convention*, 55-57.
26. *Ibid.*, 104.
27. *Ibid.*, 116.
28. *Ibid.*, 136.
29. Adams said these changes were made "to my sorrow." Massachusetts Historical Society *Proceedings*, 1873-1875, 301 (note).

representation in the lower house, Adams' proportionate formula was modified in order to give at least one delegate to every town. Yet all in all, the changes in the draft were so few that cousin Sam could write to John Adams in March with evident relief, "the fabrick of government is not materially injured." [30]

After the Constitution was engrossed, the members of the Convention apparently felt the need to recommend their handiwork to the people and explain the reasoning behind several of the articles. Such a course might seem advisable in view of the fact that about half the adult male population was asked to vote away its suffrage right (the new property qualifications were 50 per cent higher than under the Charter), that all citizens were requested to submit to taxation for religious purposes, and that the small towns were expected to be content with approximately the same apportionment of representation which they had denounced since 1776. Therefore, the Convention appointed a committee to compose an address to the people designed to reconcile them to the more unpalatable elements of the Constitution. The final draft was probably written by Sam Adams [31] and gives a unique insight into the conservative Whig mind of the Revolutionary period.

Article III of the Declaration of Rights stood perhaps in most need of justification. Without much regard for logic the *Address* insisted that its primary purpose was to guarantee freedom of conscience—a right "infinitely more valuable than all others." Public support of the Congregational church was justified in the conventional manner: "Surely it would

---

30. Harry A. Cushing (ed.), *The Writings of Samuel Adams*, 4 Vols. (New York, 1904-1908), IV, 183.

31. Dr. John Eliot attributed the *Address* to Adams and "another gentleman." William V. Wells came across fragments of a draft in Adams' handwriting. Wells, *Samuel Adams*, III, 89.

be an affront to the people of Massachusetts Bay to labor to convince them, that the Honor and Happiness of a People depend upon Morality; that Public Worship of GOD has a tendency to inculcate the Principles thereof, as well as to preserve a people from foresaking Civilization, and falling into a State of Savage barbarity." [32]

Next the committee explained the need for a two-house legislature. Reflecting the influence of Parsons, a committee member, the *Address* stated that the Senate was designed to represent property, and the House, persons; but the members did not follow Parsons in justifying the Senate veto on the basis of a "concurrent majority" in questions regarding property. Instead they cited the need of a check on hasty legislation—an explanation equally in accord with Whig theory and less likely to arouse the antagonism of relatively unpropertied citizens.

The third point requiring explanation was the restricted suffrage. "Your delegates considered that persons who are twenty-one years of age, and have no property, are either those who live upon a part of a paternal estate, expecting the fee thereof, who are but just entering into business, or those whose idleness of Life and profligacy of manners will forever bar them from acquiring and possessing property. And we will submit it to the former class, whether they would not think it safer for them to have their right of voting for a representative suspended for a small space of time, than forever hereafter to have their privilege liable to the control of men who will pay less regard to the rights of property because they have nothing to lose." [33] The assumption that many citizens who did not accumulate real property or personalty worth £60 over a period of time were idle and profligate might have had some validity in other parts of the

32. *Journal of the Convention,* 218.
33. *Ibid.*

country where land was cheap and the extent of a man's wealth depended on the amount of it he had under cultivation. Such a view certainly was not true in Massachusetts, however, as one of the towns was to point out in its return on the constitution. The eastern part of the state was quite heavily settled, and much of what land remained in the West was in the hands of speculators. The war had rendered many people destitute, and even under the best of circumstances there were many thousands of hard-working men who could never acquire personal property worth £60. It is difficult to estimate the proportion of the adult male population disfranchised by the constitution, but in view of the outcry against the suffrage qualification, it must have been considerable.

The committee justified the suspensive veto on the ground that the governor was the representative of the whole people, a theory which gained general acceptance during the Jackson administrations but which was unorthodox in the eighteenth century. To John Adams and most other conservatives of his time, the executive veto was a limited version of the royal prerogative—a discretionary power exercised for the benefit of the people rather than a response to popular will. In justifying the extensive executive patronage the reasoning of the *Address* was also somewhat in advance of its time. The committee asserted that one person would be more able to control the mass of officials than a legislative body. The point was not only sound but showed a disposition to place administration where it belonged—in the executive rather than in the legislative branch of the government. Despite lip service to the principle of separation of departments, the first constitutions had all tended to give powers to the legislatures which normally belonged to the executive. But now that the memories of Hutchinson and his clique were fading, conservatives in Massachusetts began to lose their fear of a strong execu-

tive. By 1787 conservatives everywhere would be able to view
the executive power with an equanimity impossible during
the Revolutionary period. It is important to note, however,
that democrats continued to regard governors and their
functions with suspicion.

The paragraph on representation revealed the dilemma
which faced the Convention in trying to reconcile the proportionate principle with the demand of the small towns
for individual representation. Realizing that the formula
adopted did not completely satisfy either the small interior
communities or the large seaboard centers, the committee
could only observe that "An exact representation would be
unpracticable even in a system of government arising from
a state of nature, and much more so in a state divided into
nearly three hundred corporations." [34]

During the spring of 1780 the Constitution and the *Address*
were read and debated throughout the state. In an attempt to
avoid a repetition of the failure in 1778 the Convention requested the towns to vote only on individual articles and to
give an adjourned session the power to revise those not re-
ceiving a two-thirds majority. The revised instrument would
then be put in force by the Convention without a further
popular referendum. [35] Acceptance of the proposal would
guarantee the state a constitution regardless of the amount of
opposition to individual articles, but the people would lose
some of their control over the terms of the finished instrument and the Convention would exercise more discretion
than could be sanctioned by the logic of constitutional procedures. In spite of these drawbacks, however, popular consent for the proposal was apparently secured.

When the returns on the Constitution were tabulated, it
was apparent that the very points on which the Convention

34. *Ibid.*, 219.
35. *Ibid.*, 164, 169.

sought to reconcile their constituents—taxation for religious purposes, limited suffrage, bicameralism, and the gubernatorial appointing power—were the ones which aroused the most protest. Objections to Article III of the Declaration of Rights were frequent and bitter. "The Christian religion stands in no need of the civil power for its support," wrote the Bristol town meeting, reflecting the opinions of "Philanthropos." "It is contrary to the true spirit of religion that the civil power should interfear, as Christ has declared his Kingdom is not of this world. By experience we know that religion has been greatly corrupted by its being mixt with the civil government." [36] "Christ himself is the only Lord of Conscience and King and Law Giver in his Church," declared Granville. "Teachers of religion are officers in his kingdom, qualified and sent by him, for whose maintenance he hath made sufficient provision by the laws which belong to his own Kingdom." [37] There was no sectional cleavage in the opposition to Article III. At least two towns in Suffolk—of which Boston was one—seven in Middlesex, six in Bristol, six in Worcester, and eight in Berkshire rejected it because they were opposed in principle to state interference in religion. [38] Numerically the opposition was strongest in Suffolk, probably because Boston did not lay taxes for church support. Backus and the Baptists had repeatedly asserted, both before and after the outbreak of the Revolution, that they asked no more than the privilege accorded their churches there. [39] Some towns which accepted public support of religion rejected Article III because it did not clearly define the equality of the sects. A few thought it not strict enough. Although a majority of the voters approved the article, it failed by 8,885 to 6,225 to

36. Massachusetts Archives, 276, p. 37.
37. Ibid., 49.
38. Morison, "Constitution of Massachusetts," Proceedings, 379.
39. Alvah Hovey, Memoir of Isaac Backus (Boston, 1858), 167, 190, 221.

achieve the requisite two-thirds necessary for passage.[40] Nevertheless, as will be explained later, it remained in the Constitution without amendment.

If the Convention underestimated the people's desire for the separation of church and state, it overestimated their religious tolerance. By the Constitution every officeholder was compelled to declare himself a Christian, and a test oath was drawn up which excluded papists, but presumably not recusants.[41] The members must have been surprised indeed when a large number of towns—perhaps a majority—called for a more stringent test which would exclude all Catholics from office. The menace of Rome was forcefully asserted. "We think it dangerous to have the least opening for a Roman Catholic to fill the first seat of the Government," said Norton. Lexington, citing Robertson's *Charles V.*, sent in a long historical argument against admitting Catholics to office.[42] Sandisfield declared, "Since it is a community of Protestants that are covenanting and emerging from a state of nature, it is necessary to say that not only the governor, but all executive, legislative, and military officers shall be of the Protestant religion." [43] Sectional alignment on the question was much stronger than in the case of Article III. Most of the insistence for a stronger test came from the West, from the same towns which favored democratic reform of the gov-

40. Morison, "Constitution of Massachusetts," *Proceedings*, 411.

41. The oath included a declaration that "no foreign person, prince, prelate, etc., has any jurisdiction ... ecclesiastical, or spiritual, within this commonwealth." Chap. VI, Art. I. The committee explained in the *Address*, "We have found ourselves obliged by a solemn test, to provide for the exclusion of those from offices who will not disclaim those principles of spiritual jurisdiction which Catholics in some countries have held...." *Journal of the Convention*, 221. Morison estimates that one-third of the voters demanded that the governor be a Protestant. I would estimate the figure closer to 50 per cent.

42. Morison, "Constitution of Massachusetts," *Proceedings*, 382.

43. Massachusetts Archives, 276, p. 20.

ernment. At least forty in Worcester and Hampshire counties wanted all Catholics disqualified for officeholding.[44]

The restricted suffrage was next in order of unpopularity.[45] The protesting towns based their arguments on natural rights, the principle of no taxation without representation, and the accepted function of the House as the people's representative. Two towns took issue with the reasoning of the *Address:* "Doubtless there are, and ever will be some in the commonwealth who pay little regard to the rights of property," said Mansfield. "This we readily grant, yet on the other hand how many young men neither profligate nor idle persons, for some years must be debarred from that privilege [of voting]? How many sensible, honest, and maturely industrious men, by numberless misfortunes, never acquire and possess property to the value of £60? We readily allow as we said before that there are and ever will be some who pay little regard to the rights of property; but shall it be from thence argued that thousands of good, honest members of society shall be subjected to laws framed by legislators the election of whom they could have no voice in? Shall a subject of a free commonwealth be compelled to contribute to public expenses, give his personal services where necessary, and be excluded from voting for a representative? This appears to us in some degree slavery." [46] As in the returns on the rejected constitution of 1778, most of the objections to limited suffrage based on natural rights came from the West. New Marlborough pointed to the conflict between the equal

44. Morison, "Constitution of Massachusetts," *Proceedings,* 381.

45. Morison states that the limited suffrage was accepted by more than a two-thirds majority. *Ibid.,* 390. According to my own estimate, there was something approximating an even split on the question.

46. Massachusetts Archives, 276, p. 33. The return of the ancient and wealthy town of Dorchester paralleled this reasoning. Morison, "Constitution of Massachusetts," *Proceedings,* 391.

rights guaranteed by the Declaration of Rights and restrictions on voting. Tyringham predicted, "As the people have hitherto been called upon to vote themselves independent of Great Britain and to stand forth in defense of their darling rights and privileges, we imagine they will not now give up so dear a privilege." [47] Wilbraham, in direct contradiction to the logic of John Adams, asserted that the higher the property qualifications, the less integrity one would be likely to find among the voters. [48]

By far the most incisive criticism of the limited suffrage was contained in the return from Northampton, written by Joseph Hawley. His argument was based on all three contemporary premises: natural rights, the injustice of taxation without representation, and the function of the lower house. [49] Hawley had taken little part in politics during the Revolution. Afflicted with a melancholia that approached manic depression, he led a life of retirement broken only occasionally by sallies into public life. [50] Nevertheless, his reputation was undimmed, and he exerted a great influence over the western towns. "We humbly conceive," he wrote on behalf of Northampton, "that the exclusion we complain of directly militates and is absolutely repugnant to the genuine sense of the first article of the Declaration of Rights.... By that article all men are declared 'to be born free and equal.'... The right of enjoying that equality, freedom, and liberty, is in the same article declared unalienable. Very strange it would be if others should have a right ... to take away from any indi-

47. Massachusetts Archives, 276, p. 22.
48. Ibid., p. 72.
49. Printed in full in Mary C. Clune, "Joseph Hawley's Criticism of the Constitution of Massachusetts," Smith College Studies in History, 37 Vols. (Northampton, 1915-1951), III, 13-31. Excerpts printed in Morison, "Constitution of Massachusetts," Proceedings, 408-410.
50. E. Francis Brown, Joseph Hawley, Colonial Radical (New York, 1931), 170-173.

vidual that which he himself could not alienate...." [51] He
noted the injustice of denying the suffrage to persons who
were counted for purposes of representation and who constituted the natural constituency of the House. "Indeed, Gentlemen, we are shocked at the thought that the persons of adult
men should like live stock and dead chattels be brought...
to augment the capital whereon to draw representatives for
particular towns" and after the counting be "wholly sunk
and discarded... absolutely like brute beasts. It is impossible for us to admit so black a thought, as to imagine that the
convention had an intention by their address to beguile their
constituents into a supposition that provision was made in
the frame of government for a representation of persons, as
well as property... when they were conscious that it was
not so in fact." [52] He concluded several pages of heated argument with a resounding peroration. "Shall these poor
adult persons who are always to be taxed as high as our men
of property... who have gone for us into the greatest perils
and undergone infinite fatigues in the present war to preserve us from slavery,... some of them leaving at home their
poor families, to endure the sufferings of hunger and naked-
ness, shall they now be treated by us like villains or African
slaves? God forbid!" [53]

Objections against property qualifications for officeholding
were not as numerous as those against limited suffrage. Indeed, this is understandable, for although Whigs who accepted Parsons' line of reasoning could join with democrats
in demanding manhood suffrage for the lower house, only
thorough radicals would demand a lifting of all property
qualifications for office. Nevertheless there were a number of
towns which spoke against these provisions. Middleboro,

51. Clune, "Hawley's Criticism," Smith College *Studies*, 22-23.
52. *Ibid.*, 27, 19.
53. *Ibid.*, 27.

with considerable irony, asked what would be the result if the voters' choice for governor turned out to be worth only £999. Obviously the difference of one pound would determine his ability to hold the office. The town intimated that this was rather an inadequate measure of moral and intellectual qualities. Petersham admonished: "Riches and Dignity neither make the head wiser nor the heart better. The overgrown Rich we consider the most dangerous to the Liberties of a free State." [54]

The bicameral legislature and the gubernatorial veto provoked a good deal of hostile comment from those democrats who thought that government should be no more than an agency for majority will. Some towns felt that there could be no justification for a qualification of legislative supremacy by the separation of powers. As Professor Morison explains, they had "a suspicion, which was only too well founded, that the system of checks and balances would be used to defeat the popular will." [55]

Thus Rehoboth wanted a government "similar to Hon. Continental Congress" with local officials popularly elected. Middleboro predicted that unless the towns kept a tight rein over all public servants, they "would groan under a government of the most venal and wretched set of villains." Oakham sensed the odor of monarchy in the governor's veto power and Wilbraham thought the chief executive should be denied a voice in the legislature. Cummington proposed that both houses sit together and vote in one unit, as they had done before the separation of the town delegates and assistants in the early seventeenth century. Some of the towns, alarmed at the very prospect of a governor, thought the existing government, bad as it was, preferable to that provided by the Constitution. Swansea declared the House and Coun-

54. Morison, "Constitution of Massachusetts," *Proceedings*, 392.
55. *Ibid.*, 385.

cil "more pleasing to the People in General, and Particular
to the Inhabitants of the Town Swanzey." [56]

Some of the towns which wanted a unicameral legislature
were particularly anxious that judges and other judicial officials be locally elected. As might be expected, this feeling was
strongest in the West.[57]

The Convention was accused of many crimes of omission,
among them the failure to make obligatory a constitutional
revision at some date in the near future. Adams had made
no provision at all for amendment in his draft—mute testimony to his confidence in his powers as a political scientist—
but the delegates had inserted a stipulation calling for a re-
vising convention in 1795 if two-thirds of the qualified voters
requested it. Limiting this exercise of the constituent power
to the qualified voters was a significant departure from the
practice observed since 1776 of consulting the free male population on all constitutional questions.

The basis of representation for the lower house produced
wails of anguish from the West. In the name of equal representation many towns demanded a return to the colonial
apportionment. As Washington explained it, "Each town has
an undeniable right of equal representation in General Assembly, and whereas there is a large number of delegates
from the merchantile towns and but small numbers from
the inland Towns, we have laid our objection." [58]

Following the referendum the Convention met for a final
session in June, 1780, to examine the returns, revise the articles which did not receive the requisite two-thirds majority,

56. *Ibid*. Massachusetts Archives, 276, pp. 47, 72, 19, 40.

57. Morison, "Constitution of Massachusetts," *Proceedings*, 392.

58. Massachusets Archives, 276, p. 23. See also returns of West Stockbridge, *ibid*., 24; Sunderland, *ibid*., 67. Mendon, Spencer, Sutton and
Bridgewater proposed to divide the state into districts of equal voting
strength. Morison, "Constitution of Massachusetts," *Proceedings*, 388.

and ratify the finished instrument.[59] After counting the vote, it should have been evident that the article allowing taxation for religious purposes would have to be altered, and possibly the articles on the suffrage and the religious test; yet the committee to revise and arrange the returns adopted a method of tabulation which automatically secured a two-thirds majority for every part of the Declaration of Rights and the Constitution. The town vote on each article was tabulated as below:

| Towns | Pro | Con | If Amended | |
			Pro	Con

Unfavorable votes were entered twice, once as *con* and once as *pro if amended*. The final count was then reached by adding the *pro if amended* figure to the *pro* figure for the constitution *as it stood*. Sometimes *con* votes were left out of the final tabulation entirely. Thus by creating fictitious majorities, the ratification of the constitution was assured, but at the cost of distorting and in some cases deliberately disregarding the will of a large section of the population. Middleboro, for example, rejected the Constitution as a whole 220-0, labelling it "lengthy," "unmeaning," "repetitious," and "inconsistent." The town meeting then added amendments and revisions which completely changed its character and passed the new instrument 173-3. The Convention committee, by

59. *Journal of the Convention,* 170.

listing 173-3 in every "if amended" column, translated the
220-0 vote against the Constitution into 173-3 in favor of it
as it stood.[60]

In the case of many towns, therefore, the tabulation of the
vote was plainly fraudulent. If the delegates had made even
token alterations in some of the controversial articles, they
might have justified their method. But apparently, neither
the committee nor the Convention had any such intention
from the outset. As a result, it would be impossible to tell
today how much of the Constitution was ever legally ratified
without recounting the entire vote—a tremendous task because of the complexity and frequent ambiguity of the returns. When the committee submitted its report June 15—
apparently without a sum total figure on the vote—"The
several articles of the Declaration of Rights and Frame of
Government were...read separately, and the following
question put upon each: 'Is it your opinion that the people
have accepted this article?' Which, upon every individual
article, passed in the affirmative by a very great majority."[61]
This appeal to the delegates' "opinion" testifies to the questionable nature of the entire transaction.

Possibly the members of the Convention justified their
course by the desperate need for settled government. Another
failure in making a constitution might have been disastrous.
The delegates could be fairly sure that the people would
rather have an imperfect constitution than none at all. Mis-

60. Vote of Middleboro, Massachusetts Archives, 276, p. 40. Tabulation
by Convention, *ibid.*, 59. In September the "173-3" agitated for a county
convention to overthrow "the said constitution or frame of government...
whose uncouth and unhallowed strides may crush the people into a
state of abject slavery." "Some Objections made to the State Constitution,
1780," Massachusetts Historical Society *Proceedings*, Vol. L, p. 54. Morison
gives a detailed explanation of the tabulation procedure in "Constitution of
Massachusetts," *Proceedings*, 396-399 (with notes).

61. *Journal of the Convention*, 180.

takes could be rectified in the future. Pittsfield, for example, apparently voted unanimously in favor of the instrument even though it contained many stipulations in direct contradiction to the town's demands since 1775.[62]

One factor which undoubtedly strengthened the delegates in their determination to have a constitution at all costs was the continuing threat of secession from the West. From February to May, 1780, a convention of Berkshire towns, meeting intermittently at Pittsfield, considered asking the Court "to set them off to a neighboring state that has a constitution." [63] Stockbridge, Great Barrington, and Sheffield generally opposed the proposition, but Pittsfield, Lenox, and Hancock, swayed by the eloquence of Thomas Allen, agitated for separation.[64] Possibly the movement caused disruptive internal conditions that alienated some local leaders, for there is no hint of a desire for secession in the returns on the Constitution. The issue died after ratification, but the old antagonisms remained, to crop out again in Shays's rebellion.

It is paradoxical that the first constitution formed by democratic processes should be one of the most undemocratic of its time. Although drafted by a convention elected by manhood suffrage, it was not only one of the most aristocratic of the Revolutionary period but also more thoroughly ensured government by the upper classes than the constitution of 1778 rejected by the same electorate.

There are several possible explanations of the paradox. First, and probably most important, was the fact that the need for constitutional government transcended the desire for democratic reforms. Second, the membership of the Con-

62. Smith, *Pittsfield*, 370.

63. Fred E. Haynes, The Struggle for the Constitution of 1780 in Massachusetts (doctoral dissertation, Harvard College Library, 1891), 170.

64. *Ibid.*, 172.

vention differed little from that of the legislative bodies from 1776 to 1780. Despite the distrust of the people for the General Court, they had armed most of its members with constituent powers in 1779. Whether by necessity or indifference, the people of Massachusetts depended on the Whig aristocracy for the administration of their government. From time to time there had been an influx of new men into the House of Representatives, and the leadership had passed from Warren and Adams to Hancock in 1778. Yet throughout there had been continuity of policy. Despite the Cassandra-like warnings of the Adamses, the new men had for the most part accepted the values and political science of the Revolutionary leaders.

Another important factor which explains the ratification of the Constitution was the disorganization and ineffectiveness of reform sentiment. The returns on the Constitution proved that a large number of the people of Massachusetts were dissatisfied with traditional political institutions. The censorious nature of a large proportion of the returns and the seriousness and conviction with which they were written show a deep undercurrent of unrest. But no political party was created which could have reduced the myriad demands for reform into an integrated platform, no political leader arose who could dramatize democracy and make it respectable. These developments belonged to the future; the politically active classes during the Revolution were firmly devoted to the republic in equipoise. Convinced that government should be a trust administered for the people's benefit and not an agency for majority will, they felt that the popular leader was as unnecessary as he was dangerous. At best he would make the process of government more difficult and at worst he would use the people as "stilts for his own ambition" to become a dictator. The union of mob and demagogue was the political miscegenation which gave the Whig leaders many sleepless nights, for they were convinced that it would inevitably mean the destruction of all freedom.

The equalitarianism of some Massachusetts towns, although often visionary, impractical, and marred by localism, nevertheless contained the raw material for American political democracy. The village Hampdens and Sidneys, in merging their own experience with the teachings of Locke and the English philosophers of the seventeenth and eighteenth centuries, had found a way for men to be equal yet subordinate to authority, bound by law yet free. Their object had been to invent governmental machinery which would realize the political equality and majority rule which the Whig leaders endorsed in philosophy but denied in political science. With the assistance of a relatively small number of educated men, Massachusetts townsmen had deduced the constitutional convention from the compact theory and had outlined a government elective in all its branches and based on manhood suffrage. This was a considerable achievement and quite an advance over the results of the democratic movement in North Carolina. The one element still needed was a democratic leadership and an organized party able to take over the administration of government.

TWELVE

The Attempt to Transform Pennsylvania
into a Royal Colony

DURING the years of the Regulator movement, while piedmont farmers were protesting against the depredations of courthouse rings, similar sectional and class tensions appeared in Pennsylvania which manifested themselves first in futile violence and finally, during the Revolution, in a campaign for democratic government. But while the democratic movement in North Carolina was temporarily halted by the concerted effort of the Revolutionary leaders, in Pennsylvania the campaign for equal political rights and majority rule resulted in the formation of a party which wrote a democratic constitution and dominated the government inaugurated by it.

Many factors contributed to this first triumph of democracy, not the least of which was the liberal constitutional framework of the proprietary government. The Charter of Privileges of 1701, agreed upon by William Penn and the colonists, was clearly defined fundamental law, as far as the two parties were concerned, which could be altered only by consent of the governor and six-sevenths of the Assembly.[1]

1. Francis N. Thorpe, *Federal and State Constitutions*, 7 Vols. (Washington, 1909), V, 3079.

The Assembly met at a stated time each year, sat on its own adjournments, and chose its own officers. Although not specifically empowered to do so, it granted representation to new counties by legislative act, determined the place of its meeting, and dissolved itself. Elections were held yearly under the authority of the instrument and not by royal or proprietary writ. The upper house, denied a legislative veto, was limited to administrative, judicial, and advisory functions. The executive power was exercised by the proprietor in London (always a member of the Penn family), and by his deputy governor residing at Philadelphia, both of whom possessed a legislative veto.[2] Sheriffs and coroners were popularly elected, subject to the governor's acceptance, and local taxation was imposed by county boards made up of popularly elected commissioners and assessors, the grand jury, and the justices of the peace.[3] Land was relatively easy to acquire,[4] freedom of worship for all believers in one God and the right of all Christians to hold office were written into the Charter.[5]

Thus it can be seen that on paper Pennsylvania had a remarkably democratic government. Checked only by the ex-

2. Only the deputy could exercise this veto effectively, however. All legislation signed by the governor had to be laid before the Privy Council whether the proprietor vetoed it or not, so any action the latter might take would be ineffective except as it might influence the decision of the Privy Council. William R. Shepherd, *History of Proprietary Government in Pennsylvania* (New York, 1896), 475-476.

3. E. R. L. Gould, "Local Self-Government in Pennsylvania," *The Pennsylvania Magazine of History and Biography*, VI (1882), 163-164.

4. The Penns sold tracts at a price of five to fifteen pounds per hundred acres and required a small yearly quitrent, but no concerted attempt was made to eject squatters, pre-emption rights were easy to acquire, and an attempt was made to give land for military service. Shepherd, *Proprietary Government*, 34, 70; William R. Shepherd, "The Land System of Provincial Pennsylvania," American Historical Association *Report*, 1895, 123-124.

5. Thorpe, *Constitutions*, V, 3077.

ecutive veto and the Privy Council's power of review,[6] the Assembly exercised all the powers for which lower houses in the royal colonies struggled during the eighteenth century and many which they did not dare to claim.

But in practice the Pennsylvania government was scarcely less aristocratic than those of the royal colonies. By two expedients—a high property qualification in Philadelphia and the underrepresentation of western counties—the Assembly succeeded in making itself independent of potentially radical constituencies. Of Philadelphia's taxable male population, 90 per cent was disfranchised by a suffrage qualification of £50 personalty or a fifty-acre freehold.[7] In the West, where the freehold qualification was relatively easy to meet, the effectiveness of the farmer's vote was reduced by underrepresentation. Although the population of the interior equalled if it did not exceed that of the East by 1770, the three original counties of Chester, Bucks, and Philadelphia had twenty-four representatives in the Assembly while Lancaster, York, Berks, Cumberland, and Northampton had only ten.[8] The city of Philadelphia, with an estimated eighteen or twenty thousand people in 1760,[9] also suffered discrimination by an allotment of only two representatives.

Like North Carolina, Pennsylvania contained a polyglot population. Franklin estimated that in 1766 one-third of the province's 160,000 people were Quakers, one-third Germans,

6. The Privy Council's disallowance was of limited effectiveness, for the Assembly was given five years to lay its legislation before that body. At the end of this period laws could be repealed and reenacted in different form, thus giving another period of grace.

7. Albert E. McKinley, *The Suffrage Franchise in the Thirteen English Colonies in America,* The University of Pennsylvania, *Publications,* Series in History, II, 290-292.

8. J. Paul Selsam, *The Pennsylvania Constitution of 1776* (Philadelphia, 1936), 35.

9. Evarts B. Greene and Virginia D. Harrington, *American Population before the Federal Census of 1790* (New York, 1932), 118.

and the rest Scotch-Irish and non-Quaker English.[10] The city of Philadelphia became a melting pot in which only one-seventh of the population was Quaker.[11] Again as in North Carolina, population in the frontier region grew more rapidly than in the settled East. Between 1750 and 1770 the number of taxables in York, Cumberland, Northampton and Lancaster counties increased between 100 and 300 per cent; Philadelphia and Chester counties showed an advance of about 30 per cent; the population of Bucks remained practically stationary.[12]

Party controversies between the proprietary and Assembly factions were bitter and continuous from the founding of the colony until the end of the French and Indian War and were complicated by factors of nationality and religion. The Assembly party, led by Benjamin Franklin and Joseph Galloway, was the political organ of the eastern Quakers. The Proprietary party, composed of the governor, the Anglican churchmen, and the relatively few families who monopolized executive patronage, such as the Shippens, Chews, Allens, and Tilghmans, guarded the interests of the Penn family. In normal times political activity was important only in Philadelphia and its environs, but when the Indians overran the frontier during the French and Indian War, the Scotch-Irish and German settlers there, needing help, began to give support to the Proprietary party because of the refusal of the Quaker-dominated Assembly to provide adequate defense. Pacifist Germans in the East, alarmed at Scotch-Irish militarism, rallied behind the Quaker party. In an atmosphere of hectic vituperation and recrimination political conflicts reached unprecedented proportions. Quaker and Presbyterian

10. *Ibid.*, 116.
11. Robert Proud, *The History of Pennsylvania*, 2 Vols. (Philadelphia, 1797-1798), II, 339.
12. Greene and Harrington, *American Population before 1790*, 117.

became popular designations for the Assembly and Proprietary factions.[13]

At the outbreak of the war, the governor, with the full support of the frontier settlers, had strongly urged the Assembly to raise a military force. But the members refused to do so unless the governor would submit the Penn lands to taxation—a condition to which the proprietor would not agree. Meanwhile, the frontier burned, and petitions from the West requesting military support poured in upon the government.[14] One group threatened if not given aid "to go down with all who will follow us to Philadelphia and Quarter ourselves upon its inhabitants." [15] So intense was the alarm that one observer in Chester County, which was almost adjacent to Philadelphia, reported that two thousand men there "are preparing to come to the city to compell the governor and Assembly to pass laws to defend the country." [16] Feeling against the Quakers ran so high in Reading that their lives and property were actually in danger.[17] The deadlock between the proprietor and the Assembly was broken only when the Penns agreed to contribute £5000 in lieu of

13. Charles H. Lincoln, *The Revolutionary Movement in Pennsylvania, 1760-1776* (Philadelphia, 1901), 23-39, contains the best discussion of parties in colonial Pennsylvania. See also Guy S. Klett, *Presbyterians in Colonial Pennsylvania* (Philadelphia, 1937), 245-252; Wayland F. Dunaway, *The Scotch-Irish of Colonial Pennsylvania* (Chapel Hill, 1944), 118-129. William Allen testified that in 1764, following the Paxton riots, parties formed along religious lines. William Allen to Thomas Penn, Oct. 21, 1764, Penn Papers, Official Correspondence, Vol. IX, 282, Historical Society of Pennsylvania. John Penn wrote early in 1765 that Quaker and Presbyterian had become the usual designations for the two leading parties. John Penn to ————, n.d., *ibid.*, XI, 263.

14. *Colonial Records of Pennsylvania,* 16 Vols. (Harrisburg, 1852-1853), VI, 551.

15. *Ibid.,* 667.

16. *Ibid.,* 729.

17. *Ibid.,* 705.

taxation of their lands [18]—a concession which the Assembly accepted with ill grace. The militia bill which the Assembly then passed, described as "a joke on all military affairs" by Governor Dinwiddie of Virginia, called only for voluntary service and took control of the troops away from the governor.[19]

In the succeeding years it became more apparent that the Assembly was using the distresses of the frontier to force continued concessions from the proprietor.[20] In July, 1763, a few months after the outbreak of Pontiac's Rebellion, the members voted only a paltry 700 men to defend the province,[21] and in September, although Indians were yet a menace west of Carlisle, they refused to consider a military supply bill unless it contained a legal tender clause of a type which the Privy Council had previously refused to sanction.[22] On at least two occasions the Assembly refused to reimburse localities which had raised men at their own expense and conducted campaigns against the Indians.[23] When Sir Jeffrey Amherst charged that the Assembly "tamely looked on while their Bretheren are butchered by the Savages," the members replied with an aggrieved air that they were doing all that could be reasonably expected of them.[24] As one student of the period comments, "It is evident that a large majority of the members of the Assembly, who lived in the East free from Indian attacks, were alive only to their own se-

---

18. Winfred T. Root, *The Relations of Pennsylvania with the British Government, 1696-1765* (Philadelphia, 1912), 307.

19. *Ibid.*, 308.

20. "It is clear that the Assembly played upon the exigencies of the occasion to make itself the supreme power in the provincial constitution." *Ibid.*, 319.

21. *Colonial Records*, IX, 42.

22. *Ibid.*, 53-55.

23. *Votes of the Assembly, Pennsylvania Archives*, 8th Ser., VI, 5437-5440; VII, 5508-5509.

24. *Colonial Records*, IX, 64-65.

curity and felt a gross indifference to the needs of the people of the West." [25]

Thus it is understandable that the western settlers of Pennsylvania, like those of North Carolina, turned to violence when the Assembly failed to redress their grievances. Rage against the red men had grown to such a pitch that a group of farmers in Lancaster County attacked a village of Christian Indians at Conestoga in December, 1763, murdered six of them found in the settlement, and a short time later exterminated fourteen survivors who had been given shelter in the Workhouse at Lancaster.[26] In the face of this lawless violence, the governor and the Quakers buried their quarrels and acted in concert in much the same way as did Tryon and the North Carolina Assembly. A riot act was introduced, discussed, and passed in one day by the Pennsylvania Assembly after John Penn appeared in person to request it. This merely aroused greater ferment in the back country. A growing mob at one time estimated at about a thousand settlers marched toward Philadelphia.[27] The city was thrown into panic, but in the crisis Franklin became the man of the hour. Upon the request of the governor—which gave him wry satisfaction—he went with three other men to meet the rioters at Germantown.[28] After several hours of conversation the westerners agreed to return home, but two of their number, Matthew Smith and James Gibson, remained behind to draw up a declaration of grievances. The

25. Root, *Relations of Pennsylvania with the British Government*, 326.

26. Brooke Hindle, "The March of the Paxton Boys," *William and Mary Quarterly*, 3rd Ser., III (1946), 466-467.

27. *Ibid.*, 478. "Their force, though known to be small in the beginning, continually increased as it went along." Alexander Graydon, *Memoirs of His Own Time* (Philadelphia, 1846), 47. See also letter of John Harris to Col. James Burd, March 1, 1764. Shippen Papers, Vol. VI, p. 95, Historical Society of Pennsylvania.

28. Carl Van Doren, *Benjamin Franklin* (New York, 1938), 310; Hindle, "Paxton Boys," *William and Mary Quarterly*, 480.

result of their labors was a petition read in the Assembly February 15, 1764, which marked the beginning of a bitter controversy over the Paxton murders. Party antagonisms flared as never before in the city of brotherly love, but more important, what began as a debate between prosecution and defense over an obvious crime eventuated in a discussion of basic constitutional questions.

Rather surprisingly, the Smith-Gibson petition dealt primarily with the discriminatory representation. *"First,* We apprehend that, as freemen and *English* subjects, we have an indisputable title to the same privileges and immunities with His Majesty's other subjects who reside in the interior counties of Philadelphia, Bucks, and Chester, and therefore ought not to be excluded from an equal share with them in the very important Privilege of Legislation." The authors described the existing representation as "oppressive, unequal, and unjust, the cause of many of our grievances and an infringement of our natural privileges of freedom and equality;..." [29]

The petition met as hostile a reception in the Assembly as did the Regulator papers in the North Carolina legislature. The members, intending to identify Governor John Penn with its rejection, proposed to express their disapproval at a public hearing on grievances at which he would preside. But Penn wisely refused to fall in with their plans.[30] Probably realizing that the hostility of the western settlers was not directed against himself, he held private conferences with Smith and Gibson and apparently came to some kind of agreement with them.[31] Hence the hearing was called off and the two left Philadelphia.

29. Printed in *Votes of the Assembly, Pennsylvania Archives,* 8th Ser., VII, 5542-5547.
30. *Ibid.,* 5554-5555.
31. Carl Van Doren (ed.), *Letters and Papers of Benjamin Franklin and Richard Jackson, 1753-1785* (Philadelphia, 1947), 146. In a letter to

The Smith-Gibson petition was followed by many others protesting the discrimination against the West in the allotment of representatives. Twelve hundred inhabitants of Cumberland described the existing apportionment as the source of all their suffering,[32] and groups in Lancaster, York, and Northampton asked the governor to bring pressure to bear on the Assembly for a favorable consideration of the Smith-Gibson petition.[33] Two requests for a reallotment of delegates were received from Berks.[34] The anonymous authors of the *Apology of the Paxton Men,* a paper drafted perhaps while the rioters were at Germantown, asserted that if the West had its fair share of representation, "so many of our bretheren had not been murdered or captured." [35]

The Quaker majority in the Assembly, no doubt afraid that a reapportionment of county delegates according to population would jeopardize its control of the province, disposed of the issue by postponing discussion on it until after the next elections.[36] Although western representation was increased slightly during the next decade, the newer counties were not given a fair allotment of delegates until March, 1776, when the Assembly was on the verge of dissolution.

The Paxton murders started a battle royal in the press which soon obscured the issue of representation. Franklin, sharing with Galloway the leadership of the Quaker party,

---

Thomas Penn of Nov. 15, 1763, the governor said that petitions from the West requesting the establishment of an armed force "had meant to show civility and respect." Official Correspondence, IX, 220.

32. *Votes,* VII, 5582.

33. *Ibid.,* 5608.

34. *Ibid.,* 5597, 5626.

35. MS in Historical Society of Pennsylvania. Israel Pemberton believed that the paper was written in Philadelphia. Israel to John Pemberton, Feb. 7, 1764. Pemberton Papers, XVII, 11, Historical Society of Pennsylvania.

36. *Votes,* VII, 5641.

published *A Narrative of the Late Massacres* designed to condemn, as he said, "the Action almost universally approved by the common People" and to "strengthen the Hands of the Government by Changing the Sentiments of the Populace." [37] The good Doctor described the murders in all their gruesome detail and charged that the murderers were more cruel and depraved than ancient Turks. This piece provoked a reply from Thomas Barton, an Anglican clergyman who had travelled and preached on the frontier. Without justifying the murders—for which, of course, there could be no justification—he challenged the right of the Quakers to cast the first stone. Neatly turning Franklin's assertion that the Indians would have been safer among Spaniards, Moors, or Turks than among Presbyterians, he observed that the frontiersmen would have a better chance for survival among Turks than under a Quaker government. [38]

Quaker pamphleteers viewed the march of the Paxton boys as an attempted revolution. *The Paxton Boys, a Farce,* portrayed Presbyterians inside the city as a fifth column alert for an opportunity to join hands with their brethren invading from the West and overturn the government. [39] Declared the writer of *A Looking Glass for Presbyterians,* "Presbyterianism and Rebellion are twin sitters, sprung from faction, and their affection for each other has been so strong

37. Van Doren (ed.), *Franklin-Jackson Papers,* 140. Pamphlet printed in Jared Sparks (ed.), *The Works of Benjamin Franklin,* 10 Vols. (Boston, 1840), IV, 54-78. Volumes III and IV of the Sparks edition contain in easily accessible form the essays dating from this period.

38. Thomas Barton, *The Conduct of the Paxton Men* (Philadelphia, 1764), 32. Penn wrote that the Assembly was furious over the piece and "vowed vengeance against all who have ventured to write anything that may have a tendency to expose their own iniquitous measures." John Penn to Thomas Penn, June 16, Official Correspondence, IX, 236.

39. *The Paxton Boys, a Farce* (Philadelphia, 1764). See also *The Quaker Vindicated* (Philadelphia, 1764) and *An Answer to 'the Paxton Men'* (Philadelphia, 1764).

that a separation of them could never be effected." [40] He asserted that the source of Presbyterian sedition was Princeton, haven of the "New Side," "the center of all plots, cabals, and perversion of youth." In his estimation the College of Philadelphia, under the distinguished supervision of Provost William Smith—a strong supporter of proprietary policies— was little better. Degrees there were given out so promiscuously "that leather breeches makers and gentlemen are put on the same level." [41]

Defenders of the Paxton boys replied with equal heat. One writer saw no chance of redress for the grievances of the frontier as long as Pennsylvania was under "the villainy, infatuation, and influence of a certain faction that have got the political reins in their hands and tamely tyrannize over the other good subjects of the province." [42] Another writer suggested that the best way to secure protection against the Indians would be to send all Quakers to the frontier "where they can practice as much meekness as the case requires." [43] A satirist accused the Quakers of being accessories to the Indian depredations:

> Pray, worthy Friends, observe the text,
> Get money first, and virtue next.
>
> .   .   .   .
>
> Go on, Good Christians, never spare
> To give your Indians cloathes to wear,
> Good name, good beef, pork and bread,
> Guns, powder, flints, and store of lead
> To shoot your neighbors through the head.
>
> .   .   .   .

40. *A Looking Glass for Presbyterians* (Philadelphia, 1764), 6.
41. *Ibid.*, 19-20.
42. *A Declaration and Remonstrance of the Distressed and Bleeding Frontier Inhabitants* (Philadelphia, 1764).
43. Pennsylvania *Journal*, Sept. 20, 1764.

> God knows
> To murder us you are our foes
> As he who uses eyes may note.
> The butcher often binds a goat
> And leaves his man to cut its throat.
>
> . . . . . .
>
> Change but the name,
> Quakers and Indians are the same.[44]

Besides arousing smouldering sectional antagonisms, the march of the Paxton boys caused the Assembly to consider asking the crown to take the province out of the proprietor's hands. Many members felt that royal authority was needed to keep order, but others wanted to prevent the formation of a coalition between the proprietary party and the western farmers which would threaten the Assembly position. "Violent suspicions now begin to prevail," wrote Franklin on

44. Shippen Papers, Vol. VI, 115. The verses are hand written and were apparently passed about among the members of the Proprietary party. By the fall of 1764 the pamphlet literature had degenerated to the quality of writings on outhouse walls. In a competition of vilification *The Quaker Unmasked* was followed by *The Author of the Quaker Unmasked Stripped Naked,* or *The Dilineated Presbyterian Played Hob With.* This opus inspired *Cloathes for a Stark Naked Author,* and so the race went on. The low point, perhaps, was reached in *A Dialogue Between Andrew Trueman and Thomas Zealot:*

AND. Whar ha' you been aw' this time, Tom?

TOM. Whar I ha' been? Whar you should ha' been too, Andrew, Fechting the Lord's battles and killing the Indians at Lancaster and Connestogoe!

A. How many did you kill at Connestogoe?

T. Ane and twunty.

A. Hoot, man, there were but twunty awtogether, and fourteen of them were in the Gaol.

T. I tell you, we shot six and a wee ane, that was in the squaw's belly; we sculped three; we tomahawked three; we roasted three and a wee ane; and three and a wee ane we gave to the hogs.

March 14, 1764, "that the armed mob in the country, tho' not at first promoted, has since been encouraged by the governor's party, to awe the Assembly, and compell them to make such a militia Law as the governors have long aimed at. What increases the suspicion is, that the Assembly's proposal of joining with the governor in giving answer to the remonstrance presented by the deputies of that mob was rejected, tho' intended merely to add weight to the answer, by showing that the Government was unanimous. The Proposal was approved by the moderate Part of the Governor's Council. He chose, however, to give his Answer separately, and what it was is a secret; we only learn that they went home extremely well satisfied with the governor, and are soon expected down again:... " [45] Shortly after this incident when the governor vetoed a military supply bill calling for taxation of proprietary lands, the Assembly without a dissenting vote passed twenty-six resolutions of censure which included the following declaration: "That the Proprietaries taking advantage of times of public calamity to extort privileges from the people, or enforce claims against them with the knife of savages at their throat, and not permitting them to raise money for their defense unless the proprietary arbitrary will and pleasure is complied with, is a practice dishonorable, unjust, tyrannical, and inhuman." [46]

But fulminations were unavailing, for surrender to proprietary will was inevitable. Franklin on May 1 reported rumors that the Paxton boys were ready to march on Philadelphia again: " 'tis thought they will certainly be here when the Assembly sit, the Middle of the Month." Penn wrote that 2,000 settlers were preparing to descend on the city, with the aim of forcing the Assembly to grant more representation

45. Van Doren (ed.), *Franklin-Jackson Papers*, 146.
46. *Votes*, VII, 5593.

to the West.[47] With this threat hanging over its head, the Assembly accepted a compromise on the taxation issue and rewrote the bill in accordance with the governor's wishes.[48]

After this display of power resulting from the coalition of western farmers and proprietary governor it is not surprising that the Assembly proceeded with almost complete unanimity to petition the crown to take over the province. But John Dickinson, then a promising young lawyer of large fortune and excellent connections with the wealthy Quakers, realized that the move would be literally a jump out of the frying pan into the fire. While discussion of the petition was in progress he published a memorable speech with an anonymous preface by Provost William Smith against the plan to make the province a royal colony.[49]

Dickinson did not defend the proprietors or their policy, but asserted that the Charter of Pennsylvania—which he called a constitution—was a priceless heritage, unique in the colonies, and should not be given up for transient reasons. There was no guarantee at all, he said, that the crown would continue to recognize the special privileges of the Assembly; in fact, the reverse might be expected, for the province was in very bad odor at Whitehall for its niggardliness in providing for its own defense. But Dickinson's principal argument rested on the assumption that the Charter was fundamental law: "We have received these seats by the free choice of this people under this constitution; and to preserve it in its utmost purity and vigour, has always been deemed by me a principal part of the trust committed to my care and

47. Van Doren (ed.), *Franklin-Jackson Papers*, 156; John to Thomas Penn, June 16, Official Correspondence, IX, 238.

48. *Votes*, VII, 5604, 5617.

49. Paul L. Ford (ed.), *The Writings of John Dickinson*, Historical Society of Pennsylvania, *Memoirs*, 14 Vols. (Philadelphia, 1826-1895), XIV, 11-49.

fidelity. The measure proposed has a direct tendency to endanger this constitution, and, therefore, in my opinion, we have *no right* to engage in it without *the almost universal consent of the people* expressed in the plainest manner." [50] Dickinson appeared to grasp the distinction between the constituent and the legislative power, and by implying that the people alone could give the sanction for the alteration or abrogation of a compact, made a strong case for popular sovereignty and the right of revolution. Like many other colonial leaders, however, his was a radicalism of theory only. During the Revolution he opposed the overthrow of the Assembly and the move for independence.

Galloway published a speech in answer to Dickinson with an anonymous preface by Franklin.[51] Assuring his readers that the crown would be solicitous of Pennsylvania's liberties, Galloway foreshadowed his conservatism of the Revolutionary period by asserting that king, lords, and commons, as the supreme power of the realm, could at will establish, alter, or abrogate any subordinate government. The essential reason for introducing royal authority, in his view, was the need to preserve order. In relinquishing the Charter, Pennsylvania was giving up no more than a temporary indulgence of the crown in order to obtain an internal security without which there could be no freedom whatsoever. "Surely, sir, no greater mistake was ever affirmed, than that Pennsylvania's liberties are safe now, and no truth more evident that were we to lose all our charter privileges and only enjoy those of Royal Governments, our situation would be infinitely preferable to our present state." [52]

The reasoning of both Dickinson and Galloway apparently made an impression upon the Assembly. In accordance

50. *Ibid.*, 44.
51. Preface printed in Sparks (ed.), *Works of Franklin*, IV, 100-142.
52. *The Speech of Joseph Galloway* (London, 1765), 70, 77.

with Galloway's advice, a petition to the crown was drafted and dispatched to the colony's agent in London, Richard Jackson, but Jackson was instructed not to present it until he had adequate guarantees that the liberties "under the present constitution" would be respected.[53] The members did not want royal government at any price. If they agreed with Galloway on the need for a strong administration to protect them from the incursions of western settlers, they shared with Dickinson a regard for the unique privileges of the Charter.

The Assembly had taken considerable pains to secure popular support for its cause. At Franklin's suggestion a mass meeting was held in the State House yard at which Galloway, the chief speaker, recommended "throwing off the chains of proprietary slavery and returning to royal liberty." [54] Members inspired petitions with an impressive number of signatures from their constituencies.[55] In Philadelphia the Quaker party kept open house in a tavern and conducted a house-to-house canvass which brought together such improbable companions as Thomas Wharton, the merchant prince, and "one Knowles, a barber." [56] Franklin, in a pamphlet entitled *Cool Thoughts,* presented the Assembly's case in somewhat heated fashion. For the first time he noted the argument of the West that internal peace could be secured by reapportioning the representation, but he declared that abolishing the discrimination against this section would not in itself solve the basic problem even though "more members for these [back] counties may, on other accounts,

53. *Votes,* VII, 5615.

54. John Penn to Thomas Penn, May 5, 1764, Penn Papers, Official Correspondence, IX, 220.

55. *Votes,* VII, 5604-5606; Van Doren (ed.), *Franklin-Jackson Correspondence,* 150-152, 161.

56. John Penn to Thomas Penn, May 5, 1764, Penn Papers, Official Correspondence, IX, 220.

be proper." [57] At a later date Franklin was to become an enthusiastic advocate of proportionate representation; but at the moment, he subordinated this consideration to the Assembly's grievances against the proprietor.

At first the Assembly seemed to carry all before it, but as the summer advanced, a reaction set in. Opposition to its project crystallized among three groups—the frontier farmers, the city merchants, and the strictly pacifist Quakers. In April, William Smith had published a petition against the projected change of government signed by the magistrates of Cumberland County and 1200 "of the most respectable inhabitants." [58] "The magistrates, Grand Jury, Clergy, Lawyers, and other Principal Freeholders" of Lancaster County congratulated their representative in the Assembly for opposing the change of government. "The Constitution of Pennsylvania," they said, "has for near a century been the boast and glory of our fathers and of us. We cannot therefore conceive that the freemen of this province ever empowered or gave it in charge to any of their delegates to new-frame or modle this Constitution." [59] A significant evidence of opinion among Presbyterians is contained in a circular letter signed by the Presbyterian ministers Gilbert Tennent, Francis Alison, and John Ewing. "The Presbyterians here," they said, "upon mature deliberation, are of the opinion that... our privileges by these means may be greatly *abridged*, but will never be *enlarged*.... The affair is in all probability a trap laid to ensnare the unwary.... The frontier counties are now suing for a redress of grievance, and we have the greatest reason to believe, that [the projected change of government] is no more than an artful scheme to divide or divert the attention of the injured frontier inhabitants from

57. Sparks (ed.), *Works of Franklin*, IV, 82.
58. Pennsylvania *Journal*, Apr. 12, 1764.
59. *Ibid.*, Aug. 16, 1764.

prosecuting their petitions, which very much alarm them." [60]

Some Quakers, upon reflection, realized that whatever benefits the change promised for Franklin, Galloway, and the non-Quaker members of their party, they themselves stood to lose their unique religious privileges. As early as 1756, when the abrogation of the Charter had been first envisaged, they had made overtures to the proprietor for a settlement of differences. According to one critic of their policies, they realized that their pacifism was alienating their German allies on the frontier and that under royal government they might not "stand so good a chance of having so large a share of power" as under the proprietor. [61] Nevertheless when the move for the abrogation of the Charter assumed serious proportions in the spring of 1764, most Quakers favored the party program because, as James Pemberton explained, they were alarmed at "the riotous conduct of the Presbyterians and fearful of their getting the legislative as well as the executive part of the government into their hands." [62] But by summer the attitude of the leaders had changed. Suspicious that Franklin and Galloway desired royal government primarily in order to advance their own political fortunes, they swung toward Dickinson's view of the matter. Israel Pemberton charged that the advocates of royal government originally played on the resentment of the Quakers toward the proprietor in order to obtain support for the change, "but those who kept out of the snare had not time and strength to prevent others from being taken in." He felt that a redress of grievances "was so necessary that we

60. Printed in Sparks (ed.), *Works of Franklin*, VII, 281-282 (note), and as an appendix to *A Looking Glass for Presbyterians*. See also Klett, *Presbyterians in Pennsylvania*, 257.

61. William Peters to Thomas Penn, Jan. 14, 1756, Penn Papers, Official Correspondence, VIII, 9.

62. Isaac Sharpless, *A History of Quaker Government in Pennsylvania*, 2 Vols. (Philadelphia, 1898), II, 67.

could not blame those who from the duty of their station sought it, but in doing it to endanger the loss of those liberties and privileges by which we have been distinguished appeared to us imprudent." [63] The Yearly Meeting in 1764 refused to support the Assembly's petition to the crown. Nevertheless, many Quakers, perhaps a majority, did not follow their leaders but voted with the party notwithstanding.

In the city, a few leading merchants and professional men undertook a campaign to recall the petition. George Bryan, later to become a leader of the democratic faction in the Revolution and one of the drafters of the Constitution of 1776, shared the apprehension of the Quaker leaders. He feared that in the process of replacing the Penns' government "the opportunity might be laid hold of to make many alterations not much to our liking." He claimed considerable support for this position. "Sensible of this, the measure has been received very coolly by a great majority of the inhabitants. In the country the petitions for a change of government are less liked, especially as you approach the frontier." [64] With Thomas Willing, Mayor of Philadelphia, business partner of Robert Morris and future president of the Bank of North America, Bryan started a counter-petition in the city which—according to Governor John Penn—had 12,000 signatures by September. [65] The Mayor and Corporation of Philadelphia signed a similar petition which was sent over to Thomas Penn. [66]

63. Israel Pemberton to David Barclay, Nov. 6, 1764, Pemberton Papers, XVII, 103. For more details on Pemberton's attempt to influence the Quakers against the change of government see Theodore G. Thayer, *Israel Pemberton, King of the Quakers* (Philadelphia, 1943), 203.

64. Burton A. Konkle, *George Bryan and the Constitution of Pennsylvania, 1731-1791* (Philadelphia, 1922), 47-48.

65. John Penn to Thomas Penn, Sept. 1, 1764, Penn Papers, Official Correspondence, IX, 254.

66. Burton A. Konkle, *Benjamin Chew* (Philadelphia, 1932), 105.

By midsummer it was evident that the projected change to royal government was to be the primary issue in the Assembly elections of October. Franklin and Galloway, despite their efforts, steadily lost ground in the city and in the frontier counties. A smear campaign was launched against the good doctor in which the particulars of the birth of his illegitimate son were fully aired. The Germans were reminded that he had called them "palatine boors," and the Scotch-Irish that he had labelled the Paxton boys "Christian white savages." [67] He was accused of advocating the change of government in order that he might become first royal governor of Pennsylvania and his friend Galloway the first chief justice.[68] The two were compared to the dictators who overturned the Roman constitution. In return, the Quaker party warned the Germans that their land titles would not be secure if the Scotch-Irish gained control of the Assembly. So intense were the campaigns that Governor William Franklin came over from New Jersey to hold open house at Germantown for the supporters of his father.[69]

The election in the city was a riotous affair in which both parties apparently used many of the fraudulent practices which characterized spirited contests in the nineteenth century. The suffrage qualification seems to have been ignored. On a close vote Bryan and Willing defeated Franklin and Galloway for seats in the Assembly. According to one observer, "Mr. Franklin died like a philosopher. But Mr. Galloway *agonized in Death* like a mortal Deist who had no hopes of a future existence." [70]

67. Van Doren, *Benjamin Franklin,* 315.
68. Konkle, *Bryan,* 50; "Address to the Freeholders of Pennsylvania," Pennsylvania *Journal* (supplement), Sept. 27, 1764.
69. John Penn to Thomas Penn, Oct. 19. Penn Papers, Official Correspondence, IX, 274.
70. William B. Reed, *The Life and Correspondence of Joseph Reed,* 2 Vols. (Philadelphia, 1847), I, 37.

Yet for all the fury of the election in Philadelphia, party strength in the Assembly was not greatly changed. The eastern counties had returned solidly anti-proprietary delegations which included many Quakers who had ventured back into politics with the cessation of hostilities on the frontier.[71] Dickinson and his father-in-law, Isaac Norris—an outstanding Quaker leader—were re-elected and the latter accepted the speakership. The party consoled Franklin in his hour of defeat by having him appointed colonial agent in London. When his enemies protested, he published the pamphlet *Remarks on a Protest* which revealed that his philosophic calm had been severely shaken despite appearances to the contrary. He attributed his defeat largely to the malice of his enemies and in part to "the many perjuries procured among the wretched rabble brought to swear themselves entitled to a vote." [72] If the disregard of suffrage qualifications in the city was indeed a factor in the defeat of Franklin and Galloway, this is a significant indication of the attitude of the common people toward the Quaker party and the project for the change of government.

Shortly after the election the petition for royal government underwent a second test which revealed again the sectional split over the issue. When opponents of the plan, including Dickinson, Norris, Bryan, and Willing, proposed that the Assembly recall the document or instruct the colonial agent not to present it, they were voted down by a combination of nearly all the delegates from Chester, Bucks, and Lancaster. Philadelphia County split on the issue.[73] If the West had been adequately represented, the vote would

71. The results of the elections are printed in *Votes*, VII, 5669-5670.

72. Sparks (ed.), *Works of Franklin*, IV, 147.

73. *Votes*, VII, 5682-5683. The vote on the motion to recall the petition was 22 to 10; on the motion to withhold presentation, 20 to 12.

probably have been closer. Perhaps the opponents of royal rule would have won.

Actually, the petition was in no danger of being presented in any case. The Assembly again ordered Franklin and Jackson not to take any action until maintenance of Pennsylvania's liberties was guaranteed.[74] Jackson himself was extremely doubtful whether such a stipulation would be granted,[75] and the passage of the Stamp Act soon convinced most members of the Assembly that it would be better to bear with the proprietor than trust the province to the tender mercies of royal government.

One of the most interesting aspects of the struggle is the close cooperation between Franklin and Galloway, two figures who, in view of their later careers, would seem to have little in common. Actually they supported the move for royal government for quite different reasons. Franklin opposed the proprietors because he wanted complete freedom of action for those he chose to regard as the people's representatives. Galloway, on the other hand, felt that the proprietary form was basically defective. Thus he wrote in his *Political Reflections* of 1782: "We find [in proprietary colonies] a scene of tumult and confusion.... These colonies are the perpetual scenes of parties, public feuds, broils, and breaches of the peace, which altogether destroy the public tranquillity. All that awe and respect, which are the great support of government and which are necessary to be paid by the lower class of people, to persons in office, are wanting. The Governor and Magistrates of the colony are upon a level with John the Farmer, who follows the plow for his daily subsistence, and whenever they meet, the first salutation of respect proceeds from the Governor or Magistrate; if not he loses the Farmer's vote and interest at the next election. The

74. *Ibid.*, 5683.
75. Van Doren (ed.), *Franklin-Jackson Papers*, 174-175, 191.

popular man who commands a number of votes, however undignified by morals, education, or office, is the man of rank to whom the officers of Government must pay respect and honor." [76]

The reasons of both Galloway and Franklin for wanting a change to royal government are quite clear, but it is difficult to understand how Franklin could have thought that Pennsylvania would have more freedom under the crown. Representative bodies in the royal colonies labored under much greater disabilities than the Pennsylvania Assembly. It cannot be argued that he expected the Charter to remain in force. Apparently he attached little importance to it. Perhaps the explanation of his attitude lies in a divergence between Franklin the politician, and Franklin the philosopher. His benevolent leadership of the Junto and his identification with the common man through Poor Richard tend to obscure the fact that the good doctor was a leader of an oligarchical party which was determined to rule the province in its own interest. There may be considerable truth to the assertion of his enemies that his ultimate aim was to become Pennsylvania's first royal governor. With Franklin *père* and Franklin *fils* at the head of administration in Pennsylvania and New Jersey, respectively, the Franklins would become the first family of the colonies. Even if true, however, this was an entirely legitimate ambition for a colonial liberal in 1764. The struggle between Britain and the colonies had not reached the point where a liberal could not assume office under the crown without opening himself to a charge of hypocrisy. Yet Franklin's part in the struggle over the change of government shows a certain amount of opportunism. Indeed, this factor is somewhat evident throughout his career. His principles always seemed to coincide with his interests.

76. Joseph Galloway, *Political Reflections on the Royal, Proprietary, and Charter Governments of the American Colonies* (London, 1782), 196.

Beginning his political career as an opponent of the pacifist Quakers, he became the outstanding leader of the Quaker party after a few terms in the Assembly. Although opposed to the Stamp Act, he could nevertheless secure the stamp agency for his friend and political colleague, John Hughes, and advise him, "In the meantime, a firm loyalty to the crown and faithful adherence to the government of this nation ... will always be the wisest course for you and I to take, whatever may be the madness of the populace and their blind leaders, who can only bring themselves and their country into trouble, and draw on greater burdens by Acts of rebellious tendency." [77] During the Revolution he was the best-known advocate of unicameralism and allowed his name to be used as the father of the democratic Constitution of 1776, yet at the Federal Convention he raised no objection to a form of government that was in some respects its antithesis. The fact that a funeral eulogy was pronounced by his former bitter enemy, Provost William Smith, is perhaps an indication of Franklin's talent as a politician. The remark of a Quaker acquaintance concerning him was astute, if not strictly accurate: "Friend Joseph, didst thee ever know Dr. Franklin to be in a minority?" [78]

77. Albert H. Smyth, *The Writings of Benjamin Franklin,* 10 Vols. (New York and London, 1905-1907), IV, 391-392. Original in Hughes Papers, Historical Society of Pennsylvania.

78. Quoted from William C. Bruce, *Benjamin Franklin, Self-Revealed,* 2 Vols. (New York and London, 1917), II, 98 (note). Clinton Rossiter, in his admirable *Seedtime of the Republic* (New York, 1953), presents Franklin as an outstanding representative of early American democracy (pp. 281-313). Of course Franklin, like Jefferson, was temperamentally a democrat and in his literary remains exhibits a "free and catholick spirit" very warming to present-day liberals who take their democracy seriously. Yet the fact remains that Franklin the politician did much less for the cause of democratic government from 1764 to 1776 than Franklin the philosopher has done during the twentieth century. Like other liberal Whigs of his day he made no attempt to institutionalize his democratic ideas when such a course would have involved political sacrifices. Actually,

The protest of the West, as far as it was evidenced by the Paxton boys' march and the petitions for redress of frontier grievances, did not become as articulate or comprehensive as in North Carolina during the period of the Regulator disturbances. There are perhaps two reasons for this. In the first place, the demand for reform was prejudiced from the start by the circumstances of the Paxton murders. This piece of brutality gave credence to assertions by the Quakers that the aim of the marchers was revolution. Certainly it must have seemed to the unprejudiced observer that men who condoned the savage extermination of helpless human beings could hardly be trusted with political power. As a result, the real grievance of discriminatory representation was lost among charges and counter-charges of criminality. In the second place, the western settlers had far less to complain of in normal times than the Regulators. The counties of Pennsylvania, in contrast to those of North Carolina, possessed responsible local government. Sheriffs were popularly elected and local taxes were levied by boards controlled by the people. If the piedmont farmers of North Carolina had been granted such privileges, there might never have been a Regulator movement.

When viewed in the light of their inner connections, the somewhat disparate events of 1764 present a significant picture of party, class, and sectional struggle over basic constitutional issues. Out of the struggle developed a realization of the value of free political institutions and a doctrine—somewhat hypothetical but still valid—of popular sovereignty. The West and the city of Philadelphia, by their insistence on the retention of the essentially democratic political institutions of the Charter, facilitated the attainment

---

the best designation for Franklin is one suggested by Mr. Rossiter—a political pragmatist (p. 294).

of democratic government during the Revolution. The Quaker party, by its willingness to turn for support to the British government in a time of crisis, foreshadowed its drift toward neutralism.

Actually neither of the two parties had a firm basis in public confidence. The Quaker party, stigmatized because of its refusal to provide adequate defense in time of war, had little strength with which to combat opposition, and in a crisis many of its pacifist members could be expected to resign their seats rather than participate in conflict. If there were no Galloway or Franklin to step into the breach, the party faced disintegration. The Proprietary party, composed mostly of officeholders dependent on the Penns for their positions, also had special interests which set it apart from the mass of the people. It was only the rage of the frontier that had brought this group such unexpected and improbable allies as poor Scotch-Irish and German settlers, and some city merchants. Such stalwarts as the Allens, Shippens, and William Smith had little more in common with the Presbytyrian frontiersmen than the Philadelphia Quakers. Even the party's dependence on the Charter was in itself a source of weakness. What would happen when the Charter, free as it was, became prejudiced by the British connection like the Charter of Massachusetts?

On the eve of the Revolution, while the Whig aristocracy of the royal colonies was held together by a unity of purpose, the ruling aristocracy of Pennsylvania was weakened by party dissension, religious diversities, divergent interests, and the very existence of free institutions. Would it be able to withstand the drive of unprivileged groups to utilize the Revolution as a means to bring about equalitarian democracy?

THIRTEEN

The Rise of the Whig Party
in Pennsylvania

THE years 1766-1774 were an era of relatively good feeling unparalleled in Pennsylvania's short but turbulent colonial history. With the coming of peace to the frontier, antagonism against the Quakers subsided and the Stamp Act convinced nearly everyone that a change to royal government would not be in the best interests of the colony. But if most of the specific issues which had generated party conflict were now dead, class and sectional tensions were only dormant. Merchants complained in 1765 that the Paxton boys were stopping wagons carrying trading goods to the Indians on the frontier.[1] The refusal of the Assembly to give the western counties their fair share of representation was a perennial grievance. The West was also antagonized because no effort was made to improve roads and communications.[2] At election time in Philadelphia, irritation at upper-class control of politics occasionally appeared. "A Brother

1. *Pennsylvania Magazine of History and Biography,* XVIII (1894), 41; *Pennsylvania Archives,* 1st Ser., IV, pp. 219-240.
2. Charles H. Lincoln, *The Revolutionary Movement in Pennsylvania, 1760-1776* (Philadelphia, 1901), ch. IV.

Chip" probably spoke for many voters when he advocated open nominations: "But I beg leave to ask, have not we the same privileges to preserve as [party leaders]? Have we not an equal right of electing or being elected? If we have not the liberty of nominating such persons whom we approve, our freedom of voting is at an end, and if we are too mean a body to be consulted on such a weighty occasion, our ballot is not worth throwing in on the day of election...." [3] At the election of 1772 "A. P." warned his readers to avoid choosing lawyers for the Assembly: "They are generally pricking fellows, maintainers of false suits, accustomed to let out their tongues and talents for hire, to call good evil and evil good." [4] "Citizen" condemned candidates for office who spoke slightingly of the common people. "When gentlemen of character and in office among us can dare to express themselves to this purport, men whose ancestors two generations ago were on an equality with some of the meanest of us, what may we expect? *The Laborious Farmer* and *Tradesman* are the most valuable branches of the community." [5]

Yet by 1774 unrest among settlers of the West and the lower classes of the city had not reached significant proportions, and the leadership of the Revolutionary movement was taken by upper class Whigs in Philadelphia. An astute observer, Alexander Graydon, estimated that a large proportion, "perhaps a great majority of the most wealthy and respectable" of Pennsylvania, espoused the Whig cause. "The merchants were on the Whig side, with few exceptions; and the lawyers, who, from the bent of their studies, as well as their habit of speaking in public, were best qualified to take the lead in the various assemblies...." [6] But upper-class

3. Quoted from *ibid.*, 81 (note).
4. Quoted from *ibid.*, 94.
5. Quoted from *ibid.*, 93 (note).
6. Alexander Graydon, *Memoirs of His Own Time* (Philadelphia, 1846), 117.

Whigs differed sharply over the proper methods of opposing British imperial legislation and over the extent to which resistance should be carried. These issues divided the party into four fairly distinct factions. The first, and most conservative, was composed of some of the influential members of the Proprietary party—men like James and Andrew Allen, Edward Shippen, Jr., Edward Tilghman, Jasper Yeates, and Provost William Smith. After 1776 some of these men were suspected of Toryism. The second faction contained most of the liberal members of the Quaker party who controlled the Assembly from 1774 to 1776 and was exemplified most perfectly by John Dickinson. The third was made up of an active, younger group of business and professional men who had played a subordinate part in politics during the years preceding 1774 but who rapidly took over leadership of the Whig movement afterwards. Among their number were Charles Thomson, Thomas Mifflin, Joseph Reed, George Clymer, Thomas McKean and James Wilson.

Thomson, a wealthy self-made merchant, was called by John Adams "the Sam Adams of Philadelphia." As Secretary of the Continental Congress from 1774 to 1789 he was tremendously influential in national politics. Thomas Mifflin, a merchant of distinguished lineage but popular among all classes in Philadelphia, was elected four times to the Assembly between 1772 and 1776 by large majorities. Although a Quaker, he became Quartermaster-General in the Continental army from 1775 to 1777 and served three terms as governor between 1790 and 1799. Joseph Reed, born of a wealthy New Jersey family, studied law at the Middle Temple and returned to practice in Philadelphia. Appointed Adjutant-General of the army by Washington in 1775, he later resigned from military service to become President of Pennsylvania from 1778-1781. George Clymer, another prosperous merchant, was one of the relatively few original Whig leaders to favor independence in 1776. He was prominent in public life until his retirement in 1796. Thomas McKean, a well-known lawyer from Delaware, became an outstanding figure in both Delaware and Pennsylvania politics during the Revolutionary and early national periods. A bitter opponent of the democratic Constitution of 1776 and an outstanding Federalist until 1792, he later became a strong supporter of Jefferson. Elected Governor of Pennsylvania in 1800, he organized conservative Republicans and Federalists into an enduring political machine. James Wilson was the only important Whig leader to come from the West. After emigrating from Scotland, where he received a good education in philosophy at the Universities of St. Andrews, Glasgow, and Edinburgh, he practised law in Carlisle. Another consistent and unsparing critic of the Constitution of 1776, he occupied a position at the Federal Convention of 1787 second in importance only to Madison's. Appointed a justice of the Supreme Court by Washington, his promising career was blighted by an inordinate passion for land speculation.[7]

On the left wing of the Whig party was a small group of doctrinaire democrats—not influential as yet—which included George Bryan, James Cannon, Timothy Matlack, Tom Paine, and David Rittenhouse. More will be said of them later.

The history of the Revolutionary movement in Pennsylvania from 1774 to 1777 is largely the record of the conflicts between the four distinguishable factions to secure the leadership of the protest movement. When news of the Boston Port Bill arrived, Thomson, Mifflin, and Reed sponsored a series of meetings in Philadelphia to publicize the Whig

7. Biographical data taken from *D.A.B.;* J. Thomas Scharf and Thompson Westcott, *History of Philadelphia,* 3 Vols. (Philadelphia, 1884), Vol. I; Graydon, *Memoirs;* and Louis A. Biddle (ed.), *A Memorial of Benjamin Rush* (Lanoraie, Pa., 1905).

cause. They also established committees in the counties and called a convention for July 18 which they hoped could command enough support throughout the province to elect delegates to the Continental Congress. From the outset their activities were regarded with suspicion by the conservative provincial leaders, many of whom had attended the Philadelphia meetings in order to exercise a moderating influence. Aware that a convention might inject an unwelcome radical note into the protest movement, the conservatives prevailed upon Governor Penn to call a special session of the Assembly which could undertake to keep the opposition to Britain within legal bounds. This body, upon convening, chose a congressional delegation headed by Galloway, and he himself drafted instructions which charged the members "to avoid everything indecent and disrespectful to the mother state." The intentions of the conservatives are probably well illustrated by Galloway's Plan of Union, which, although initially commanding a good deal of support, eventually aroused hostility in Congress because it did not provide for the local autonomy which most Whigs were anxious to secure.[8]

Although the radicals connected with the committees and the conservatives in the Assembly distrusted each other, their differences were ones of means rather than ends. Both desired a peaceful and speedy reconciliation with Britain. This agreement on objectives gave a certain surface cordiality to relations between the various factions of the Whig party during the rest of 1774. When the Massachusetts delegates to Congress arrived in Philadelphia, they were met at the outskirts by a group of the radical Whigs including Benja-

8. A detailed account of the conflicts between radicals and conservatives in the summer of 1774 will be found in E. P. Douglass, Democracy in the American Revolution (doctoral dissertation, Yale University, 1949), Part IV, ch. 2.

min Rush, Mifflin, and Bayard, and were warned not to utter a word in favor of independence, "for the idea ... is as unpopular in Pennsylvania as the Stamp Act itself." [9] At a dinner given by the Assembly to the members of Congress on October 20, all joined heartily in the toast, "May the sword of the parent never be stained with the blood of her children." [10] On December 10 the Assembly became the first of the colonial legislatures to adopt and confirm the proceedings and measures of the Congress.[11]

Other factors tended to promote a temporary lull in the conflicts among the Whigs. In the first place, John Dickinson had now become the acknowledged leader of the radical group, a position for which he had been carefully groomed by Thomson, Mifflin, and Reed. His *Farmer's Letters,* by treating the issue with Britain in a calm, reasonable, and dignified fashion, constituted a standard to which most honest Whigs could repair—for the moment at least. In the second place, Galloway, long regarded with the deepest suspicion by the radical faction, retired from politics after the failure of his plan of union [12] and the conservative group in and out of the Assembly which shared his ideas ceased to have much influence. Finally, Dickinson, Mifflin, and Thomson all won seats in the Assembly at the October elections. Edward Biddle, a staunch Whig from Berks, replaced Galloway as speaker. Biddle was the first westerner ever to serve in that capacity.

But from the moment the leaders of the radical Whigs

9. Charles F. Adams (ed.), *The Works of John Adams,* 10 Vols. (Boston, 1850-1856), II, 512.

10. *Ibid.,* 400.

11. *Votes of the Assembly, Pennsylvania Archives,* 8th Ser., VIII, 7162.

12. Oliver C. Kuntzelman, *Joseph Galloway, Loyalist* (Philadelphia, 1941), 125, 127-128; Julian P. Boyd, *Anglo-American Union; Joseph Galloway's Plans to Preserve the British Empire, 1774-1788* (Philadelphia 1941), 44-45.

took their seats they became more cautious and a rift developed between them and the Philadelphia committee, their original vehicle. Dickinson began to incline toward Galloway's view that internal tumult with its threat of anarchy and civil war was the greatest danger facing the colonies.[13] In his *Farmer's Letters* he had felt that there was more to be feared from the unlimited taxing power of Parliament. The extent of his conversion to Galloway's type of conservatism is illustrated by his draft of the Articles of Confederation drawn up in the summer of 1776 which somewhat resembled Galloway's proposals of 1774 in its emphasis on centralized authority.[14]

The growing dissension within the Whig party became evident when the Philadelphia Committee, now chosen by city-wide election,[15] called a second Provincial Convention to meet in January, 1775. The encouragement of domestic manufacturing was the ostensible reason for the gathering, but the underlying objective was the raising of a military force and possibly the dissolution of the Assembly. Joseph Reed was elected president, much against his inclinations.[16] When the intentions of the Committee became known, Dickinson, Mifflin, and Thomson met privately with some of its members, and "by pointing out ... the fatal consequences that might and would inevitably ensue," prevailed upon

13. Galloway's fear of anarchy which led him to desire royal government in 1764 pervades his pamphlet of 1775, *A Candid Examination of the Mutual Claims of Great Britain and the Colonies* (New York, 1775).

14. See the discussion of the Dickinson draft of the Articles of Confederation in Merrill Jensen, *The Articles of Confederation* (Madison, 1941), ch. V.

15. Pennsylvania *Journal*, Nov. 2, 9. Returns of the election are in *ibid.*, Dec. 28.

16. William B. Reed, *The Life and Correspondence of Joseph Reed*, 2 Vols. (Philadelphia, 1847), I, 97.

them to avoid extreme measures.[17] Probably as a result of this pressure the Convention limited itself to restating the Whig position on colonial rights and passed measures encouraging home manufactures. The members listened to a rousing speech by James Wilson which suggests that he favored armed resistance,[18] complimented the Congress on its work, and bound themselves to carry out its orders.[19]

According to an account published in Rivington's Tory *Gazetteer*, some of the Whigs, alarmed at reports that "the farmer had deserted the committee," got Dickinson to attend the Convention. The correspondent asserted that Dickinson maintained a stony silence throughout the proceedings and later declared that "he was really alarmed at the Proceedings of our Committee." [20] A few weeks later an informant in the same paper recounted a conversation with a former Committee member. "My friend observed that though he had heretofore been active in the measures of the Committee, yet their conduct now appeared to him so inconsistent and absurd, that he was determined never more to countenance them; said he was well convinced they aimed at a general revolution and were promoting the measure to overthrow our excellent Constitution;—drunk with power they had usurped, and elated with their own importance, they were determined on nothing so much as to increase discord and confusion. By these they had risen to power—from these they derived their whole consequence; they knew full well if the present troubles should subside, they must again sink into

17. New York Historical Society *Collections*, 75 Vols. (New York, 1868-1942), XI, 284.

18. Printed in Bird Wilson (ed.), *Works of James Wilson*, 3 Vols. (Philadelphia, 1804), III, 247-269.

19. *Pennsylvania Archives*, 2nd Ser., III, 627. Minutes printed in *ibid.*, 623-631.

20. *American Archives*, 4th Ser., I, 1211.

native obscurity." [21] Even though these reports are perhaps colored by wishful thinking on the part of the Tories, they nevertheless offer good illustrations of that fear of the new men thrown to the top by the Revolutionary ferment which seized Whig leaders in Massachusetts and elsewhere.

The Convention of 1775 marked the beginning of a protest against the manner in which the Assembly was conducting the opposition to Britain. Henceforth the authority of the legal government waned and the committees became the real government of the colony.[22] They were in a position to enforce the injunction of one newspaper editorialist: "Let every man be governed by the resolves of the city and county where he resides; every city and county by the resolves of the provincial committee (in this case the writer was obviously referring to the Philadelphia Committee); and finally every province by the determination of the whole in a general Congress." [23] The Assembly apparently had no place in this organizational chart of revolutionary bodies.

After news of Lexington and Concord arrived, the martial spirit which swept through Pennsylvania again temporarily united the factions of the Whig party. Voluntary militia units called associations were formed in each county under the sponsorship of the local committees, and the Assembly assumed leadership of them through a committee of safety headed by Franklin.[24] The legal legislature of Penn-

21. *Ibid.*, 1232.

22. Lincoln, *Revolutionary Movement in Pennsylvania*, 186.

23. Pennsylvania *Gazette*, Aug. 31, 1774.

24. See proclamations and oaths of association in Gratz Collection, Historical Society of Pennsylvania. Reports on the formation of associations are printed in *Pennsylvania Archives*, 2nd Ser., XIII. "The Martial Spirit throughout the Province is astonishing," wrote John Adams. "It rose all of a sudden, since the news of the Battle of Lexington. Quakers and all are carried away with it." *Warren-Adams Letters*, 2 Vols. (Boston, 1917, 1925), Massachusetts Historical Society, Collections, LXXII, LXXIII, Vol. I, 51. Christopher Marshall, a radical Philadelphia merchant, also

sylvania, like those in most of the royal colonies, functioned both as a constitutional and a revolutionary body.

But as in the case of the reaction to the Boston Port Bill a year before, the general support given to measures of resistance did not indicate unanimity of motive. James Allen, scion of the proprietary family, probably expressed the view of many of his friends when he declared that he was induced to join an association because "A man is suspected who does not; and I chuse to have a musket on my shoulders, to be on a par with them; and I believe discreet people mixing with them may keep them in order." [25] When the Assembly refused to equalize the burden of defense preparations by making military service compulsory or by imposing special taxes on conscientious objectors, associators began to suspect that the members were more concerned with maintaining the unique privileges of the Quakers than with a vigorous defense of colonial rights. Resentful associators in Lancaster county attacked Mennonites who refused either to join companies or allow themselves to be taxed for support of military measures, and threatened to resign unless the pacifists were compelled to assume a fair share of the burden. The committee of inspection there, headed by Shippen and Yeates, feared that a military coup would result from the riots and urged conciliatory measures toward Great Britain.[26] Philadelphia associators unanimously refused to serve as minute men [27] on the grounds that the pay was too low and that Quakers were

---

noted the bellicose attitude of the people. William Duane (ed.), *Extracts from the Diary of Christopher Marshall, 1774-1781* (Albany, 1877), 23.

25. "Selections from the Diary of James Allen," *Pennsylvania Magazine*, IX (1885), 186.

26. Committee of Inspection to Pennsylvania Congressional Delegates, June 3, 1775. Yeates Papers, Historical Society of Pennsylvania.

27. On June 30 the Assembly resolved to take the associations into the pay of the province when and if needed and recommended that a corps of minute men be formed in each county. *Votes*, VIII, 7245-7249.

exempt from either special taxation or service. The officers
of the three city battalions, no doubt realizing the difficulty
of inducing the Assembly to lay extra burdens on pacifists,
resolved at a special meeting "to wait on the honorable Congress to know whether they have not formed some plan for
the regulation of the people who have voluntarily associated
in defense of their country." [28]

When the Assembly reconvened in September, the officers
of the Philadelphia associators notified it of the refusal of the
privates to serve and asked that a tax be laid on conscientious
objectors. They declared that people *"sincerely* and *religiously* scrupulous are but few in Comparison to those who
upon this occasion, as well as others, make conscience a con-
venience;—that a very considerable share of the property
of the province is in the hands of people professing to be of
tender conscience in military matters; that the associators
think it extremely hard that they should risk their lives and
injure their fortunes in defense of those who will not be of
the least assistance in this great struggle;..." In conclusion
they requested that the associations be transformed into a
provincial militia. [29] The outcry against Quakers and other
pacifists became so great that the Assembly was finally forced
to lay a special tax of £2 and 10 shillings on all non-associators. [30] Yet apparently this concession did not satisfy all the
military organizations. Associators of Berks asserted that the
tax still did not equalize the burden of supporting military
preparations in view of all the extra expenses of the associators and their loss of earnings. [31]

28. MS Minutes of Philadelphia Associators' Meetings, Peters Papers,
VIII, Historical Society of Pennsylvania.

29. *Votes,* VIII, 7259-7260. For further details on the growing hostility
of associators for Quakers, see *ibid.,* 7262, 7334-7343; Duane (ed.), *Marshall
Diary,* 49-50.

30. *Votes,* VIII, 7382.

31. *Ibid.,* 7399.

As in 1756 and 1763, the Assembly, by its inability to cope with military problems, was inviting a demand from non-Quakers for greater participation in the government. In 1764 the western counties had wanted increased representation; in the spring of 1776 the resentful associators, ridiculed for allowing their lives to be rated "at 50 shillings apiece," [32] demanded even more—an extension of the suffrage. As the Committee of Privates declared to the Assembly on February 23, "Your Petitioners beg Leave to represent, that it has been the practice of all countries, and is highly reasonable, that all persons (not being mercenaries) who expose their Lives in defense of a country, should be admitted to the enjoyment of all of the rights and privileges of a citizen of that country which they have defended and protected." [33] When the Assembly not only ignored the request but presumed to choose general officers for the military establishment, the associations repudiated the authority of the legal government entirely. Declared the Committee of Privates, "Many of the associators have been excluded by this very House, from voting for the members now composing it, though this House was applied to on their behalf. Therefore, they are not represented in this House.... The counties, which have the greatest number of associators, have not a proportional representation; and therefore cannot be considered as having an equal voice..." [34]

In Pennsylvania, as in Maryland and Massachusetts, military service appeared to breed a desire for equal political rights. To deny a voice in the council of the province to those who were willing to shed their blood in her behalf seemed contrary to elemental justice. In a period when the safety of

32. Quoted from J. Paul Selsam, *The Pennsylvania Constitution of 1776* (Philadelphia, 1936), 86.
33. *Votes,* VIII, 7406.
34. *Ibid.,* 7546.

society depended primarily on the courage and determination of its members, it is understandable that possession of an equity in the visible assets of the corporation no longer appeared to be the sole criterion of responsible citizenship and the badge of status. The man who shouldered a gun in defense of his country would certainly seem to have a greater attachment for it than the man who continued to devote himself to accumulation. The coming of the war to Pennsylvania inescapably brought with it a change of values favorable to political democracy. Massachusetts democrats deduced manhood suffrage from the compact theory of government and natural law: in Pennsylvania the military organizations viewed the right of every armed man to vote as a self-evident proposition. The political procedures of the individual companies also fostered the spirit of democracy. Officers were elected by the men who were to serve under them, and in some cases military decisions were also subject to majority will. The associations served as a kind of school for democratic processes.

Thus by 1776 the breach in the Whig party had widened dangerously. Many of the former radicals were pursuing a moderate course and were striving to uphold the authority of the Assembly. A new and much more virulent radicalism had sprung up in the county committees and in the associations characterized by a resentment at what appeared to be the Assembly's half-hearted defense of American rights and its oversolicitude for the privileges of pacifist groups. The question of independence finally completed the split between the moderate and radical factions and made possible the attainment of a democratic constitution.

Not least among the objections to independence on the part of many Revolutionary leaders was the fear that it would lead to social upheaval. Thus Dickinson, in a speech before Congress on the subject of independence, is reported to have declared the restraining power of the King and Parliament "indispensable to protect the colonies from disunion and civil war." Even if successful in a revolution, "they would have to dread, should the counterpoise of monarchy be removed, that the democratic power would prostrate all barriers, and involve the state in ruin." [35] James Wilson, in an address written for delivery before the Continental Congress, admitted the seriousness of the grievances against Britain but asserted, "We are too much attached to the English laws and constitution, and know too well their happy tendency to diffuse freedom, prosperity, and peace ... to desire an independent empire. If one part of the constitution be pulled down, it is impossible to foretell whether the other parts of it may not be shaken, and perhaps overthrown." [36] As late as June 8 he was still arguing against independence, but he changed his mind in time to sign the Declaration. In the summer of 1776 Robert Morris wrote to Reed, "I have uniformly voted against and opposed the Declaration of Independence," and Reed himself declared that he would have been entirely satisfied with local autonomy and exemption from parliamentary taxation.[37]

The remnants of the Proprietary party were even more confirmed in their opposition to independence. Joseph Shippen was "shocked" at *Common Sense.* "God forbid we should be driven to the Necessity of adopting a Measure so apparently fatal to America," he declared.[38] "Absolute necessity alone should ... justify an innovation on the constitu-

35. Quoted from a report of the speech by Thomas F. Gordon, *The History of Pennsylvania from Its Discovery ... to ... 1776* (Philadelphia, 1829), 535-537.

36. *Journals of the Continental Congress, 1774-1789,* 34 Vols. (Washington, 1904-1937), IV, 145. Speech printed pp. 134-146.

37. Reed, *Reed,* I, 201, 203.

38. Joseph Shippen to ――――, Jan. 15, 1776. Shippen Papers, VII, Historical Society of Pennsylvania.

tion," wrote Jasper Yeates to Col. James Burd.[39] James Allen confided to his diary that if the advocates of independence prevailed, "All may bid adieu to our old happy constitution and peace.... I love the cause of liberty; but cannot heartily join in the prosecution of measures totally foreign to the original plan of resistance. The madness of the multitude is but one degree better than submission to the Tea-Act." [40] Quakers opposed independence not only because it would make war inevitable, but, as Thomas McKean wrote Adams much later, "they foresaw the consequences of an equal representation." [41]

The openly conservative Whigs joined the Tories in bitter denunciations of independence after the appearance of *Common Sense*. Feeling the foundations of society shaking beneath their feet, they extolled the virtues of the British constitution and stressed the need of separation of powers in government in order to preserve the state from anarchy. William Smith, as "Cato," quoted Montesquieu effectively to demonstrate that the English form of government provided the best guarantee of liberty.[42] As a kind of *mea culpa* for his past Whiggish activities he declared in a published eulogy of General Montgomery, "God forbid that any professions of mine...should inflame men's minds to the purposes of wild ambition or mutual destruction." [43] "What constant scenes of blood and devastation does history present to us in democracies," lamented one newspaper writer, "the multitude in a perpetual ferment like an ocean in a storm...." [44] Charles Inglis, an Anglican clergyman, stressed

39. March 7, 1776, Shippen Papers, VII.

40. *Pennsylvania Magazine*, IX, 186, 187.

41. Adams, *Works*, X, 75.

42. Pennsylvania *Gazette*, Apr. 3, 10, 1776.

43. *An Oration in Memory of General Montgomery* (Philadelphia, 1776), 21.

44. Pennsylvania *Gazette*, Feb. 28, 1776.

the need of monarchical and aristocratic, as well as democratic elements in a stable constitution. He said that Paine
"for want of knowing the nature of real liberty...busied
himself in pursuing an imaginary one; he built a Chalcedon
although he had before his eyes Byzantium." [45] The author
of *Plain Truth,* a pamphlet dedicated to Dickinson and possibly written by Smith or George Chalmers,[46] reviewed the
arguments against Paine, again with the help of Montesquieu, and declared the great error of *Common Sense* to be
the author's inability to realize that "mankind can bear none
but imperfect laws." [47]

During the spring radical publicists—among them James
Cannon, as "Cassandra," and Paine, as "Forrester"—lashed
back at Smith, Inglis, and other conservatives, but they did
not probe as deeply into basic political problems as their opponents. Yet there were a few indications in the press of a
deeper radicalism. When "Civis" attacked the demands of
the associators for the vote on the grounds that "minors, apprentices, and immigrants who knew not the happy form of
government of Pennsylvania" would come to control the
province,[48] "Elector" replied by declaring that the present
high suffrage qualifications gave an advantage to "the profligate and corrupt." He asserted that the sentiment for independence would seem infinitely greater if the common
people were allowed to vote.[49] "Always remember that rich
men derive no right to power from their wealth," declared
another writer. "Recollect how often you have heard the

45. *The True Interest of America Impartially Stated* (Philadelphia,
1776), 18, 54.
46. See Paul L. Ford, "The Authorship of Plain Truth," *Pennsylvania
Magazine,* XII, 421-425.
47. *Plain Truth* (Philadelphia, 1776), 9, 12, 16, 129.
48. Pennsylvania *Gazette,* May 1.
49. *Ibid.,* May 15.

first principles of government subverted to the calls of Cato and other Catalines to make way for men of fortune to declare their sentiments upon the subject of independence, as if a minority of rich men were to govern the majority of virtuous freeholders of the province." [50] Some editorialists writing in this vein considered the right to vote as consideration for military service rather than a normal perquisite of citizenship. As one writer put it, "Every man who pays his shot and bears his lot" should have the right to vote while "every non-associator and stickler for dependency ... should be kept from our councils."

Although the sentiment for independence rose steadily in the West and among the lower classes in the city, the Assembly resolutely refused to entertain the idea. As long as it constituted the legal government of the province, the radicals could expect that it would strive for a reconciliation with Britain. Therefore, in the spring of 1776 after the Assembly had refused to allow its Congressional delegates to vote for independence, the radical leaders began to plot internal revolution. In the royal colonies no such necessity existed because the governors had departed and revolutionary bodies were in control. Also, many of the Whig leaders of normally conservative convictions there favored independence by the spring of 1776. But in Pennsylvania the Assembly was functioning adequately both as a revolutionary and a constitutional body. Bills on routine matters were being sent to the governor for signature while the defense of the province was handled by resolutions carried out by the Committee of Safety.

In the fulfillment of their designs the Pennsylvania radicals received considerable assistance from the Continental Congress, whose radical members were also alarmed at the

50. Pennsylvania *Packet,* June 24.

tendencies of the Assembly.[51] On May 10 and 15 Congress by resolutions invited the people of the colonies to suppress all governments deriving authority from the crown on the theory that they were not equal to the exigencies of the times. The resolutions could only have been directed against the existing regime in Pennsylvania, for every other colony was controlled by a revolutionary body. The fact that the Philadelphia Committee called a meeting on the evening of May 15 to discuss "the taking up and forming of new governments" suggests an understanding with the radicals in Congress. The committees had always been the executors of congressional orders; what more natural than that they should consider a congressional resolution as a command to overturn the government of their own province?

In spite of the protests of conservatives that the resolutions could not apply to the Assembly, since it was certainly equal to the exigencies of the times and had severed its connections with the crown to the extent of raising an army for defense,[52] the revolutionary process swung into high gear. At a tumultuous gathering in the State House yard, May 20, the Philadelphia Committee demanded the calling of a constitutional convention and received enthusiastic approval from an estimated 4,000 to 5,000 people who attended the meeting. According to an observer from South Carolina, "The people behaved in such a tyrannical manner that the least opposition was dangerous." [53] A Provincial Conference

51. Elbridge Gerry complained that the provincial government held back the whole continent, and Richard Henry Lee declared "The Proprietary colonies do certainly obstruct and perplex the American machine." Edmund C. Burnett (ed.), *Letters of Members of the Continental Congress,* 8 Vols. (Washington, 1921-1936), I, 442, 459-460.

52. See "Address and Remonstrance of Inhabitants of the City and County of Philadelphia," *Votes,* VIII, 7524-7526.

53. "Extracts from the Diary of Dr. James Clitherall, 1776," *Pennsylvania Magazine,* XXII (1898), 470.

of Committees was set for June 18 in order to get a mandate from the province as a whole and decide upon representation and suffrage for the convention.[54] The response among the associations was an enthusiastic endorsement of the Philadelphia Committee's action.[55] The Assembly recognized the handwriting on the wall. After June 10 no quorum could be obtained, and on June 14 the few members present voted to allow the congressional delegates to cast their ballots for independence.[56]

The composition of the Provincial Conference showed how completely the location of political power in the province had shifted. Of the 108 members, 58 held military titles and probably many others were privates in the associations.[57] No members of the great proprietary families and no recognizable Quakers appeared on the list of delegates. But even more noticeable was the lack of well-known Whigs. The names of Thomson, Mifflin, Reed, Dickinson, Clymer, and Wilson were conspicuous by their absence. This was because almost the entire Whig leadership had either become discredited or had engaged in patriotic activities outside the arena of local politics. Dickinson, Wilson, and Morris were under a cloud because of their refusal to support independence in Congress; Mifflin and Reed were with the army, and Thomson was Secretary of Congress. Franklin's name headed the Philadelphia delegation, but he never attended meetings. The most active members were Thomas McKean, President, Christopher Marshall, Timothy Matlack, and Benjamin Rush. These men, with the addition of Cannon, Paine,

54. Minutes of the meeting and pertinent documents are contained in *American Archives*, 4th Ser., VI, 517-523.
55. See Selsam, *Pennsylvania Constitution*, 126-129.
56. *Votes*, VIII, 7542-7543.
57. Selsam, *Pennsylvania Constitution*, 137; Members listed in *Pennsylvania Archives*, 2nd Ser., III, 635-637.

and Rittenhouse, were now directing the Philadelphia Committee.

The Provincial Conference fulfilled its purpose with dispatch. By unanimous vote, the Assembly was declared "not competent to the exigencies of our affairs" and a constitutional convention was decided upon "for the express purpose of forming a new government in this province on the authority of the people only."[58] The suffrage was given to all adult associators and to the legal voters, provided the latter were prepared to take an oath which acknowledged the competency of the convention and which repudiated allegiance to the King of Great Britain.[59] The suffrage was denied to all who had been published as Tories and not recanted their error. All professing Christians who repudiated British rule and were qualified to vote for members of the Assembly could be elected as delegates to the Convention. With some qualms the Conference took over administration of the associations and exercised legislative powers, with the understanding that the arrangement was only temporary and did not imply a claim of sovereignty. A committee which included Dr. Rush prepared an address to the people urging them to bind their delegates by instructions.[60]

Representation at the Convention was to be heavily weighted in favor of the West. Under the pretext that population figures were unavailable, and that "the number of taxables in the counties respectively does not differ so much as to make it of any probable disadvantage to allow an equal representation,"[61] each county was given eight delegates. Actually, lists of taxables drawn up in 1770 were available for all the counties except the three newest—Westmoreland,

58. *Pennsylvania Archives,* 2nd Ser., III, 639.
59. *Ibid.,* 640.
60. *Ibid.,* 656-657.
61. *Ibid.,* 642-643.

Bedford, and Northumberland [62]—and since the population of these was known to be small,[63] it would not have been difficult to determine a proportionate ratio. Certainly it could not be doubted that Philadelphia county, with 10,000 taxables in 1770, deserved more representatives than Northampton with 2,800. Yet the Conference, some of whose members had led the fight for proportionate representation in years past, ignored any such considerations. As a result the three eastern counties, with about the same population as all those of the West, had only twenty-four delegates while the West had sixty-four. Ironically, the underrepresentation of the East in the Convention was greater than the underrepresentation of the West in the Assembly.

Apparently the question of popular ratification of the constitution was never even raised. It was assumed that the Convention would both draft the instrument and put it in force.

The object of the Conference was not so much to pave the way for democratic reform of the government as to insure control by the radical Whig faction. The provisions on suffrage were plainly designed to give the vote to as many radicals as possible and deny it to as many moderates as possible. The justification for the Convention was not the conviction, as in Massachusetts, that only a special act of constituent power could establish a legitimate government, but the fiction that the Assembly was unequal to the exigencies of the times. In other words, the Convention in Pennsylvania was a political expedient and not, as in Massachusetts, the cornerstone of constitutional government. Of course, the Convention did succeed in bringing democracy to Pennsylvania, but it was a democracy of circumstance rather than

62. See Evarts B. Greene and Virginia D. Harrington, *American Population Before the Federal Census of 1790* (New York, 1932), 117.

63. In 1779 Bedford had 1200 taxables, Northumberland and Westmoreland 2100 apiece. *Ibid.*

of theory. Where Massachusetts succeeded in the creation of democratic doctrine but failed in the formation of a democratic party, Pennsylvania was to succeed in the formation of a party but fail in the task of providing democracy with a firm theoretical basis.

The course of the Whig movement in Pennsylvania is unique because of its deviation from the pattern set in the royal colonies. There the dissolution of assemblies and the subsequent ending of legal government provided an overpowering grievance which unified resistance behind the assembly parties. The issue was plain—American liberty *vs.* British slavery, and the assembly leaders appeared as natural leaders of the popular cause. Whatever internal grievances existed were overshadowed by the threat from without. Therefore the Revolutionary leaders were in a better position to combat any radicalism which arose during the transition from colonies to commonwealths. But in Pennsylvania the Whigs were put in an equivocal position from the outset. The government they dominated was intact, if slightly stigmatized by the British connection. Extreme measures of resistance were unnecessary either to keep order in the province or to press the campaign for local autonomy. Most of the royal colonies were already at war with Britain and had therefore committed themselves almost irrevocably to independence, but Pennsylvania, up to the actual signing of the Declaration, had the power of choice.

It was this very necessity of choice that split the Whig party. One by one as the colonial leaders saw the hour of decision approaching, they retired from politics, aware, perhaps, that such a course invited disaster but helpless to find an alternative. The most conservative were the first to go— Galloway, Wharton, the strict Quakers, Smith and the proprietary families, and finally Dickinson. Of the moderates among the new men, Willing, Morris, and Wilson stayed in politics but lost their influence. Thus by the spring of 1776 the moderate majority in the Assembly was left leaderless and discredited while their administration was coming to share the hatred felt for the British government. A *coup* by the radical party was inevitable.

But in the meantime the radical party itself had also undergone alteration. The original leaders, Thomson, Mifflin, and Reed, had apparently lost interest in committee politics and had devoted their energies to other tasks; as a result the mantle fell on a new group of relatively unknown men like Cannon, Matlack, Young, and Paine. When the blow came that destroyed the Assembly, these men were suddenly thrust into leadership at the crucial moment when a constitution had to be drafted.

The internal revolution had created an internal vacuum in Pennsylvania, and, as events were to prove, the underprivileged rushed to fill it. Equal representation of all counties regardless of population, and suffrage qualifications which prohibited all but rebels from voting, meant that the West would now dominate the state. The stage was now set for the formation of a democratic party which would take over the administration of government.

FOURTEEN

The Creation of a Democratic Party, 1776

THE ninety-six delegates who met at the State House on July 15, 1776, to draft the fundamental law of the state bore little resemblance to the some thirty-six gentlemen who had guided the destinies of the province during the colonial period.[1] Most were farmers and artisans who had been active in the associations. Outside of the Philadelphia delegation— which included Franklin and Clymer—there were very few men of prominence or previous experience in governmental affairs. Franklin himself, although elected President of the Convention, took little or no interest in the course of events. "As to the political concerns of the State he was apathy itself," wrote Graydon, "and like King Lear it was obviously his fast intent to shake all cares and business from his age." An acquaintance later informed Graydon that it did not appear that the good doctor had even read the Constitution after its publication.[2] The effective leadership appears to have been supplied by George Bryan, David Rittenhouse, James Cannon, Timothy Matlack, and Dr. Thomas Young.

1. List of delegates and minutes of the convention printed in *Pennsylvania Archives*, 3rd Ser., X, 755-784.
2. Alexander Graydon, *Memoirs of His Own Time* (Philadelphia, 1846), 286-287.

Bryan, the Philadelphia merchant who had opposed the projected change of government in 1764, was not a member of the Convention, but he was frequently consulted by the members and has been credited along with Cannon and Matlack as one of the drafters of the Constitution. According to Graydon, his politics were far to the left. "It was his passion or policy to identify himself with the *people* in opposition to those who were termed the *well born*." As for Cannon, a mathematics teacher at Philadelphia College, Graydon wrote, "It may not be uncharitable to presume that having little knowledge of man, and scholastic predilection for the antique in liberty, which generally falls to the lot of a pedagogue, he acted accordingly."[3] David Rittenhouse, the celebrated mathematician and astronomer, had little or no previous experience in politics.[4] Matlack, a relapsed Quaker, had been outstanding in the rough-and-tumble committee politics, but his chief interest appears to have been horseracing, cock-fighting, and bull-baiting.[5] According to a popular anecdote, the Quaker, James Pemberton, who had once bailed him out of debtor's prison, asked Matlack one day as he was girding his sword, "What is that thing at thy side for?" "That is to defend my property and my liberty," replied Matlack. "Why Timothy," rejoined Pemberton, "as for thy property we know thou has none, and as for thy liberty, thou owest that to me."[6] Dr. Young was not a member of the Convention but exercised considerable influence over the Philadelphia Committee. Described as "a certain bawling New England man of noisy fame," by Edward Shippen, he

3. *Ibid.*, 287-288.

4. Biographical sketch in *Pennsylvania Magazine*, IV (1880), 229-230, and in *D.A.B.*

5. See Asa M. Stackhouse, *Col. Timothy Matlack, Patriot and Soldier* (Privately printed, 1910), 5-7.

6. J. Paul Selsam, *The Pennsylvania Constitution of 1776* (Philadelphia, 1936), 207.

was later instrumental in securing the adoption by Vermont of a constitution modelled after that of Pennsylvania.[7]

As for the membership of the Convention, "Not a sixth part of us ever read a word on the subject [of government]," wrote Thomas Smith, of Bedford, one of the few educated men present.[8] He noted sarcastically that during the sessions a member asked that all documents under consideration be printed, because some delegates "could read print better than writing.... Our principal seems to be this: that any man, even the most illiterate, is as capable of any office as a person who has had the benefit of education; that education perverts the understanding, eradicates common honesty, and has been productive of all the evils that have happened in the world.... We are resolved to clear every part of the old rubbish out of the way and begin upon a clean foundation."[9] Smith's description of his colleagues and their intentions was probably quite accurate.

Nominations and elections for the Convention appear to have been closely controlled by the radical faction. The Philadelphia delegation was nominated at a meeting called by the Committee of Privates at which speeches were made by Cannon, Matlack, and Doctor Young.[10] The vote was light, and, in view of the discriminatory suffrage qualifications and the fact that moderates and Quakers did not participate, probably did not represent the will of the people as a whole. The county of Northampton, for example, had elected James Allen to the Assembly in May by a vote of 853-14,[11] thus in-

7. *Ibid.*, 121, 184 (note).
8. William H. Smith (ed.), *The St. Clair Papers*, 2 Vols. (Cincinnati, 1882), I, 371.
9. *Ibid.*, 373-374.
10. William Duane (ed.), *Extracts from the Diary of Christopher Marshall, 1774-1781* (Albany, 1877), 81.
11. "Diary of James Allen," *Pennsylvania Magazine*, IX (1885), 186.

dicating a strong moderate sentiment which could hardly have been reflected in the choice of the Convention delegates, even allowing for a considerable change in public sentiment since that time.

Little is known of the work of the Convention, for the minutes are very sketchy. On July 27 the draft of a bill of rights was reported by a committee which included Cannon, Matlack, and Rittenhouse, and after two days of discussion it was ordered to be printed.[12] There was nothing to distinguish it from other contemporary documents of its type except the last article: "An enormous proportion of property vested in a few individuals is dangerous to the rights, and destructive of the common happiness of mankind; and therefore every free state hath a right to discourage possession of such property." [13] This article, which has almost a New Deal ring, is one of the very few instances in the Revolution where democratic political doctrines were used to qualify the absolute right of property. During the period there was considerable antipathy on the part of the poorer segments of the population for those who gained political power by means of their wealth, but apparently few responsible persons ever suggested that the state interfere with the existing distribution of property in order to deprive the wealthy of their influence. The article was apparently too radical for the majority of the Convention, for it did not appear in the final draft of the bill of rights.

Considerably more time was spent on the frame of government, for a draft was not ready until September 5.[14] In the interim there was some discussion of constitutional issues in the newspapers and in pamphlets, mostly on the composi-

12. *Pennsylvania Archives,* 3rd Ser., X, 762.

13. *An Essay of a Declaration of Rights,* Broadside, Historical Society of Pennsylvania.

14. *Pennsylvania Archives,* 3rd Ser., X, 764-765.

tion of a legislature. Conservatives condemned unicameralism because they thought it would leave the people at the mercy of factions which could command a majority in the single house. Democrats countered by pointing out the possibility of deadlock in a bicameral legislature, and they noted the propensity of upper houses to use obstructionist tactics to defeat popular will. One commentator declared that the existence of faction provided the strongest argument for the unicameral legislature; the collection of all conflicting interests under one roof would necessitate compromises whereas bicameralism made reconciliation more difficult.[15]

Proposals by the conservatives had little effect on the Convention. The farmers, associators, and Philadelphia radicals who composed it were apparently determined to establish a completely democratic form of government. On August 2 they resolved that "the future legislature of the state shall consist of one branch only, under proper restrictions." [16] When George Clymer and a delegate from Lancaster, George Ross, attempted to reopen debate on the question— possibly in the hope of securing a bicameral legislature— their motion was defeated.[17] Although there is no further evidence of opposition to the plans of the majority, twenty-

---

15. *Four Letters on Interesting Subjects* (Philadelphia, 1776), 20. For another example of the democratic point of view see Pennsylvania *Packet,* July 1. Bicameralism .was advocated by "Demophilus" in *The Genuine Principles of the Ancient Saxon, or English Constitution* (Philadelphia, 1776). The traditionalism of this pamphlet gives it a Jeffersonian coloring. The pamphlet, *An Essay of a Frame of Government for Pennsylvania* (Philadelphia, 1776)—perhaps the work of Dickinson—advocates the republic of equipoise in the conventional manner. Adams' *Thoughts on Government* and Carter Braxton's *Address to the Convention of Virginia* were published in Philadelphia in the spring of 1776 and undoubtedly exerted some influence on local opinion regarding the Pennsylvania constitution.

16. *Pennsylvania Archives,* 3rd Ser., X, 763.

17. *Ibid.,* 765.

three members did not vote in the otherwise unanimous acceptance of the Constitution on September 28.[18]

The instrument which the Convention had drawn up could scarcely have been more democratic. Every freeman twenty-one years of age who paid public taxes could vote for members of the Assembly and the Council and be eligible for any public office in the state (Sect. 6).[19] The Council, as under the Charter, was limited to executive and administrative duties, but it had rather extensive powers of appointment. The President of the Council, elected by joint vote of both houses, was only *primus inter pares*. Complete local self-government was secured by the local election of justices of the peace, sheriffs, coroners, commissioners, and tax assessors (Sects. 30, 31). Judges of the Supreme Court of Judicature, denied tenure during good behavior, were chosen by the Council for seven-year terms and were "removable for misbehavior at any time by the general assembly" (Sect. 23). Given adequate salaries, they were forbidden to accept fees or perquisites of any kind. Although this stipulation did not extend to the judges of the lower courts, the Constitution indicated disapproval of the fee system by declaring the emoluments of public office to be compensation for services and not the returns from investment. Thus, "whenever an office, through increase of fees or otherwise, becomes so profitable as to occasion many to apply for it, the profits ought to be lessened by the legislature" (Sect. 36). Any official who took greater fees than allowed by law "either directly or indirectly" would be disqualified from ever holding public office in the state again (Sect. 26).

18. Selsam, *Pennsylvania Constitution*, 164.

19. Since poll taxes were to account for part of the state revenue for some time to come, this meant that all heads of families had the right to vote. The sons of freeholders were given the suffrage by separate provision. Therefore, the only free males who could not vote were sons of non-freeholders living with their parents.

Plural officeholding was entirely forbidden. All foreigners residing in the state for one year would be given the right to vote as "free denizens," and after two years' residence would be eligible for public office (Sect. 42). Although the Constitution endorsed religious freedom, it stipulated a religious test for office which required acknowledgment of the divine character of the Old and New Testament. This might have barred Deists and other unorthodox Christians from office and obviously barred Jews. Under terms of the oath, however, it is important to note that Catholics were eligible to hold office (Sect. 10). Imprisonment for debt was abolished, except in cases where there was presumption of fraud, and stiff penalties were decreed for candidates who attempted to buy votes at elections. It is significant that by the Constitution of 1776 democrats in Pennsylvania achieved nearly the entire program of reforms desired in North Carolina and Massachusetts.

One of the most interesting provisions of the Constitution was a stipulation that bills passed by the legislature could not become effective "except on occasions of sudden necessity" until they had been printed for public consideration and passed by the next Assembly (Sect. 15). Apparently this process of suspending laws until the will of the people could be ascertained, constituted one of the "proper restrictions" which the Convention meant to impose upon the Assembly. Democrats everywhere felt that constituents could restrain a legislature more effectively than other organs of government operating according to the principle of checks and balances. But whatever the theoretical benefits of suspended legislation, it was so obviously impractical that Assemblies uniformly disregarded the constitutional provision and put laws into effect immediately after passage.

A somewhat more effective check on the legislature was the Council of Censors. Once every seven years this body would be elected "to enquire whether the Constitution has been preserved inviolate in every part; and whether the legislative and executive branches of government have performed their duty as guardians of the people, or assumed to themselves, or exercised other or greater powers than they are entitled to by the constitution:..." (Sect. 47). If the Council should find any article of the constitution "defective," it was empowered to call a convention to amend it. Although the wording of the article is confusing, apparently the Council was designed to be a court of judicial review as well as an initiating body for the amending process. At first glance, the idea seems impractical and eclectic,[20] but if given time to develop, the Council might have realized the expectations of its originators. Since it was elected only once during the fourteen years in which the Constitution was in effect —and then under unfavorable political circumstances—the body never received an opportunity to prove its value. Theoretically, at least, the Pennsylvania plan has some merit. Judicial review of legislation by a specially elected body also empowered to initiate constitutional amendments might be considered a process at once more democratic and efficient than judicial review by the courts alone.

The democracy introduced by the Constitution was not so much a radical innovation, as charged by conservatives, as a fulfillment of the democratic potentialities of the Charter of Privileges. In establishing a unicameral legislature, an administrative Council, and local self-government, the Convention was maintaining the traditional institutions of the province. With the exception of the Council of Censors and the provision for suspensive legislation—neither of which ever became effective—the only important alterations in the

20. Lewis H. Meader, in "The Council of Censors," *Pennsylvania Magazine*, XXII (1898), 265-300, has analysed the institution and traced it back to origins in ancient history.

Charter government outside of the abolition of the proprietorship were the reapportionment of representation and the
extension of the suffrage. These changes were in reality not
"innovations" at all but a return to the spirit of the Charter
itself.

But if the Constitution was outstandingly democratic, the
political methods of the Convention and the procedure by
which the instrument was adopted were not. The Convention acted as the sovereign government of the state and was
recognized as such by the Continental Congress. But perhaps
as an indirect acknowledgment of the impropriety of assuming legislative powers, the Pennsylvania body published its
legislation as ordinances and resolves, and not as laws. Of
course, the exercise of sovereign power was certainly necessary because of the impotence of the legal Assembly; nevertheless the necessity for the assumption of such power was
created by the Convention itself. Some of the legislation it
passed was quite arbitrary and discriminatory, even with
allowances for war conditions. Non-associators were fined
at the high rate of twenty shillings for every month of exemption from military service, and four shillings per pound
of assessed valuation was added to their normal property
tax.[21] By an ordinance of September 25, justices of the peace
could take into custody and hold indefinitely any person
"who shall by advisedly speaking or writing, obstruct or
oppose, or endeavor to do so, the measures carrying on by
the United States of America." The accused could appeal
only to the Council of Safety.[22] The ordinance made no provision for habeas corpus or jury trial and endowed a political body with judicial functions.

The Constitution, as presented to the people, amounted
almost to an ultimatum. Although published "for public

21. Pennsylvania *Gazette*, Sept. 18.
22. *Ibid.*, Sept. 25.

perusal," no attempt was made to obtain public reaction to it and the instrument was ratified by the Convention only eighteen days after appearance in the newspapers.[23] The unfair representation by which the West was able to dominate the Convention was to be continued for a time in the new government. Although representation in proportion to taxables was endorsed by the Constitution and was to be put in force after 1778, in the meantime the counties and the city of Philadelphia were apportioned six representatives apiece (Sect. 17). But the most arbitrary act of the Convention was to draft an election oath by which each voter was compelled to accept the Constitution before he could cast a ballot for assemblymen and councillors: "I, ——————, do swear (or affirm) that I will be faithful and true to the commonwealth of Pennsylvania, and that I will not directly or indirectly do any act or thing prejudicial or injurious to the constitution or government thereof, as established by the Convention." [24] Thus, reversing democratic procedure, the Convention prevented the people from rejecting or altering the handiwork of their own representatives. In view of the treason ordinance, even criticism was dangerous. Ironically enough, Pennsylvania received her democratic institutions from a body which barred a possibly large proportion of the population from participation in politics.

The Constitution got a stormy reception despite a mollifying *Address* written by Cannon, Matlack, and Rittenhouse,[25] and the members of the Convention were subjected to sometimes severe criticism by conservatives and some of the Revolutionary leaders. Charles Thomson probably spoke for others beside himself when he wrote to Dickinson, August 16, "I cannot help regretting ... that you have thrown the

23. Selsam, *Pennsylvania Constitution,* 162-163.
24. *Ibid.,* 164.
25. Printed in *American Archives,* 5th Ser., II, 581-587.

affairs of this state into the hands of men totally unequal
to them [by retiring from politics]. I fondly hope, however,
that Divine Providence ... will restore you ... to your country to correct her errors, which I feel those now bearing rule
will through ignorance, not intention, commit in settling
the reform of government." [26] Other observers were not so
charitable to the Convention. James Allen probably voiced
the conviction of most conservatives when he declared that
the members delayed writing a constitution because of a
desire to retain sovereign powers and only relinquished
them when "the voice of the people, i.e. the Whiggist part,
obliged them to frame a government and dissolve themselves." [27] "Scipio" composed a bill of indictment: "What
body has disposed of our liberty, property, and lives without
our consent, by cruel and tyrannical ordinances? The Convention. What body of men paid themselves above three
thousand pounds for sitting above two months for doing
business which might have been transacted in ten days? The
Convention." He concluded by accusing the members of securing to themselves "a perpetuity of their power, by fencing
it in with oaths unprecedented in any free country." [28]
The Assembly, which had continued to meet without a
quorum until September 25, when it dissolved itself for the
last time, ended its journal with a series of resolves which
condemned the treason ordinance and the imposition of
fines on non-associators.[29] Robert Proud, the historian of
Pennsylvania, flayed the members of the Convention in
verse:

> Of all the plagues that scourge the human race,
> None can be worse than *upstarts*, when in place;

26. Dickinson Family Papers, Historical Society of Pennsylvania.
27. *Pennsylvania Magazine*, IX (1885), 188.
28. *American Archives*, 5th Ser., II, 940.
29. *Votes of the Assembly, Pennsylvania Archives*, 8th Ser., VIII, 7586;
printed in Pennsylvania *Gazette*, Oct. 2.

Their power to shew, no action they forebear;
They tyrannize over all, while all they fear;
No savage rage, no ravenous beast of prey,
Exceeds the cruelty of the Servile Sway! [30]

Asked "Brutus" in a dialogue with "Camillus": "Must gentlemen, who have ruled society for a century past, be trampled down to the level of common mechanics in an instant and be obliged to consult their humors before they can have the least chance of filling a department of government?" "Camillus" sadly replied that this was indeed the case. "In a word, the new system of government...gives a part of the people, particularly those who frequent public houses where the laws are always posted up for consideration, a negative upon the proceedings of the whole state." [31]

Supporters of the Convention replied with equal heat. They asserted that the Constitution represented the will of the people, despite any irregularities in its adoption, and that critics of the instrument revealed themselves as Tories or self-seeking aristocrats. Thus one editorialist declared it a patriotic duty to abide by the Constitution.[32] "Consideration" asserted that the underlying reason for opposition to the instrument was that "gentlemen will not be governed by leather aprons." [33] He parried the argument that the document should have been submitted to popular ratification by pleading the haste necessitated by war conditions. Dr. William Shippen, himself a member of a first family, took wry pleasure from the discomfiture of his aristocratic friends. He wrote to his brother Edward in somewhat pointed fashion, "I don't wonder to see more of our friends offended and full of resentment upon the change who have been hereto-

30. *Pennsylvania Magazine*, XIII (1889), 435-436.
31. Pennsylvania *Packet*, Oct. 15.
32. *Ibid.*, Oct. 22.
33. Pennsylvania *Gazette*, Oct. 30.

fore at the head of affairs, in short have in many instances behaved as though they thought they had a sort of fee simple in them and might dispose of all places of honor and profit as pleased them best, now to be ousted or at least brought down to a level with their fellow citizens." [34]

Much of the specific criticism of the Constitution was directed against the voter's oath and the unicameral legislature. "Brutus" observed that Parliament "held up slavery to us, but never enacted a law to forbid our complaining of it." [35] "A Friend to Truth" replied that the oath to support the Constitution was no more than an affirmation of fidelity to popular sovereignty.[36] This was a rather subtle but misleading rejoinder. Actually, those who took the oath swore to uphold the Convention's interpretation of popular sovereignty rather than the principle itself. If the people had been given an opportunity to ratify the Constitution, a pledge of loyalty might have been justified. But in this instance representatives demanded that their constituents accept without question a decision on fundamental law made in their behalf. In a way the procedure of the Pennsylvania Convention was more arbitrary than that of the Revolutionary congresses in other states which drafted constitutions with little or no mandate from the people. These documents, considered as legislative enactments, could be altered from the moment of adoption in response to popular pressure, but the Pennsylvania Constitution could not be amended for seven years. Nearly every critic of the Convention cited the oath, and the defenders of the Constitution were usually silent in the face of the attack.

34. *Pennsylvania Magazine*, XLIV (1920), 286.

35. *American Archives*, 5th Ser., II, 865. See also "W" in Pennsylvania *Packet*, Oct. 22, who found a precedent for the oath in Cromwell's order that all members of Parliament pledge their loyalty to him before taking their seats.

36. *American Archives*, 5th Ser., II, 865-866.

The objections to the unicameral legislature in general followed the line laid down by Adams—that because of the depravity of human nature and the resultant propensity of liberty to run to license, checks and balances must be written into any stable plan of government.[37] Benjamin Rush described in more detail the need for upper houses. Although active in the campaign to call the Convention, Rush noted with approval that many of his friends thought the Constitution "rather too much upon the democratical order" and commented that if the governor and council had possessed a legislative veto, "the government would have derived safety, wisdom, and dignity from it." [38] Others had often pointed out that the propertyless might legally rob the rich by gaining control of a unicameral legislature, but Rush explained in a pamphlet of 1777 [39] that it was just as likely that the rich, by using their wealth to corrupt the people's representatives, might rob the poor of their liberty. In his opinion bicameralism, by diverting the rich to an upper house, would thereby insure the integrity of the lower. "The government of Pennsylvania has been called most improperly a government for poor men," he wrote. "It carries in every part of it a poison to their liberties. It is impossible to form a government more suited to the passions and interests of

37. As one writer put it, "If men were wise and virtuous as angels, a single legislative assembly would be the best form of government that could be contrived for them.... But since this is not so, the inhabitants of free states in every age have found it necessary to perpetuate their liberty by compound legislatures." Pennsylvania *Packet*, Sept. 24. See also "Demophilus" in Pennsylvania *Journal*, Sept. 25; "Casca" in Pennsylvania *Evening Post*, Oct. 31.

38. Benjamin Rush to Anthony Wayne, Sept. 24, Wayne Papers, Historical Society of Pennsylvania. Printed in Lyman H. Butterfield (ed.), *The Letters of Benjamin Rush*, 2 Vols. (Princeton, 1951), I, 114-115.

39. *Observations on the Government of Pennsylvania in Four Letters*, reprinted in Dagobert D. Runes (ed.), *The Selected Writings of Benjamin Rush* (New York, 1947), 54-84.

rich men." [40] Although apparently reconciling bicameralism with democratic ideals—in contrast to the conceptions of Adams and Parsons—Rush's argument had serious weaknesses. If the rich were indeed intent on corrupting the people's representatives, the presence of an upper house—where they would presumably employ their energies by trying to corrupt each other—would scarcely divert them from their objective. But even if we assume that Rush was correct in supposing that the potential corrupters of the people's representatives would flock to the upper house and ignore the lower, the result would be that the potentially corrupt would have a collective veto over the will of the potentially virtuous.

Two opposing parties formed rapidly after the publication of the Constitution. A real issue was at stake—equalitarian democracy vs. eighteenth-century republicanism. The democrats, or "Constitutionalists" as they came to be called after the election of 1776, included a majority of the yeoman farmers of the western counties, the lower classes of Philadelphia, and a few doctrinaire democrats like Cannon, Matlack, Paine, Rittenhouse, and Bryan. The "Anti-Constitutionalist" or "Republican" party, as it was sometimes called, included almost the entire Whig organization which had led the Revolution in its earlier stages. The list of signatures on a memorial to the Council of May, 1777, calling for a new constitution, is a roster of the heroes of this period. [41] After

40. *Ibid.*, 63.
41. Original with signatures in Gratz Coll., Historical Society of Pennsylvania. There is ample evidence in the composition of the Anti-Constitutionalist party. James Allen noted that the Constitution "split the Whigs to pieces." *Pennsylvania Magazine*, IX, 189. Graydon declared that most lawyers were in the Anti-Constitutionalist ranks. Graydon, *Memoirs*, 332. Mathias Slough in a letter to Jasper Yeates spoke of the almost universal disapproval "of men of property and understanding" for the Constitution. March 28, 1777, Provincial Delegates Letters. Yeates himself wrote, "Whenever I reflect on the times, I am seized with the blue devils and walk

the war the Quaker aristocracy and the former proprietary families soon added their strength to this group.

The Anti-Constitutionalist party was organized by the same methods which had proved so effective against the Assembly in 1776. "A large number of respectable citizens," called by handbill to a meeting at Philosophical Hall on October 17, discussed the shortcomings of the Constitution and unanimously passed thirty-two resolutions against it which were probably drawn up in advance by those who promoted the gathering.[42] The Convention was accused of acting *ultra vires* in assuming legislative powers and of departing "unnecessarily" from traditional forms. "It is the sense of this meeting that the people did not desire such *strange innovations*, but only that the kingly, proprietary, and parliamentary powers should be totally abolished and only such alterations made as would thereby be rendered necessary...." Chief among the specific criticisms of the constitution was the lack of separation of powers as taught by "The Baron de Montesquieu, whose name...all Europe reveres."[43] The oath and the Council of Censors were denounced and a resolution adopted that the Constitution was "disrespectful to religion,"[44] possibly in the hope of secur-

---

around the room in a sweat." To James Burd, March 29, 1777, Shippen Papers, VIII. "Honest" John Morton, an assemblyman from Chester for many years before the Revolution, supposedly died of grief "at the prospect of the misery which he foresaw would be brought on Pennsylvania by her present form of government." Butterfield (ed.), *Letters of Rush*, I, 151.

42. Duane (ed.), *Marshall Diary*, 97. Broadside of the minutes in Historical Society of Pennsylvania.

43. Rush declared in his *Observations*, "Mr. Locke is an oracle as to *principles*, Harrington and Montesquieu are oracles as to *forms* of government." Runes (ed.), *Selected Writings of Rush*, 78.

44. A few clergymen, among whom were William Smith and Henry M. Muhlenberg, had objected that the religious tests were not strict enough. Selsam, *Pennsylvania Constitution*, 216-221. "Consideration," a

ing support from those who wished a more stringent religious test. Voters were urged to refuse the oath and elect an Assembly which would resolve itself into a convention for the revision of the Constitution. Presumably, this convention would also exercise the legislative powers the Anti-Constitutionalists had so strongly condemned in the hands of the last Convention. Before the meeting broke up, all members subscribed to an oath of their own, later published, which was designed to absolve them from any suspicion of Loyalism.[45]

The meeting at the Philosophical Hall was followed by a mass meeting in the State House yard on October 21 designed to gain an ostensible mandate for the resolves and get the counter-revolutionary movement under way in the counties. Estimates of attendance varied with the sympathies of the observers. Marshall, by now a thorough Anti-Constitutionalist, placed the number at 1,500, but a democratic editorialist estimated 200 or 300.[46] Apparently there was no such unanimity as characterized the meeting which had called the Provincial Conference. An army officer—perhaps Dickinson, who was in Philadelphia after a short military career—led off the discussion by accusing the Convention of pushing through its schemes while the state leaders were away at war. McKean also spoke and criticized the Constitution. Then rebuttals were delivered by Cannon, Matlack, Dr. Thomas Young, and James Smith of York County. They defended the "innovations" on the grounds that there were no adequate precedents at hand on which to base a popular government and that the members of the Convention were

democratic editorialist, claimed that the resolution regarding religion was included purely for propaganda purposes. Pennsylvania *Gazette*, Oct. 30.

45. "At a Meeting Held at the Philosophical Society Hall, Oct. 17." Broadside, Historical Society of Pennsylvania.

46. "Consideration," in Pennsylvania *Gazette*, Oct. 30.

determined to wipe out every vestige of royal or proprietary forms.[47] Because of the length of the debate, it was necessary to hold a second meeting the next day to vote on the resolves agreed upon at Philosophical Hall. According to Marshall, these were then affirmed by a large majority. Committees were appointed to "carry the proceedings into each county and request...concurrence." [48]

With the forwarding of the proceedings to the counties —a procedure similar to a trip made by Dickinson, Mifflin, and Thomson in 1774 to gain support for the radical faction —the Whig revolutionary process which had so effectively aroused opposition against the British government was repeated against the Constitution. But the idea of a new convention met a much chillier reception in the hinterland than had the call for the overthrow of the Assembly. The Committee of Correspondence in Cumberland reported that most of its members were satisfied both with the oath and the Constitution,[49] and the Chester Committee decided unanimously to "disregard" the letter of the Philadelphia Anti-Constitutionalists.[50] There is no unqualified endorsement of the resolutions of the Philadelphia mass meeting on record.

Indeed, opposition to the plan of calling another convention may have been greater than available evidence indicates, for the Philadelphia group felt compelled to publish an elaborate statement of intentions: "You have been told that we are connected with the Tories and that we are aiming to bring back the late royal and proprietary power of this state. We deny the charge...and we call upon those

47. *Ibid.;* Duane (ed.), *Marshall Diary,* 98.
48. *Ibid.,* 99.
49. Robert L. Brunhouse, *The Counter-Revolution in Pennsylvania, 1776-1790* (Harrisburg, 1942), 19; Selsam, *Pennsylvania Constitution,* 228.
50. *American Archives,* 5th Ser., III, 463.

men who have propagated this calumny to prove that we have ever aimed at anything else than the establishment of a free and consistent government on the authority of the people." [51]

The issue of a new convention was decided by the elections of November 5. The western counties, whose enthusiastic support had enabled the Philadelphia radicals to reach their objectives in the campaign from 1774 to 1776, now broke decisively with the old leadership. Although both the city and county of Philadelphia elected Anti-Constitutionalist tickets,[52] the great majority of the western delegates came prepared to put the Constitution into effect. Of the seventy-two members of the Assembly, twenty-six had served in the Convention and thirteen in the Provincial Conference.[53]

Frustrated in their plan to turn the legislature into a convention, the Anti-Constitutionalists were at least able to prevent the functioning of the government. By absenting themselves from the Assembly, they made it impossible to obtain a quorum. In the meantime, however, the deteriorating military situation made the establishment of legal authority absolutely necessary. Dickinson—now a member from Philadelphia County—suggested a compromise whereby the minority would agree to attend the sessions if the majority would promise to vote for a new convention in January.[54] Perhaps this offer was accepted, for enough conservatives appeared in December to allow the Assembly to organize and elect a speaker. Shortly afterwards, however, an attempt to call a convention was defeated. Dickinson and his friends, believing they had been betrayed, retired for many years

51. *Ibid.*, 483. Copy of original broadside in Historical Society of Pennsylvania.

52. Duane (ed.), *Marshall Diary*, 102.

53. Selsam, *Pennsylvania Constitution*, 230.

54. Charles J. Stillé, *The Life and Times of John Dickinson, 1732-1808* (Philadelphia, 1891), 208-209.

from politics and the Assembly was again unable to muster a quorum.

Between the imminent danger of a British invasion and the near paralysis of the government, Pennsylvania was in chaos for most of the winter. Congress fled to Baltimore in December and Philadelphia was put under martial law.[55] Nevertheless the Constitutionalists slowly gained strength. By March a quorum could be obtained because special elections held to fill the vacant seats had resulted in an increase of their majority. George Bryan was returned as councillor from Philadelphia.[56] The Constitution was formally put into effect on March 4 when Thomas Wharton, Jr., was elected President of the Council, Bryan, Vice-President, Matlack, Secretary of the state, and Rittenhouse, Treasurer. Wharton, although disliking the Constitution, was willing to serve because of the pressing need for stable government.[57] He had made an excellent record as head of the Council of Safety and was universally esteemed.

Thus a democratic party was firmly in control of the government. It had succeeded in capturing control of the Whig movement, imposing a democratic constitution on the state, and in organizing an administration. Its monopoly of the state patronage assured a tenure of power for many years to come. As Graydon pointed out, although the Republicans had the support of all the men of wealth and education, the Constitutionalists had "prothonotaryships, attorney-generalships, chief justiceships, and what not to dispose of." [58] The history of third party movements in America has shown, if nothing else, that patronage is the political staff of life.

---

55. Selsam, *Pennsylvania Constitution*, 236.
56. *Ibid.*, 241; Brunhouse, *Counter-Revolution in Pennsylvania*, 22.
57. See Wharton's letter to General St. Clair printed in Anne H. Wharton, "Thomas Wharton, Jr.," *Pennsylvania Magazine*, V (1881), 436.
58. Graydon, *Memoirs*, 332.

The wealth of the Republicans, ample as it was, could not equal the sums the Constitutionalists were prepared to distribute to deserving party members. Jasper Yeates indicated the measure of the democrats' success when he wrote to Colonel Burd, "The Clamors of the Red-Hot Patriots have subsided into easy places and offices of Profit." [59]

But the Constitutionalists were weakened by the intense antagonism their methods had aroused. Moreover, they could never produce leaders who could match the ability of the Whig aristocracy. Hence the cause of democracy slowly declined in the years following the Revolution. Discredited by inefficiency, intra-party squabbles, and jobbery, the party was unable to meet the tremendous challenge to its majoritarian ideals posed by the Federal Constitution. In 1789 the foes of democracy finally succeeded in calling a convention which wrote a constitution of the conventional type. [60]

Why was it that in Pennsylvania alone the politically unprivileged succeeded in turning the Revolution into a movement for internal reform? The basic reason, perhaps, was the failure of the Whig leaders to exercise control over the Constitutional Convention. At the moment when their interests stood in the greatest need of protection they practically disbanded their party and turned the state over to their political opponents. Dickinson and other conservatives such as Wilson and Morris made the great mistake of retiring from public life when the fight seemed to be going against them—first, when the movement for independence became irresistible and second, when the campaign to call a second convention failed. The radical leaders—Thomson,

59. Yeates to Burd, March 29, 1777. Shippen Papers, VIII.
60. The excellent book by Brunhouse, *Counter-Revolution in Pennsylvania*, covers the history of the period from the Revolution to the adoption of the new constitution.

Mifflin, and Reed, made an equally grave error in leaving the arena of local politics. The Whig leaders seem to have been totally unaware of the danger in allowing men whose interests and political ideals were quite different from their own to write a constitution. Through the shortsightedness of the leaders the Convention had been given an opportunity to work its will unopposed. The attempt of the conservatives to start a counterrevolution in the fall and winter of 1776 possibly came too late to be effective, and in any case, the stigma of Toryism attached to them and their lack of determination doomed it to failure. The Revolutionary aristocrats recognized too late that their allies among the farmers of the West and the artisans of the city were as interested in democracy as in fighting the British.

The Whig leaders in other states realized that the establishment of proper constitutions was as necessary to protect their interests and preserve freedom as was the expulsion of the British from the colonies. Thus in the southern states fundamental law was drafted as soon as the decision for independence was made; when democratic opposition developed in Massachusetts, the leaders still maintained their control over the state government and succeeded in postponing decisions on constitutional matters until they could secure an instrument in accordance with their wishes.

The existence of legal government in Pennsylvania from 1774 to 1776 also weakened the Whig party. The dissolution of assemblies in the royal colonies strengthened radical sentiment, acted as a solvent for internal tensions, and united all classes behind the Whig leadership. With the opening of hostilities in the spring of 1776 reconciliation became impossible short of absolute submission, so under the circumstances there was little that the leaders could do except seize the sovereignty and establish independent governments. But none of the compulsions to independence were present in

Pennsylvania. Here there was no necessity for revolutionary government and the seizure of sovereignty because the Assembly was in session and the Whig party controlled it. Imminent class and sectional conflict naturally drove the upper classes to conservatism, and the absence of open hostilities with Britain gave the Whig leaders a chance to act as mediators between the mother country and the other colonies. The risks of war for most Pennsylvania Whigs greatly outweighed any advantages which could accrue from it. Therefore, moderate sentiment among Pennsylvania leaders grew in the same proportion as radical sentiment in the royal colonies. Unwilling and unable to face the challenge of independence, the original Whig party disintegrated with the downfall of the Assembly and the affairs of the state were taken over by democrats.

The absence of a tradition of separation of powers in the colonial government was also embarrassing. The function of checking majority will, exercised by governors and councils in the royal colonies, was accomplished in Pennsylvania by the proprietorship, discriminatory representation, and high suffrage qualifications. Since all three were thoroughly discredited and since Pennsylvania had no bicameral traditions, conservatives had little material with which to build a system of checks and balances. The political institutions of Pennsylvania were basically democratic; therefore—in contrast to the situation in the royal colonies—tradition worked to the benefit of those who sought to revive the equalitarianism of the Charter.

Under these circumstances it can be seen that the coming of democracy to Pennsylvania was rather the result of circumstances than of political planning. Democratic protest here in the years before the war was less violent than in North Carolina, and during the framing of the Constitution less articulate than under similar circumstances in Massachusetts. There was apparently no understanding of democratic theory to match that exhibited by some of the Massachusetts towns. But the important fact is that here was created the first political party devoted to equalitarian democracy which was able to take over the administration of government.

FIFTEEN

Thomas Jefferson and Revolutionary Democracy

NO DESCRIPTION of democracy in the Revolution would be complete without an examination of Jefferson's drafts of a constitution for Virginia in 1776 and his subsequent reform bills. Jefferson has displayed himself for posterity in voluminous literary remains as a friend of the common man and the champion of democratic principles in government. He is revered as the founder of the Democratic party and the philosopher whose ideals of freedom have played a tremendously important part in the shaping of the American tradition. Splendid personal qualities, such as humanitarianism, lack of prejudice, candor, generosity, and versatility, have accorded him a host of admirers down through the years. It is no exaggeration to say that today no other figure in American history—with the possible exception of Lincoln—enjoys such affectionate regard.

On the basis of personal writings Jefferson would certainly qualify as a democrat by eighteenth-century standards. He repeatedly testified to the conviction that all men should be equal in political rights and that the ideal republic was a representative government in which the will of the majority of citizens constituted the ultimate authority for legislative decision.[1] Yet it is just as apparent that Jefferson was a different type of person than the equalitarian democrats with whom this book has been concerned, and a closer study of his career reveals many points of affinity with the conservative Whigs of his day which set him apart from the democrats of the Revolutionary period.

Thomas Jefferson was by tastes, education, and inheritance an aristocrat, far removed from the yeoman farmers, so often nameless, who demanded reform of the state governments. Even though he could write to DuPont de Nemours that he loved the people "as adults whom I freely leave to self government," he tacitly regarded them as an objective entity apart from himself, as did other Revolutionary leaders. Although an informal manner led some of his more rigidly class-conscious colleagues to consider him something of a leveller, he never quarrelled with the social distinctions maintained in the eighteenth-century American republic. Democracy to him was more an enlightened philosophy than a program of action against a political system characterized by privilege, as was the case with the lower-class Revolutionary democrats. Nowhere in Jefferson's writings do we find the sense of injury and urgency and the dominant note of protest which characterized the emanations from the democrats with whom this book is concerned. He usually held himself aloof from the bitter political contro-

1. It would be impossible and unnecessary within the following chapter to do justice to Jefferson's conception of democracy as illustrated in his personal writings. Among the many special treatments of the subject, the following may be cited for particular attention: Carl Becker, "What Is Still Living in the Philosophy of Thomas Jefferson?" *American Historical Review*, XLVIII (1942-1943), 691-707; Charles M. Wiltse, *The Jeffersonian Tradition in American Democracy* (Chapel Hill, 1935), particularly ch. X; Adrienne Koch, *The Philosophy of Thomas Jefferson* (New York, 1943); Richard Hofstadter, *The American Political Tradition and the Men Who Made It* (New York, 1948), ch. II.

versies of the day, seldom levelling charges at enemies and
never indulging in billingsgate. He preferred to leave this
phase of political operations to others while pursuing his
objectives by quiet and effective back-stage maneuvering and
persuasion.

Perhaps the most striking difference between Jefferson and
the Revolutionary democrats lay in his acceptance of the
basic political relationships established by eighteenth-century American constitutions and in the strain of conservative
thinking which appears in his constitutional and legislative
proposals. Jefferson never evinced much interest in altering
the institutions of Whig government in such a way as to
realize equalitarian and majoritarian ideals. Instead he appeared to accept without serious reservation a political science
which in many respects made impossible the realization of
his political philosophy. To some degree this may be explained as the unavoidable concession of a practical politician
compelled to work in a milieu completely dominated by a
ruling class drawn from the upper strata of society, but when
he actually went out of his way on occasion to endorse institutional arrangements specially designed to qualify political equality and erect barriers against majority will, then
his attitude shows undoubted inconsistencies which are difficult to explain. The fact that in 1788 he described the Federal Constitution—then far from a democratic instrument—
as "a good canvas, on which some strokes only want re-
touching" [2] is difficult to reconcile with his statement that
the ideal republic was one in which the majority ruled. *The
Federalist* papers were certainly not designed to propagate
democratic notions, yet Jefferson referred to them as "the
best commentary on the principles of government which

2. Paul L. Ford (ed.), *The Works of Thomas Jefferson*, 12 Vols. (New
York, 1904-1905), V, 426. Referred to as "Federal Edition."

ever was written." [3] Even John Adams' slashing attacks on democracy in his *Defense of the Constitutions of the United States* evoked no protest from Jefferson. He felt that the book "was formed to do a great deal of good." [4] It is difficult to escape the conclusion that Jefferson frequently drew a sharp line between speculative and practical thought, between ideal solutions for human problems and solutions which could be reached with the means at hand.

In addition to his acceptance of conventional political science, there was a strain of traditionalism in Jefferson's thinking—particularly during his early years—which set him apart from lower-class democrats. He fully shared the Whig conviction that the purpose of opposing British imperial legislation was to rescue traditional British rights from the attacks undertaken by an omnipotent, and therefore revolutionary Parliament. Study of history and philosophy had given him a sense of the growth and continuity of institutions and an admiration for many of those which had developed in the motherland over the centuries. Therefore, unlike the more unsophisticated democrats of the day, he attached great value to precedent and did not expect that freedom could be secured or maintained without utilizing accumulated experience. In his early plans for the American future Jefferson was looking backward to the English past for guidance; only later, after contacts with contemporary French thinkers, did his horizons widen to include more cosmopolitan sources of inspiration.

Reliance on the English tradition first appears in one of his earliest writings, the *Summary View of the Rights of British America* (1774). The object here was to find an ethical and legal basis for the autonomy which the Whigs desired after 1773. Efforts by Dickinson and Dulany to effect

3. *Ibid.,* 434.
4. *Ibid.,* 349.

a compromise between Parliamentary supremacy and independence by a distribution of the taxing power between the local and central legislatures had failed to arouse much interest in Britain. With the passage of the Boston Port Bill and the Massachusetts Government Acts, Whig leaders felt that their only safety lay in securing sovereign legislative powers for the colonial assemblies. But it was considerably more difficult to justify the claim of autonomy than to assert it. The Whigs were sincerely anxious to avoid secession from the empire. Hence some way had to be found to reconcile colonial self-government and the British constitution.

This was the problem to which Jefferson addressed himself.[5] His solution was to demonstrate historically and legally that the "true" British constitution rested on a compact between the colonists, acting through their legislatures, and the king. He asserted that the first settlers, like the ancient Saxons who left Germany for Britain in the sixth century, had expatriated themselves when they left the homeland, bringing with them their own laws, customs, and rights. Once established in America—entirely at their own expense—amity and consanguinity induced them to re-establish relations with England by voluntarily acknowledging the sovereignty of their former king. Parliament was not included in this reunion for the colonists owed allegiance only to the king, and only to the extent of the implied compact freely entered into after settlement.[6]

Jefferson's theory of the process of colonization and the relationship between the colonies and the mother country is certainly ingenious, but it is, of course, quite unhistorical.

5. James Wilson took up the same problem independently of Jefferson and arrived at much the same conclusions. See his "Considerations on the Nature and Extent of Legislative Authority of the British Parliament," in Randolph G. Adams (ed.), *Selected Political Essays of James Wilson* (New York, 1930), 43-83.

6. Ford (ed.), *Works of Jefferson* (Federal Edition), II, 64-68.

Yet it would be unfair to condemn him for his lack of critical and impartial analysis. Like most of his contemporaries, he used history as a means of demonstrating the truth of certain generally accepted philosophical propositions. As Bolingbroke expressed it, history was philosophy teaching by example. Therefore, if the Whig conception of the constitution was "true" (and who in their party could doubt it?) the facts of settlement must demonstrate this truth. Jefferson's philosophy was therefore the determinant of his historical analysis. The distortion of the *Summary View* illustrates the intellectual processes of the age.

But the importance of the *Summary View,* for our purposes, lies not in its illustration of Jefferson the historian, but in its description and analysis of the traditional rights of British subjects. The most important of these, which Jefferson resurrected from the dim past of Saxon England, were the rights to establish legislative bodies, to hold lands in allodial ownership, and to be free from the arbitrary exercise of the royal prerogative. These rights were part of the true heritage of Englishmen which had been obscured from view by the dark cloud of feudalism which had settled over England after the Norman conquest. The object of Americans should be to purge the dross of this unenlightened age and return to the pristine purity of original English institutions.[7]

This was the spirit in which Jefferson approached the problem of a constitution for Virginia in the spring of 1776. In the *Summary View* he had isolated a few of the essential British rights denied by the Crown and Parliament. In his draft constitutions he hoped to merge these rights with the principles subsequently enunciated in the Declaration of Independence and make the whole the foundation for a

7. *Summary View,* in *ibid.,* 78-88. Jefferson's traditionalism has been pointed out in Gilbert Chinard, *Thomas Jefferson, the Apostle of Americanism* (2nd ed.: Boston, 1946), ch. II.

republican government. For most Whigs, the drafting of
constitutions was an unpleasant necessity; for Jefferson it
was a glorious opportunity. Therefore, when the Virginia
Convention instructed its delegates in the Continental Congress to propose independence and then appointed a committee to draft a plan of government, Jefferson suggested
that he be recalled from congressional service in order to
participate in the adventure. "In truth," he wrote to Thomas
Nelson, "the drafting of a constitution is the whole object
of the present controversy; for should a bad government be
instituted for us in future it had been as well to have accepted
at first the bad one offered to us.[8]

The Convention did not accede to Jefferson's wish, possibly because he was considered more valuable in Philadelphia, but more probably because there was already enough
talent at work on constitutional projects. George Mason was
drawing up a draft, and Adams' *Thoughts on Government*
had elicited wide approval. Undaunted by the failure to consult him, Jefferson composed three drafts in the weeks that
followed, and George Wythe, also a delegate to Congress,
took them to Williamsburg when he returned in June. Their
influence was small, however, for the Convention, after long
and acrimonious debate, had progressed so far towards the
attainment of an acceptable instrument that the members
did not want to reopen discussion on points already decided.
They did agree, however, to attach to the Constitution Jefferson's preamble of grievances against the king.

In the provisions regarding the organs and powers of government, Jefferson's drafts bear considerable resemblance to
Adams' *Thoughts on Government*. Executive, legislative,
and judicial departments were carefully separated; the legislature was to be bicameral, with the lower house electing

8. Julian P. Boyd (ed.), *The Papers of Thomas Jefferson* (Princeton,
1950), I, 292. See also Mr. Boyd's editorial note, 329-337.

the upper for an extended term.[9] In the first draft suffrage
was given to all taxpayers, and in later drafts the privilege
was extended to freeholders not resident of the counties,
thus giving extra votes to landholders with tracts in more
than one county. By further provision to give fifty acres of
land to every able-bodied man who desired it, Jefferson went
far toward securing manhood suffrage for the lower house.
The governor—styled administrator—and his council would
be appointed by the lower house. There were no property
qualifications for office, and representation was to be proportionate to population. The constitution might be amended
by vote of the inhabitants in two-thirds of the counties. Cast
in the form of a legislative bill, it would be put in force by
the Convention then sitting.[10]

Jefferson's drafts differ from the Constitution subsequently
adopted for Virginia mainly in the manner of electing the
senate, the extent of the suffrage, the basis for representation,
the lack of property qualifications for office, and the provision for amendment. By the Virginia instrument senators
were to be elected directly by the voters; the suffrage was
restricted to free, white males who owned real property, as
in the colonial period; each county was allotted two delegates regardless of population, all officials of the government
were required to own real property, and there was no process
stipulated for amendment.[11]

The Virginia Constitution, although obviously not demo-

9. By the first draft senators would be elected for life, but this term
was lowered to nine years in the second and third drafts. Jefferson favored
long terms of years without possibility of re-election, "Yet I could submit,
though not so willingly, to an appointment for life." Boyd (ed.), *Jefferson Papers*, I, 341, 348-349, 359, 504.

10. Jefferson's drafts are printed in *ibid.*, 337-365.

11. The Mason Plan, the Mason Plan Revised, the committee report,
and the text of the Constitution as finally adopted are printed in *ibid.*,
366-386.

cratic, nevertheless approached democracy more closely than
some contemporary instruments insofar as it made both
houses of the legislature directly responsible to the qualified
voters. Yet it was this very provision which provoked the
most criticism from Jefferson. "I have ever observed," he
wrote to Edmund Pendleton, "that a choice by the people
themselves is not generally distinguished for its wisdom. The
first secretion from them is usually crude and heterogeneous.
But give to those so chosen by the people a second choice
themselves, and they will generally chuse wise men. For
this reason it was that I proposed the representatives (and
not the people) should chuse the senate, and thought I had
notwithstanding that made the senators (when chosen) perfectly independent of the electors." [12] Here Jefferson showed
an affinity for Whig rather than democratic constitutional
theory. Democrats everywhere strenuously opposed the election of the upper house by the lower, first, because a body
so chosen would not be responsible to the electorate, and
second, because the people's delegates should have no power
to redelegate their authority. But, like Adams, Jefferson
hoped to make the upper house a check on the people and
their representatives. His "independent" senate, by definition, was to be nonrepresentative, a body of men divorced
from the electorate and thus able to veto popular legislation
with impunity if they thought it advisable. Jefferson wanted
no senators who would "curry favor with" the voters, as he
once phrased it. His proposal to lower the suffrage qualifications in elections for the House of Delegates and reappor-
tion representation in accordance with population would
indeed have made that body more representative of the
people, but as long as its bills were subject to the veto of an
independent upper house, the people could never be sure
that their will would be translated into law.

12. *Ibid.*, 503.

In 1776 Jefferson thought that the purpose of the upper house should be to give more thorough deliberation to legislation than was possible in the lower house and revise it, if necessary, in accordance with higher standards of wisdom and justice. But by 1782 he apparently veered around to the more usual Whig view that the senate should be the representative of property as opposed to persons. "The purpose of establishing different houses of legislation," he wrote in the *Notes on Virginia,* "is to introduce the influence of different interests or different principles. In some of the American states the delegates and senators are so chosen, that the first represent the persons, the second the property of the state. But with us, wealth and wisdom have equal chance for admission into both houses. We do not, therefore, derive from the separation of our legislature into two houses, those benefits which a proper complication of principles is capable of producing. . . ." [13]

By the close of the Revolution, many of the state politicians came to look upon the upper house as the guardian of accumulated wealth against the encroachments of the propertyless. Hence the maintenance of its independence became even more vital. Such thorough conservatives as Theophilus Parsons, of Massachusetts, were quite willing to allow a broad suffrage and proportionate representation for the lower house as long as the upper was secure from popular control. Indeed, two state constitutions gave the vote to taxpayers and apportioned representation in accordance with population. [14] Constitutional plans formulated after 1778 showed a tendency to divide society into two components—property and persons—and give each a veto on the other in the legislature. It is important to note that Jefferson appeared to accept this Whig dualism rather than the democratic

13. Ford (ed.), *Works of Jefferson* (Federal Edition), IV, 19.
14. New Hampshire and New York.

principle that only persons were entitled to representation in governing bodies.

Jefferson was more in accord with democratic theory, however, in his omission of property qualifications for office, in the provision for amendment, and the advocacy of popular conventions to frame fundamental law. Although his draft constitutions are cast in the form of a bill, Edmund Randolph asserted that Jefferson questioned the competence of the Virginia legislative convention to write a constitution.[15] We have no evidence from Jefferson himself in 1776 to support this assertion—possibly because he considered the Constitution temporary—but in *Notes on Virginia* he pointed out that the instrument was defective because of the method of its adoption.[16] In recognition of the need for amending procedures, later emphasized by his conviction that constitutions should bind only the generations that made them,[17] Jefferson stood squarely on the side of democrats. It will be recalled that Adams made no provision for amendment in any of his constitutional plans.

As previously indicated, the most strikingly original sections of Jefferson's drafts are those delineating the rights of citizens. At his hands the ancient and honorable rights of Englishmen now became basic rights for an American republic. The essential reason for a constitution, he explained in his third draft, was "to re-establish such ancient principles as are friendly to the rights of the people, and to declare certain others which may cooperate with and fortify the same in future." [18] The primary task was to strip the executive of the prerogative powers by which the English mon-

15. "Edmund Randolph's Essay on the Revolutionary History of Virginia, 1774-1782," *Virginia Magazine of History and Biography*, XLIV (1936), 43-44.

16. Ford (ed.), *Works of Jefferson* (Federal Edition), IV, 23-28.

17. *Ibid.*, XII, 12-13.

18. Boyd (ed.), *Jefferson Papers*, I, 357.

archs had been able to encroach on the rights of the people. The first state constitutions kept governors weak by failing to make grants of power; Jefferson, fearful of strong executives at this period of his life, accomplished the same objective by specifically depriving his "administrator" of the elements of prerogative exercised by royal governors. Saxon heritage would be realized by expanding fee simple tenure into allodial ownership and by abolishing primogeniture. As "cooperative" rights, perhaps, he specified freedom of speech and religion and freedom to bear arms.[19]

The America of his dreams was in some respects a picture of what England should have been but never was. He felt that the basic British political and legal institutions, purged of monarchy and hereditary status, constituted an adequate foundation for free government. Through these the people could achieve ultimate supremacy in the exercise of the constituent power; on the legislative level checks and balances would guard against precipitant action on the part of either the people or their representatives which might constitute a danger to freedom. Like Locke, Jefferson felt that the proper function of a majority of the people was to guard human rights rather than to formulate political policy.

Frustrated in the desire to reform Virginia government by the failure of the Convention to consider his constitutional proposals, Jefferson attempted to gain the same ends through legislation. So important did this task appear to him that he refused an appointment as a congressional emissary to France in order to take a seat in the House of Delegates.[20] Between 1776 and 1780 he presented a series of bills,

19. *Ibid.,* 343-345, 362-364.
20. Jefferson's ostensible reason for refusing the appointment was the delicate health of his wife; however, in view of his subsequent career in the House it is probable that the opportunity to foster his reforms weighed more heavily with him. See *ibid.,* 483, 524.

the most important of which were designed to eradicate "every fiber ... of antient or future aristocracy" from Virginia.[21]

Jefferson's many and capable biographers have uniformly considered these bills to be landmarks along the path of democratic reform, and have accepted without much question Jefferson's belief that the bills accomplished their objective. Actually they were by no means radical or unprecedented for the times. They certainly did not break the control of the planter aristocracy over state politics nor to any significant degree make government more responsive to the will of the whole people. For the most part the measures were reforms which represented the spirit of the times and cut across party lines which formed on the issues of political equality and majority rule. Democrats in other states supported Jefferson's proposals, but so did all Whigs of liberal persuasions.

Before analyzing Jefferson's bills it is necessary to understand the meaning he attached to the word "aristocracy." Since he and his friends were obvious aristocrats within the commonly accepted meaning of the term, the word must have had some special connotation in his mind. Unfortunately, neither Jefferson nor his contemporaries ever defined it during the Revolutionary period, but judging from the way they applied it, "aristocrats" were Tories or Tory sympathizers from the upper strata of society who admired monarchy and hereditary status and wished to maintain an equivalent for them in the succession governments.[22] Small in

21. Ford (ed.), *Works of Jefferson* (Federal Edition), I, 77.
22. For an example of what were considered "aristocratic" ideas at the time, see the pamphlet by Carter Braxton, "Address to the Convention of Virginia," *American Archives,* 4th Ser., VI, 748-754. Braxton, a blueblood connected by marriage with the Carter family, was a Virginia delegate to the Continental Congress when he wrote the pamphlet in the spring of 1776. Richard Henry Lee sent a copy of it to Edmund Pendleton with

numbers and weak politically—in the South at least—"aristocrats" never enjoyed as much influence as Jefferson apparently imagined. Some, like John Randolph, Attorney General of Virginia, fled to England at the outbreak of the war; most took no part in the struggle; a few, like Carter Braxton of Virginia and Joseph Galloway of Pennsylvania, even participated in the Whig movement during the earlier phases of the struggle primarily to bring about a reconciliation.

A failure to appreciate the limitations of the term "aristocracy" therefore can result in distorting the purpose of Jefferson's bills. He certainly did not intend to act the part of a leveller; his object was to eradicate the political and economic influence of a small number of families whose Tory views were incompatible with a republican state and to prevent the rise of a new aristocracy with claims based on hereditary status.

Jefferson conceived the abolition of primogeniture and entail to be the best method of opening the attack on "aristocracy." By making land freely alienable he expected to annul economic privileges and make an opening for those whom he regarded as aristocrats of virtue and talent.[23] Historians, following Jefferson, have generally viewed primogeniture and entail as bastions of special privilege and have, therefore, considered the abolition of these privileges to be a signal victory for democracy. It has been assumed that since entails prevented the division of large estates they made land difficult to acquire and therefore promoted tenantry among the mass of the yeoman farmers. There can be little

---

the comment, "This contemptible little tract betrays the little knot or junto from which it proceeded." James C. Ballagh (ed.), *The Letters of Richard Henry Lee,* 2 Vols. (New York, 1911-1914), I, 190-191. Braxton later lost his seat in Congress, possibly because his authorship of the "Address" became known.

23. Ford (ed.), *Works of Jefferson* (Federal Edition), I, 58.

doubt that historically entails had led to this result in Britain and on the continent, but there is little evidence to show that in America the tying up of land in this manner in itself militated against the prospective small freeholder. Outside of New York, the great land speculators of the late colonial period acquired their grants in order to resell in smaller plots at a profit. The moderate quitrents imposed by the crown created a burdensome overhead on the large landholder; unless he disposed of his lands quickly he would face serious loss. If tenants had been easy to secure no doubt speculators would have been tempted to create a permanent income for themselves by entailing their grants and giving leases to farmers, but since newcomers to America usually found it easy to acquire fee simple holdings from the crown, there was little possibility of interesting them in a life of tenantry. The entail and lease system could only be maintained in areas where all available land was occupied; American conditions did more to prevent the perpetuation of feudal practices than did legislation.

If Jefferson's bill to abolish entail had offered any serious threat to the planter class, we might expect that the Whig aristocrats who controlled the House of Delegates would oppose it. But such was not the case. It passed with ease in October, 1776. Richard Bland, a blueblood with well-known conservative leanings, was a member of the committee which framed it.[24] Unfortunately we have no direct evidence to indicate why Virginia planters agreed so readily to the free alienability of land. Perhaps the considerations just cited carried some weight with them, but, judging from what

24. The legislative history of the bill may be followed in *Journal of the House of Delegates, 1776* (Richmond, 1828), 10, 18, 23, 36. Jefferson's draft, subsequent amendments, and excellent notes will be found in Boyd (ed.), *Jefferson Papers*, I, 560-562. See also the discussion by Dumas Malone, *Jefferson the Virginian* (Boston, 1948), 247-260, and by Nathan Schachner, *Thomas Jefferson*, 2 Vols. (New York, 1951), I, 146-148.

would be the results of free alienability in their case, it is not unreasonable to assume that they expected financial profit from such a policy. The removal of entails would liquidate frozen assets; indeed, it would amount almost to a cash gift from the legislature. Only bankrupts would have any reason to oppose Jefferson's bill, for entails protected realty and personalty against judgments. It is no wonder · that lawyers "were enclined to look on entail with disfavor," [25] for it probably limited the scope of their activities. There is probably considerable truth in the statement by Henry Lee, Jr., that free alienability "was of obvious necessity from the form of our institutions and the prevailing temper of the people, and had only to be proposed by any member in order to be adopted by a large majority,..." [26]

Jefferson's abolition of entail was by no means a radical or unprecedented measure. "Even in the tidewater, where entail was most prevalent, it was not a universal custom by any means, in fact not as prevalent as has been commonly supposed." [27] Colonial courts would sometimes set entails aside,[28] the fictitious action of common recovery was often used to circumvent them, and the dockings by the Virginia House of Burgesses were common. The Georgia Common Council in 1750 enlarged all entailed grants to absolute inheritance and made subsequent grants in fee simple. South Carolina aristocrats did away with entail by the constitution of 1778. By 1790 entails were prohibited or modified almost

---

25. Richard B. Morris, "Primogeniture and Entailed Estates in America," 27 *Columbia Law Review*, 34.

26. Quoted from Malone, *Jefferson*, I, 256. Mr. Malone discounts the judgment on the ground that Lee was a political enemy of Jefferson.

27. Clarence R. Keim, "The Influence of Primogeniture and Entail in the Development of Virginia," University of Chicago, *Abstracts of Theses, Humanistic Series*, V (1926-1927), 289-292.

28. Morris, "Primogeniture and Entailed Estates in America," 27 *Columbia Law Review*, 31.

everywhere by law or constitutional provision. All the evidence suggests that free alienability of land was a policy on which most Americans, regardless of political orientation, could agree. In promoting his bill Jefferson was representing the liberal thought of the times.

Jefferson considered that the measure abolishing primogeniture, incorporated in the Revision of the Laws which he helped draft, struck another telling blow at aristocracy. This is very doubtful, however, for his measure applied only in cases where a devisor died intestate. Since very few wealthy men failed to leave wills, obviously the bill did little or nothing to change the processes of inheritance. The great planters both before and after Jefferson's time could leave all their property to the eldest son and thus keep large estates intact. Like the free alienability of land, partible inheritance was not new to America. It had been generally observed in New England and Pennsylvania since the seventeenth century.[29]

The remaining parts of Jefferson's legislative program likewise did not greatly affect the social system of Virginia. For the historian they are important primarily as illustrations of prevailing liberal thought; for the biographer they reveal a curious juxtaposition or traditionalism and individualism inherent in Jefferson at this time.

This characteristic of his appears plainly in the Bill for Proportioning Crimes and Punishments. Influenced to some degree by Beccaria, he proposed to limit the death penalty and abolish cruel and unusual punishments, particularly those involving the barbarous *lex talionis*. In common with the enlightened men of his generation he believed that the

---

29. George L. Hoskins, "The Beginnings of Partible Inheritance in America," 51 *Yale Law Journal*, 1281. Jefferson's bill is printed in Boyd (ed.), *Jefferson Papers*, II, 391-393. For an exhaustive and definitive account of his participation in the Revision, see editorial note, 305-324.

object of punishment should be to reform the criminal rather than inflict upon him the vengeance of society. Yet again his accomplishment scarcely does justice to the intention. In his bill the law of retaliation, sometimes in its most gruesome form, often becomes the basis for punishment. Thus, "Whosoever committeth murder by poison shall suffer death by poison"; a challenger who killed his opponent in a duel was to be gibbeted; "Whosoever shall be guilty of rape, polygamy, or sodomy, with man or woman, shall be punished, if a man, by castration; if a woman, by boring through the cartilege of her nose a hole of one-half inch in diameter at the least." Anyone guilty of disfiguring another was to be disfigured in like manner "or if that cannot be, for want of the same part, then as nearly as may be in some other part of at least equal value and estimation." [30] This was indeed a refinement worthy of a medieval legist.

The footnotes to the bill would delight the legal historian. Long and involved, they cite authorities as far back as Saxon chroniclers. The fact that Jefferson was so solicitous of tradition, even when it led to such unpalatable results, indicates again his desire to maintain the English heritage. Indeed, he opposed the proposal by Pendleton, the alleged traditionalist, to "abolish the whole existing system of laws and prepare a new and complete institute." Jefferson conceived the entire Revision as an adaptation of British precedent to American conditions. Although he disapproved of the *lex talionis* at the time of writing the bill and hoped it would be stricken out at some later date, the fact that he included it at all is mute evidence of an ingrained conservatism which contrasts strongly with the liberalism of his personal papers.

30. Bill printed in Boyd (ed.), *Jefferson Papers*, II, 492-504. See also editorial note, 504-507, and Jefferson's letter of transmittal to Wythe, 292-301. Jefferson's doubts and hesitations regarding the *lex talionis* are discussed in Schachner, *Jefferson*, I, 151.

In old age he professed surprise that he could ever have accepted such a "revolting principle" as retaliation. His perplexity was no more than a recognition of the gulf one so often finds in the eighteenth century between enlightened thought and unenlightened practice, between liberal social philosophy and traditional social institutions.

But if Jefferson the traditionalist wrote the sections of the bill incorporating the law of retaliation, Jefferson the individualist was responsible for the following: "And where persons, meaning to commit a trespass only, or larceny,... and doing an act from which involuntary homicide hath ensued, have heretofore been adjudged guilty of manslaughter, or of murder, by transferring such their unlawful intention to an act, much more penal than they could probably have in contemplation; no case shall hereafter be deemed manslaughter, unless manslaughter was intended, nor murder, unless murder was intended." Jefferson was here attacking the doctrine of constructive intent by interpreting intent as motive. Legal reformers since his time have often repeated his proposal, but it has never been adopted. Everywhere in America today homicide is adjudged intentional if it is perpetrated during the commission of a felony, and motive has no legal relevance.[31]

Jefferson's proposed Bill Concerning Slaves, in the Revision of the Laws, was a practical and Spartan attempt to solve the race problem in Virginia. He shared the dislike for slavery common in the upper South during the eighteenth century.[32] The growing conviction that it was an inefficient

31. "Motive is not intent, motive is not an essential element of crime. A bad motive will not make an act a crime nor will a good motive prevent an act from being a crime." Justin Miller, *Handbook of Criminal Law* (St. Paul, 1934), 54.

32. For a sampling of opinion on this matter, see: Moses C. Tyler, *Patrick Henry* (Boston and New York, 1899), 388-389; Kate M. Rowland, *The Life of George Mason, 1725-1792,* 2 Vols. (New York, 1892), I, 127;

labor system which would hamper the rise of industries and the realization of its inconsistency with the natural rights philosophy fostered a desire for its abolition. Virginians were greatly angered when, just before the Revolution, the Board of Trade disallowed a law prohibiting the further importation of slaves, and Jefferson listed this action in his first draft of the Declaration of Independence as a major grievance against the King. When Governor Dunmore in 1776 called on slaves to rebel against their Whig masters, the fear of servile insurrection provided an even greater incentive to solve the Negro problem than had economic or humanitarian factors heretofore. Jefferson's proposals reveal little of his humanitarianism and in many ways anticipate the notorious "black codes" of the ante bellum South. Although personally he desired that the children of slaves be freed upon reaching maturity, the bill gave freedom only to slaves who should hereafter be imported into the state. Moreover, the boon was accompanied by a condition. Unless the freedmen left the state within a year they could be impressed back into servitude. Slaves could not move from place to place without passes, could not keep arms, and could be punished without trial for various misdemeanors by whipping.[33]

Jefferson's solution of the race problem was the deportation and resettlement of Negroes. Although kindly disposed toward his black brethren, he considered them generally inferior to whites and was as unable as others of his genera-

---

Moncure D. Conway, *Omitted Chapters of History Disclosed in the Life and Papers of Edmund Randolph* (New York, 1888), 49; Howard R. Marraro (ed. and tr.), *Memoirs of the Florentine, Philip Mazzei* (New York, 1942), 221. Practical Landon Carter did not share the enthusiasm of some of his friends for abolition. "Much is said of slavery of negroes," he wrote in his diary, "but how will servants be provided in these times?" "Diary of Landon Carter," *William and Mary Quarterly,* XX (1912), 182.

33. Boyd (ed.), *Jefferson Papers,* II, 470-473.

tion to envisage the two races living side by side on a basis of equality. "Nothing is more certainly written in the book of fate than that these people are to be free," he wrote in his autobiography, "nor is it less certain that the two races, equally free, cannot live in the same government. Nature, habit, opinion, has drawn indellible lines of distinction between them." [34]

Jefferson's Bill for the more General Diffusion of Knowledge, a very advanced piece of social legislation for the time, exhibits his liberalism in a more favorable light. The measure would establish elementary schools to give three years' education to all white children at public expense and grammar schools which would charge tuition. By means of competitive scholarships for these grammar schools "twenty of the best geniuses will be raked from the rubbish annually" for further education, and ten of these would be sent by the state to the College of William and Mary after graduation.[35]

In Jefferson's mind the educational purpose of these scholarships was primarily vocational. He hoped to train over a period of time "best geniuses" for public service; he wanted to recruit an aristocracy of virtue and talent which would eventually replace the aristocracy of wealth.[36] As for those not so fortunate as to be born into the genius class, their education would be sufficient if they could "recognize ambition under all its shapes" and thus avoid the traps set for them by demagogues. "It suffices us," he wrote in 1813, "if the moral and physical condition of our own citizens qualifies

34. Ford (ed.), *Works of Jefferson* (Federal Edition), I, 77.
35. Bill with editorial note in Boyd (ed.), *Jefferson Papers*, II, 526-535. See also Jefferson's description of it in *Notes on Virginia*, Ford (ed.), *Works of Jefferson* (Federal Edition), IV, 60-65.
36. "By that part of our plan which prescribes the selection of youths of genius from among the classes of the poor, we hope to avail the state of those talents which nature has shown as liberally among poor as rich...." Ford (ed.), *Writings of Jefferson* (Federal Edition), IV, 64.

them to select the able and good for the direction of their government...." [37] There is little evidence that Jefferson thought that the mass of the people could ever become capable of administering their own affairs.

The provision for competitive scholarships illustrates Jefferson's primary philosophic trait—individualism. He felt that the state should allow all men the opportunity to achieve their diverse objectives in life. The social and economic hierarchies of eighteenth-century America should be opened to all who had the talents to qualify for admission. Status was only wrong when it suppressed the fit and exalted the unfit. Jefferson did not mean to do away with aristocracy in the broad sense; he only wanted to recruit its ranks from below and base its status on talent and service rather than heredity. His present quarrel was with those whom he regarded, in his own limited definition, as aristocrats, and not with the institution itself.

Jefferson was, of course, not alone in his desire for a system of public education. The constitutions of Georgia, North Carolina, Pennsylvania, Massachusetts, and New Hampshire either endorsed the principle or actually established some kind of limited school system. The idea of public education was almost 150 years old. In 1647 the Massachusetts Bay Colony had led the way by requiring the towns to establish schools.

Jefferson's Bill for Establishing Religious Freedom was always his particular pride, and for good reason. Compulsive conformity in religious matters he always regarded as the worst kind of intellectual tyranny. A bill to abolish it once and for all would be a great social service and would provide an opportunity to give practical application to his individualist creed. Three-fourths of the bill is devoted to an explana-

37. *Ibid.,* XI, 349.

tion of the philosophical and ethical reasons for the separation of church and state. The crux of the enactment itself was a provision that no one "shall be compelled to frequent or support any religious worship" and that "opinions in matters of religion ... shall in no wise diminish, enlarge, or affect ... civil capacities." [38] Actually the bill made no great change in the religious life of the state and certainly did not introduce freedom of worship, as the title suggests. The Bill of Rights attached to the Constitution contained a categorical statement on religious freedom attributed to Madison, and the Virginia legislature, under Jefferson's leadership, had suspended the subsidies to the Anglican clergy in December, 1776. Thus in fact if not by express enactment the Anglican church was disestablished before Jefferson introduced his bill.

Jefferson's measure might therefore seem unnecessary were it not for the fact that some supporters of the Anglican church and even some dissenters wished to impose taxation for the support of all churches. This "General Assessment" scheme, which bears some resemblance to the religious settlement of Massachusetts and Connecticut, provoked considerable controversy in the Virginia House. It was to settle the issue that Jefferson introduced his bill, but so strong was the opposition to his measure that it was not adopted until 1786.[39] Jefferson apparently wished that the bill might be considered a part of fundamental law, but since the Constitution itself was only a legislative statute and since it did not provide for amendment, the only way he could give special status to his measure was by labelling its provisions natural rights. To obviate the possibility of repeal, therefore, the bill declared that if "any act shall hereafter be passed to

38. The bill is printed in Boyd (ed.), *Jefferson Papers*, II, 545-547.
39. For a summary of the facts of the religious controversy and the legislative history of the bill, see *ibid.*, I, 525-530; II, 547-553.

repeal the present or narrow its operation, such act will be an infringement of natural right."

If Jefferson did not single-handed bring religious freedom to Virginia, he was certainly instrumental in inducing the legislature to endorse the principle of the separation of church and state. Nearly all the first constitutions or bills of rights made declarations in favor of religious freedom, and the Anglican church was disestablished everywhere during the Revolutionary period by law or constitutional provision. But religious freedom, to most Whigs, meant only freedom of worship and the equality of the Protestant sects; it did not mean the separation of church and state or the abolition of religious tests for office which discriminated against non-Christians and sometimes Catholics. As we have seen in Massachusetts, the support of religion was often identified with the maintenance of public morality. Of course Jefferson did not deny the moralist value of religion. As a sincere Deist he held the precepts of the Great Teacher in high esteem. But from his study of the Stoics he became convinced that morality flowed from the love of virtue as much as from the love of God. Combined with this conviction was his inordinate suspicion of institutionalized religion, so common among eighteenth-century liberals. Hence to his mind state support of religion was not only needless, but very dangerous, for it would give an opportunity for clerics to use the coercive power of the state in their perpetual campaign to enforce conformity. He believed that the freedom of the individual to follow his conscience would never be safe until churches were completely separated from the secular arm. The purpose of his Bill for Establishing Religious Freedom, therefore—like many of his other proposals—was not primarily to give new rights but to gain acceptance of a principle by which those in existence might be protected.

In view of Jefferson's projects and achievements during

the Revolutionary period, what place does he occupy in the democratic movement described in this book? How democratic is "Jeffersonian democracy"? There can be no doubt that in his literary remains Jefferson repeatedly endorsed political equality and majority rule, but conclusions about him based solely on what he said about himself can be somewhat misleading. The trouble is that he wrote with varying degrees of seriousness, sometimes indulged in hyperbole, and often, as a true philosopher, explored ideas without commitment in order to satisfy his curiosity as to their ultimate implications and results. But an evaluation—at least for the early period of his life—can be made with more accuracy when his constitutional and legislative plans are given equal consideration.

From this brief survey of Jefferson's activities in the field of reform during the Revolutionary period it would appear that on the whole he leaned more toward eighteenth-century Whiggism than toward eighteenth-century democracy. In common with democrats he held no palpable fear of the people and was optimistic for the future of free government. In criticising the constitutions established by legislative enactment and in advocating easy amendment processes he joined with democrats in attempting to institutionalize the constituent power in the people. His disregard of property qualifications (he never specifically attacked them, however, until well into the nineteenth century) and his provision for proportionate representation in his constitutional drafts amounted to an endorsement of political equality. Yet, even after these factors have been taken into consideration, his personal tastes and manner of living, his failure to make political issues of his more radical proposals, his traditionalism and his acceptance of the Whig political science all combined to set him apart from the yeoman farmers who strove for democratic government in the Revolutionary period. Although in his constitutions of 1776 he would give the people political equality, they could exercise their equal rights only under the paternalism of an "independent," non-representative legislative house whose members held their positions for long terms of years. In the *Notes on Virginia* Jefferson voiced the fear that rule by the people's representatives alone would become "an elective despotism" as oppressive as the tyranny of a dictator.[40]

The celebrated Virginia reforms, while ostensibly undertaken as a means of diminishing the privileges of aristocracy, broadening economic and political opportunity, reforming the criminal law, and safeguarding the rights of conscience either failed to achieve the decisive results Jefferson later claimed for them or lack the particular importance he attached to them. The abolition of entail placed no obstacle to the accumulation of wealth on the part of the great planters nor diminished their political power. The Bill Concerning Slaves, as it stood, offered freedom under harsh terms and appeared to be motivated more by a desire to rid Virginia of the blacks than to rid the blacks of their chains. The Bill for Proportioning Crimes and Punishments was in some respects a legal retrogression. The Bill for Establishing Religious Freedom by contrast was indeed a vital measure in the main stream of democratic reform, but its importance lies in separating church and state rather than in guarding the rights of conscience. Paradoxically, however, the measure actually ran counter to the desires of most yeoman farmers who desired majoritarian and equalitarian constitutions during the Revolution because it would have prevented the imposition of religious tests for office.

In the last analysis, Jefferson's ideal government was aristocracy in the sense of government by the best—the best

40. Ford (ed.), *Works of Jefferson* (Federal Edition), IV, 20. See also Hofstadter, *American Political Tradition*, 28-31.

morally, spiritually, and intellectually. He felt those in authority should be checked by the people, it is true, but only because all humans needed checks. Lord Acton's famous phrase, "All power corrupts and absolute power corrupts absolutely" might well have come from Jefferson's lips. To keep the natural aristocracy pure and capable he thought that it must be continually revitalized by new recruits from the mass of the people, geniuses "raked from the rubbish" of the untalented.

The rule of virtue meant rule by the virtuous, and these would always be in a minority. Jefferson's optimism for the future of society rested as much on a faith in those who had the capacity to rise above the people as on the people themselves. It was the duty of government to keep the channels of advancement clear. Every opportunity must be allowed for the individual to develop himself according to his own particular capacities. Jefferson's individualism was inherently rugged.

His philosophy, therefore, was liberal rather than democratic. Although liberalism has wider connotations today, in the eighteenth century it could be defined as acknowledgment and respect for reasonable diversities in human affairs, and could be found in different political systems. If a democratic state protected and maintained these diversities, it could be called liberal; if it allowed majority will to enforce conformity it would be obviously authoritarian, but at the same time, no less democratic. In the eighteenth century, democracy designated who should exercise political power and liberalism prescribed the manner of its exercise.

As previously indicated, the Whigs believed that the primary purpose of government was to maintain the natural rights without which free society could not exist. The liberals among them, like Jefferson, felt that this would not be a difficult task, for mankind was naturally good and disposed to be cooperative. Therefore government could afford to be lenient and restrict the sphere of its operations as much as possible. Conservatives like Adams who took a dimmer view of mankind felt that stricter controls were necessary. In order to protect society against the centrifugal forces set loose by the inherent selfishness in human nature, they asserted that government must adhere rigidly to the principle of separation of powers. Both liberals and conservatives were agreed, however, that rights must be guarded against any manifestation of will, whether majority or minority. It was here that conservatives came into direct conflict with democrats, who believed that the only purpose of government was to implement majority will. Democrats did not deprecate the importance of rights; the possibility of a conflict between these and majority will never occurred to them. Their faith in mankind was so complete that it never needed explicit formulation. This naiveté made much of their political planning ineffective and visionary.

Revolutionary liberalism as opposed to Revolutionary democracy was conservative on two counts: first, because it elevated rights above will, and second, because these rights were largely traditional. Liberals like Jefferson of course believed that there were some natural rights not yet translated into the statutes and political usages of England and the colonies, but for the most part the freedom they wished could be obtained without an appeal to philosophy. They preferred to rest their case against Britain on the solid ground of the rights of Englishmen, which embodied the most important of natural rights. This explains in part why three-fourths of the Declaration of Independence is devoted to the enumeration of specific violations of English rights by the sovereign. The famous preamble, which we value so highly today, may have been in 1776 the least important part of the document. Its primary purpose was to inform the world that the rights of Englishmen had a universal quality which made them indispensable for freedom everywhere.

If "Jeffersonian democracy," considered both in theory and practice, contains more of the elements of liberalism than democracy, why is the term still common currency today? Possibly one reason is a propensity on the part of biographers to make Jefferson the standard for democracy rather than the reverse. But even more important is the fact that democracy today is primarily concerned with the same values which Jefferson so strikingly exemplified. In combatting fascism and communism we are fighting on a different field the same battles which he carried on against the authoritarianism of his own day. Similar enemies promote similar ideologies of defense; since we are upholding Jefferson's rights it is inevitable that his philosophy should provide tremendous inspiration.

This conception of democracy as value is of relatively recent origin. During the nineteenth century democracy was concerned primarily, but not exclusively, with the processes designed to implement majority will first demanded during the Revolution. But with the passage of the seventeenth amendment and the adoption in some states of such reforms as direct primaries, initiative, referendum, and recall, interest in majoritarian processes began to wane. The element of value in democracy, formerly minor, grew in importance as it was seen that the implementation of majority rule was not alone sufficient to suppress economic privilege and bring the measure of freedom expected from political reforms. "Social democracy" and "economic democracy" entered the political vocabulary. The onslaught of the new authoritarianism exemplified by fascism and communism did even more to elevate value over process in current conceptions of democracy. Today, primarily concerned with the protection of human rights, democracy bears the coloration of eighteenth-century liberalism, the essence of which was the acknowl-edgment and protection of reasonable diversities. Hence, paradoxically, Jefferson, as the greatest eighteenth-century exponent of liberalism, becomes more democratic by con-temporary standards than by eighteenth-century standards. The problem of "Jeffersonian democracy" is therefore pri-marily one of definition. When democracy is construed as political processes establishing political equality and majority rule, Jefferson cannot be considered a democrat to the same extent as the dissident groups in the Revolutionary era. But when democracy is considered to be a symbol of the values of human freedom about which world controversy rages today, then Jefferson emerges as a democratic philosopher and statesman of primary importance.

SIXTEEN

Democracy and Liberalism in the Revolution

IN the preceding chapters we have followed the course of the first democratic movement in America from its beginnings in the sporadic protests against the aristocratic domination of provincial governments up to its emergence as a political force during the formation of the first state constitutions. But this survey has left at least one important question unanswered: Why did democracy make so little progress in the nation as a whole during the Revolution? As we have seen, the desire for democratic reform made a significant recorded appearance in Massachusetts, Pennsylvania and North Carolina. Although the scanty materials available on New Hampshire and Georgia suggest similar activity there, less than half of the new states were affected by movements to place the sovereign legislative power in the hands of the whole people. Why did the protest against political privilege, often heard in the years before the war, not lead to widespread social revolution when the confusion and dislocations attendant upon civil strife offered an opportunity for it to do so?

Unfortunately the materials available for this study do not make possible definitive answers which can be documented, yet certain conclusions emerge which point toward a solution of the problem. In the first place, the agitators for democratic reform usually lacked leadership. In colonial America it was relatively easy for ambitious and able yeoman farmers or artisans to acquire the property and education necessary for admission into the ranks of the gentlemen. Thus the natural leaders of the people rose to become lawyers, merchants, or planters. Witness the careers of Patrick Henry, Edmund Pendleton, Benjamin Franklin, and John Adams. In a more rigid and static society which placed serious obstacles in the path of personal advancement, men of this type would have been compelled to throw in their lot with the lower classes and would have exercised their talents—in Eugene Debs's phrase—to rise with the people instead of from them. In the second place, the wide dispersal of the population and poor communications so weakened the authority and scope of government that its impositions were not keenly felt. Also, the attraction of abundant, cheap land took the farmer's mind off politics. Whenever he felt himself oppressed by the privileged few, he found it easier and more profitable to move outside the range of their influence than to stand and give battle for his right to equal consideration. Certainly the tide of westward migration beginning about 1770 removed much of the pressure for democratic reform in the thirteen original states. Only where the population was more firmly settled, as in Pennsylvania or Massachusetts, or where the aristocracy was very weak, as in New Hampshire and Georgia, did democracy score notable advances.

In the third place, the agrarian interests of the vast majority of Americans minimized economic conflict between the rich and the poor. In an agrarian, as contrasted with an industrial economy, inequalities of wealth do not necessarily entail differences of economic interests. Most agrarians are debtors, regardless of their wealth, and all share the desire for low taxes, low tariffs, cheap money, and high prices for agricultural commodities. The history of the ante bellum South, for example, shows how agrarian ideas can provide cohesiveness, stability, and even contentment in a hierarchical society containing a wide gap between the rich and the poor. In eighteenth-century America, the harmony of economic interest between small farmers and the owners of large agrarian enterprises undoubtedly played a large part in reconciling the former to upper-class leadership in the new state governments. The yeoman farmer could be reasonably sure that his essential interests would be protected by the aristocrat. It is significant, in this connection, that the two states which experienced the most insistent demands for democratic reform—Massachusetts and Pennsylvania— contained powerful commercial groups which exercised considerable political influence.

Finally, and perhaps most important, the degree to which the ideals of the Revolution were achieved was sufficient to remove most of the incentive for social revolution. The Whig political science, although erecting barriers to majority will, nevertheless designed governments more responsive to the whole people than could be found anywhere else in the world. For the first time in modern history the political function was to be exercised primarily in the defense of freedom, limited though the definition of freedom might be by our standards. Bills of rights established a standard of liberty equally central to all classes and conditions, placed the stamp of illegitimacy on arbitrary rule, and set strict limits to the sphere of government. The constitutions themselves made it plain that even within this limited sphere government must be conducted according to law.

If the democratic movement failed in most instances to reach its objectives, it nevertheless defined the areas in which controversies on constitutional issues were to take place in the coming years and forced both conservatives and radicals to reflect on the problems of balancing liberty with order, stability with flexibility, administrative efficiency with responsiveness to the will of the people. During the struggles over the first state constitutions the instinctive conservatism of the Whig leaders and the instinctive radicalism of the politically unprivileged took substantive form. Conservatives became aware of the values, relationships, and processes which they wanted to preserve, and their radical opponents achieved a degree of consensus as to what they wanted changed and how much. We can see today that in translating attitudes toward change into philosophical ideas and institutional frameworks, both antagonists discovered vital truths about the nature of political freedom.

Perhaps the most valuable contribution of the conservatives was the principle that individuals have absolute rights against government entitling them to self-expression and the achievement of their diverse purposes. In this repudiation of authoritarianism in human relationships, the Whigs developed a liberal political philosophy which has become the hallmark of American ideology and has served as a cohesive force throughout the nation's history. During the Revolutionary period, however, the effectiveness of this philosophy was somewhat lessened by the inordinate institutional protection given to property and by the archaic and somewhat reactionary nature of Whig political science. The first of these factors probably arouses more hostility from present-day observers than it did from the mass of the people at the time. Rich and poor were agreed in the eighteenth century that the protection of property was a desirable objective. Wealth was more evenly distributed than it is now, and most of it was in the form of real estate and chattels rather than intangibles. Even the wealthiest businessmen personally supervised their establishments and the finance capitalist had not as yet appeared on the scene. Since there were very few "idle rich" in the new nation, the protection of property could be viewed as safeguarding the rewards of effort rather than as insuring the continuance of unearned increment. Insofar as the conservatives opposed the paper money experiments desired by the debtor class, their policies were entirely sound and laudable, regardless of whether their personal interests were involved. As we combat communism today, it is well to remember that the economic ideals we associate with free enterprise are very similar to the economic ideals of eighteenth-century conservatives. It is important to note, however, that the gulf between the ideals and prevailing practice is considerably wider today than it was in the eighteenth century.

Under the conditions of the eighteenth century, then, the elaborate constitutional guarantees designed to maintain the existing distribution of wealth did not work as much injustice as they would today. A more serious criticism of the Whig political science was its static and mechanistic nature which to some extent rendered it incompatible with dynamic, expanding American society. In their anxiety for the safety of rights, the Revolutionary leaders tended to resist all change which would bring the new state governments more into harmony with the fluid conditions of the times. Merging colonial traditions and precedents with leading concepts gleaned from political philosophers, they tried to construct political systems like the cosmic universe of Newton in which all the elements of society would revolve endlessly in unvarying orbits, each held to its path by universal forces of attraction and repulsion. The ideal political society for most Whigs was a solar system in microcosm in which infinite power was held in check by infinite law; this was the republic in equipoise, a copy of the divine plan as revealed by eighteenth-century science.

It was obvious to most Whigs, however, that their own planning would fall short of such an ideal. Inevitably the social universe would generate certain meteoric and cometic forces which, veering uncontrollably among obedient stars and planets, would threaten chaos by disrupting the rhythm of attraction and repulsion. Some Whigs thought a misguided people would be the greatest threat, others viewed "aristocrats" with more suspicion, all feared the demagogue whose magnetic personality could draw to himself the reservoir of latent revolutionary power lodged in the people. Upon reflection, many concluded that the danger to be expected from power lay not so much in its source as in its exclusive possession; therefore the task of political architects should be to make the exercise of power difficult, dangerous, and unprofitable. It apparently never occurred to most Revolutionary leaders that by making change hard to secure through legal and constitutional channels they might force it to take place by violence. Their theories might have made inevitable the very eventuality they sought so hard to avoid. It is significant that Massachusetts, which had a constitution closest to the Whig ideal, was the only state to experience armed insurrection during the Confederation period.

It was the gradual adoption of the type of reforms advocated by democrats which harmonized American constitutional government with American conditions. The development of amending procedures, the lowering and final abolition of property qualifications, the establishment of proportionate representation and upper houses responsible to electorates, made the state, and concurrently the national government, flexible enough to meet the needs of a rapidly expanding nation. Slowly the mechanistic ideal disappeared and the modern conception emerged that the primary purpose of government was to serve the people rather than control them. Succeeding generations of politicians recognized that systems must bow before the claims of the people expressed in legal processes. The contention of the democrats that the will of majorities expressed through elections provided better protection for human rights than automatic checks and balances was gradually acknowledged. The separation of powers was used as democrats hoped it would be— as a means of curbing officeholders and not as method of separating the people from sovereign power.

Time has demonstrated that rights held in trust by the few tend to degenerate into privileges exercised for the benefit of the few. Yet time has also dispelled the corollary notion of the Revolutionary democrats that majority will and public welfare are one and the same thing. In a world where human relationships are continually marred by greed and violence there can be no impregnable haven for human rights. We have all too often seen unworthy men elected to office and kept there by a majority of their constituents. The policies of Hitler were probably supported by most German citizens, and it is likely that the present rulers of Russia would be confirmed in their offices by free election if they chose to allow it. A lynching mob often contains most of the inhabitants of a small community. Faith that majorities will devote themselves to public welfare must rest, in the last analysis, upon the premise that the average man will govern his actions by reason and that he will bear regard for the interests of others as well as himself. Modern psychology has shown that reason is often submerged by nonrational motivations, and experience has demonstrated that men acting together in a mass often show less regard for moral principles than would each acting separately. Dictators in control of totalitarian states can over a period of time evoke any response they wish from their people merely by applying the proper stimulus. Political bosses in this country often make majority will their creature by the use of favor and fear. But though instances can be multiplied to show misuse of majority power and therefore demonstrate the falsity of the axiom that majority will and public welfare are identical, yet these instances do not represent the standard pattern of American political behavior. In most cases, in most places, under most circumstances, majorities have not prostituted human rights, and certainly we can say today that the democratic reforms of the last 150 years have not brought the chaos which our Revolutionary forefathers would confidently have expected from them.

The identification of majority will with public welfare prevented the democrats from fully realizing that freedom in political society is determined rather by the manner in which political power is exercised than by its location. The mere assumption of sovereign powers by a revolutionary body will only mean the exchange of one tyranny for another—regardless of slogans, programs, and political orientation of the revolutionists—unless certain ethical principles of conduct are acknowledged to be of paramount importance. We may criticise the attempt by conservatives in Massachusetts to retain a state church, but we would have to agree with their premise that free government cannot exist without the acceptance of certain standards of morality. If there is a difference of opinion as to whether Christianity provides the only medium for the teaching of ethics, at least we are coming to realize that moral education is as necessary as vocational training. We may smile at John Adams' scholasticism in beginning a pamphlet on republican government with the Aristotelian *cliché* that all republics depend on virtue, but in our hearts we know that Adams, regardless of his philosophical method, had seized on a profound truth. Our quarrel today would be with the application of these Whig principles rather than with the principles themselves.

Perhaps the most important of the ethical values which the Revolutionary leaders sought to infuse into government was justice. No doubt the attainment of perfect justice is impossible, for groups holding political power will always tend to identify justice with the advancement of their own interests. Yet there are certain generally acknowledged standards which cross the barriers of party and interest and are respected by all men who give thought to the welfare of others. Although some Whigs, like Parsons, tended to identify justice with the maintenance of the existing distribution of wealth, others, like Jefferson, could apply it in political decisions with less thought for their own interest. All were aware that operations of will, whether majority or minority, had in the past often flouted moral sanctions and could be expected to do so again. This was the basic reason for the mechanisms of restraints which Whigs built into their republics of equipoise.

As in the case of the Whig belief in the primacy of moral principle, we would agree with their premise that rights must be protected against will, but placing more faith in majorities, we could not accept the means they devised to provide the necessary safeguards. Had their rigid political frameworks not been altered in order to lessen, and finally abolish privilege, future generations of leaders would undoubtedly have succumbed to the temptation of serving their own interests exclusively and human rights would have eventually been used to protect minority privileges. The Whig governments were prevented from becoming narrow, selfish oligarchies only by the gradual recognition of equality demanded by the democrats.

The programs of the Revolutionary Whigs and democrats are therefore complementary to each other. Neither eighteenth-century liberalism nor eighteenth-century democ-

racy was capable by itself of providing political freedom.
Each without the other might have degenerated into tyranny. It was fortunate for the future of the nation that both
liberalism and democracy became potent forces during the
Revolutionary period.

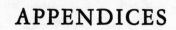

APPENDICES

APPENDIX 1

Note on Constitutional Struggles

in New Hampshire, 1776-1783

THE Revolutionary movement in New Hampshire was similar in many respects to that of Massachusetts—particularly in the growth of democratic sentiment in the western towns. This is not surprising, for political, economic, and social conditions in the two colonies were much alike. In both, the large measure of autonomy accorded the small towns fostered a spirit of independence, and frontier conditions promoted the growth of an equalitarian attitude. During the Revolution the same sectional cleavage appeared in New Hampshire as in Massachusetts: the western towns resented domination by the mercantile East and strove to introduce democratic reforms into the various constitutional plans proposed between 1776 and 1783. Unfortunately, the sources for a study of Revolutionary democracy in New Hampshire are meager in comparison with those of her southern neighbor, but the available materials indicate that the democratic movement was of significant proportions and that the less privileged citizens were able to secure the adoption of more of their program than was the case with their brethren in Massachusetts.

After the collapse of royal government in 1774 and 1775

the Whig leaders of New Hampshire, like those of Massachusetts, attempted to check the growth of anarchy by establishing a *de jure* government. Since the colony had no charter which could be "resumed," the Continental Congress, at the urging of the New Hampshire delegation on November 3, 1775, advised the calling of a "full representation of the people" which would draft a temporary constitution to be in effect until the end of the dispute with Britain.[1] Shortly thereafter, similar advice was sent to South Carolina at the insistence of John Rutledge.[2]

The Provincial Congress immediately laid plans for a constituent congress to meet in December, 1775, but, like the Revolutionary leaders of South Carolina, they did not consider that a "full representation" required extending the suffrage to all free, adult males. The possession of a freehold worth £20 was stipulated for voters and a freehold worth £300 for delegates. Many towns which had not hitherto enjoyed the privilege were invited to send delegates, however, and an attempt was made to establish proportionate representation.[3] At the outbreak of the Revolution,

1. Nathaniel Bouton and others, eds., *Provincial and State Papers of New Hampshire*, 40 Vols. (Concord, 1867-1943), VII, 642.

2. See above, p. 40.

3. During the colonial period the governors had claimed the right of giving representation to new communities as a function of the prerogative power, but the Assembly, noting the procedure followed in Massachusetts under the Charter, protested that it should be accomplished by legislative act. A long struggle over the issue ensued in which the governors, supported by the Privy Council, were ultimately successful. Realizing that a small house made up mostly of delegates from seacoast towns would be easier to control than a larger body with considerable western representation, they issued writs of election very reluctantly to the growing communities of the interior. For a full discussion of the controversy over representation, see William H. Fry, *New Hampshire as a Royal Province* (New York, 1908), 152-168; Leonard W. Labaree, *Royal Government in America; A Study of the British Colonial System before 1783* (New Haven, 1930), 179-183.

only 36 of the 155 towns in the colony were entitled to send delegates to the Assembly. Among those without representation were such considerable places as Concord, with 1,052 taxables, Brentwood with 1,100, and Epping with 1,569. Nor was the representation proportionate among the privileged towns. Although Portsmouth, by far the largest, had four delegates, Hampton with 862 inhabitants had two, while Londonderry with 2,590 had but one.[4]

The arrangements on suffrage and representation apparently caused a strong protest, because on November 10 the Congress decided to reconsider both matters.[5] Four days later it gave the vote in the coming elections to all taxpayers, lowered the property qualifications for officeholding from a £300 to a £200 freehold, and reapportioned the representation to benefit the smaller at the expense of the larger towns.[6] Plymouth and Portsmouth were now given only three representatives apiece, and some small interior towns with only one-tenth their population were allotted one each. Many small communities were required to combine to obtain representation, but in making allotments the proportionate principle was completely disregarded. Some inhabited places with 300 or 400 taxables would be "classed" (i.e. combined for purposes of representation), while others of equal population were given individual representatives. The resolutions of November 14 were significant concessions to the western towns, but they failed to silence all protests. Sectional controversy over suffrage and the apportionment of representation continued throughout the Revolutionary period.

Conflict between conservatives and democrats over the na-

4. Richard F. Upton, *Revolutionary New Hampshire* (Hanover, 1936), 28.

5. *Provincial Papers*, VII, 651.

6. *Ibid.*, 657-659.

ture of the instrument to be drafted was not long in appearing. Josiah Bartlett and John Langdon, delegates to the Continental Congress, probably spoke for most Revolutionary leaders when they advocated a government as much like that of Massachusetts as possible, with the lower house electing a council which would exercise executive as well as legislative functions.[7] In sharp contrast were the ideas of General John Sullivan, formerly a lawyer from the interior of the state. He favored a government directly dependent upon the people and, like eighteenth-century democrats everywhere, felt that popular sovereignty would provide a better check on the people's representatives than the separation of powers. "No danger can arise to a State from giving the people a free and full voice in their own government," he wrote. "And that, what is called the prerogative of the Crown, or checks upon the licentiousness of the people, are only the children of designing and ambitious men, no such thing being necessary; for though many states have been overturned by the rage and violence of people, yet the spirit of rage and violence has ever been awakened in the first place by the misconduct of their rulers. And, though often carried to the most dangerous heights, so far from being owing to too much power being lodged in the hands of the people, that it is clearly owing to their having too small, and their rulers too extensive a power.... I would therefore advise such a form of government ... that one interest should unite the several governing branches, and that the frequent choice of the rulers, by the people, should operate as a check upon their conduct ... or disgrace them for betraying the trust reposed in them."

Unlike many democrats, Sullivan was not obsessed by a fear of the executive power. Along with his democratic legis-

7. *Ibid.,* 642. See also the instructions of Portsmouth to its delegates, *ibid.,* 701-702. These stress the necessity of reopening the courts.

lature he recommended a governor possessing a suspensive veto and control of military appointments.[8] Sullivan's conception of good government approached more closely the modern American democratic state than did the ideas of most of his contemporaries.

The instrument adopted by the constituent Congress was vague and sketchy, obviously intended to be temporary, as the long justificatory preamble explicitly stated. The Congress declared itself to be a House of Representatives and assumed power to choose a council. All patronage was placed in the hands of the two houses. After one year the council would be elective. No property qualifications for voting or officeholding were specified, nor was there any provision against plural officeholding or mention of representation. It was obviously the intent of Congress to leave these matters *in status quo* and deal with them when and if necessary by legislation.[9]

The Constitution evoked protest from all quarters. As in South Carolina, moderate Whigs who opposed constitutions in principle because they made reconciliation with Britain more difficult cited the lack of a popular mandate and the impropriety of allowing the people's delegates to enlarge their own powers.[10] Portsmouth, like Boston, objected particularly to the lack of a prohibition against plural officeholding, possibly because the reapportionment of representation had greatly increased the weight of the western towns in the government. Some of these communities, like the inland towns of Massachusetts, protested against the undemocratic features of the instrument. Sixteen of them memorialized the House in December, 1776, demanding—

8. *Ibid.*, 686-688.
9. Constitution printed in *State Papers*, VIII, 2-4.
10. *Ibid.*, 14-17, 33; Upton, *Revolutionary New Hampshire*, 68, 179; Lawrence S. Mayo, *John Langdon of New Hampshire* (Concord, 1937), 105.

in the aggregate—individual representation, abolition of property qualifications for office, election of senators on a state-wide basis rather than from the counties, abolition of the upper house veto, and a bill of rights.[11] They suspected that the government was falling into the hands of a new aristocracy. Chesterfield charged that "it is our candid opinion that the state of New Hampshire, instead of forming an equitable plan of government, conducing to the peace and safety of the state, have been influenced by the iniquitous intrigues and secret designations of persons unfriendly, to settle down upon the dregs of monarchical and aristocratical tyranny, in imitation of their late *British* oppressor." [12]

Like some of the towns of Berkshire County in Massachusetts, many of the inland communities felt their grievances so strongly that they proposed to secede from the state rather than submit to a government designed more in accordance with the desires of the mercantile East than their own. Giving only partial recognition to the Portsmouth regime, they considered joining the putative state of Vermont, but after long and somewhat disillusioning negotiations with the Allen brothers they returned rather sullenly to their allegiance after the war.[13]

When the Declaration of Independence made reconciliation with Britain extremely improbable, if not impossible, the demand for a new constitution came from many parts of the state. The Portsmouth town meeting continued to ask for a ban on plural officeholding, and the interior towns were so dissatisfied with the existing government that the House sent Meshech Weare and Benjamin Giles on a tour

11. *State Papers,* VIII, 421-426.

12. *Ibid.,* 424. Dartmouth College became a center for the dissatisfaction voiced by the West. See Alice M. Baldwin, *The New England Clergy and the American Revolution* (Durham, 1928), 149-153.

13. For details on the ˙secession movement, see Upton, *Revolutionary New Hampshire,* chap. XIV.

through the region to do what they could to alleviate the discontent.

As in Massachusetts, the lower house during the fall of 1776 had come under the control of a faction opposing the existing constitution. The fact that the body allowed delegates to the Continental Congress to be elected by the qualified voters [14]—the only instance of this procedure in any of the states during the Revolutionary period—throws some light on the trend of its policies. Several resolutions to hold a constitutional convention were passed, but the Council, stronghold of the conservatives, always refused to concur, showing a reluctance similar to that of the upper house in Massachusetts. Finally in 1778 it agreed to the proposals of the representatives, and a convention was called. There was no limit on the number of delegates who could be sent by the individual towns, and acceptance by three-fourths of the electorate was necessary to ratify the instrument.

Unfortunately we know almost nothing about the work of the Convention, for no journals remain. Many western towns, refusing to have anything to do with the Portsmouth government, failed to send delegates. The instrument completed in 1779 was not much different from its predecessor and was rejected by a vote of 1,700 to 1,100.[15] It is impossible to state conclusively the reasons for the rejection because the returns from the towns have been lost, but the raising of property qualifications for office and the maintenance of the previous apportionment of representation may have been factors of importance.

In 1781 the House of Representatives, with the concurrence of the Council, called a second convention. Several ex-

14. *State Papers*, VIII, 699.
15. The constitution and a list of Convention delegates is printed in *Town Papers*, IX, 834-842. The vote on the constitution is given in Mayo, *Langdon*, 179.

pedients were adopted at this time and later in order to avoid another failure like that of 1779: the majority necessary for ratification of the Constitution was reduced from three-fourths to two-thirds; the instrument was not to be submitted to the rebellious towns; and—following the example of Massachusetts—the Convention was empowered to stay in session in case of another rejection in order to revise the instrument in accordance with the wishes of the electorate.[16] It is important to note, however, that unlike the procedure followed in Massachusetts, a revised instrument had to be re-submitted to the people for ratification. This precaution made chicanery like that perpetrated in the Bay State by the Convention of 1780 impossible.

Despite well-laid plans, however, the chances of success appeared to diminish at the outset when only 55 delegates appeared from the 103 towns to which precepts had been sent—eight of them from the large eastern centers of Portsmouth, Exeter, and Londonderry. Conservatives undoubtedly dominated the Convention completely, for the instrument submitted to the people was quite aristocratic in character. Ostensibly to solve the problem of representation, the House of Representatives was to be nominated by an electoral college chosen by the tax-paying freemen; senators would be directly elected by citizens worth £100, the governor by tax-paying freemen. Property qualifications for office were high: members of the electoral college and representatives must be worth £200, senators £400, and the governor £1,000. The governor was given a suspensive veto which could be overridden only by a three-fourths vote of both houses. He could prorogue the General Court for ninety days and order it to convene away from its usual habitat in case "infectious distempers" prevailed there—perhaps political as well as physical. The long Bill of Rights made a religious settlement

16. *State Papers*, VIII, 897-898.

much like that of Massachusetts by empowering communities to lay taxes for the support of religion.[17]

The Convention was apparently quite proud of its handiwork, particularly the electoral college. In an address to constituents the members pointed out that all towns, regardless of population, would now have representation in the legislature, yet the size of the House of Representatives would be kept within manageable limits. The General Court would contain only sixty-two members—fifty representatives and twelve senators—and as a result would be inexpensive, efficient, "devoid of party spirit" and "interested views," and devoted to "higher and better principles." [18]

Although the proposed constitution might satisfy the Convention which drafted it, the document failed to win approval from constituents. Obviously citizens not worth £100 would not want to vote away the right to elect senators, and the desire for direct representation on the part of the small towns would not be satisfied by depriving all towns of it. Also, the extensive gubernatorial patronage, the suspensive veto, and the power to prorogue and to change the meeting place of the legislature probably recalled memories of royal prerogative. It is no wonder that the proposed constitution was overwhelmingly rejected.

Unfortunately, the returns from the towns on this instrument, as well as those on the proposed constitution of 1779, have been lost, but from subsequent revisions it is plain that the people objected also to the limited suffrage for the senate and to the property qualifications for office. The Convention, again compelled to alter the instrument, submitted a new version to the people which reinstated direct representation, gave the vote for both houses to tax-paying free-

17. The list of delegates to the Convention and the proposed constitution are printed in *Town Papers*, IX, 842-844; 852-877.
18. *Address* printed in *ibid.*, 845-852.

men, and cut all property qualifications for office at least in half. The members refused, however, to diminish the governor's powers and carefully explained the need for a strong executive in an Address accompanying the new instrument.[19]

But the townsmen refused to accept the Convention's logic. They rejected the proposed constitution of 1782 as decisively as they did those of 1779 and 1781. Bowing to the inevitable, the Convention in a third revision then deprived the governor of his suspensive veto and changed his title to president in an evident attempt to eradicate the last trace of the hated prerogative power. The provisions against plural officeholding were also strengthened.[20] Apparently satisfied at last, the constituents accepted this instrument in 1783.

Thus it seems apparent from the results of these constitutional controversies, even though we have little evidence to demonstrate it, that the desire for democratic government was as strong, if not stronger, among the people of New Hampshire than among those of Massachusetts. In their demand for a broad suffrage which would include nearly all adult males, a legislature with both houses dependent upon this electorate, and an executive deprived of the legislative veto, they struck at the heart of the Whig ideal—the republic in equipoise. Although the Constitution of 1783 transformed these desires into fundamental law, nevertheless the document did not signify a complete democratic victory. The smaller towns were still compelled to accept the classification scheme and county representation in the senate was apportioned on the basis of tax receipts, thus giving the East complete predominance in the upper house. But though accumulated wealth did receive protection, the fact that this house was directly dependent upon a wide electorate considerably diminished, both in theory and in fact, its value

19. *Ibid.*, 877-882.
20. Constitution printed in *ibid.*, 896-919.

as a bulwark against radical legislation promoted by unpropertied majorities.

Apparently the towns accepted without protest the principle of taxation for religious purposes. The fact that they did again illustrates the indifference, if not hostility, of many of the humbler townsmen to the separation of church and state. Living in small communities out of touch with metropolitan centers, they were unaffected by the religious liberalism common among the Whig leaders.

APPENDIX 2

Note on a Democratic Revolution in Georgia

1775-1777

RELATIVELY little is known about the Revolutionary movement in Georgia, but from the available evidence it would appear that it was accompanied by an internal revolution comparable to that of Pennsylvania. The most recently settled of the thirteen colonies, Georgia had a population of only 50,000 in 1776, most of which was spread out along the coast and on the banks of the tidal rivers. Savannah, the main seaport, was a town of only 300 or 400 houses. A few men like James Habersham, Governor James Wright, John Graham, and Noble Jones possessed vast tracts of land and hundreds of slaves, but most of the settlers were yeoman farmers, usually very poor and of the most diverse origins. The British government, anxious to make the province a bastion against the Indians and—previous to 1763, the Spaniards—gave land very liberally to immigrants, often remitted taxes for long periods of years, and undertook the support of the government. During the colonial period it spent approximately £215,000 on the development of Georgia.[1]

1. Albert B. Saye, *A Constitutional History of Georgia, 1732-1945* (Athens, 1948), 72; E. Merton Coulter, *A Short History of Georgia* (Chapel Hill, 1933), 93-96.

At the outbreak of the Revolution, radical sentiment was much weaker in Georgia than to the North because of close economic connections with the mother country and the proximity of Indians on the West and British garrisons in Florida.[2] The colony does not appear to have been troubled by sectional or class controversy, possibly because of its diminutive size and because the Commons House accomplished certain reforms of the type often demanded by yeomen farmers elsewhere. In the years preceding the Revolution the legislature prevailed on the governor to extend representation to newly settled regions on the plea that representation should accompany taxation;[3] taxes were laid on property as well as polls and ballot voting was introduced.[4] Although the property qualifications were approximately the same as in the other southern colonies—50 acres for voters and 250 for representatives—the ease of acquiring land put the suffrage, at least, within the reach of every able-bodied man.

The news of the Boston Port Bill and the Massachusetts Government Acts produced no reaction comparable to the protests from the other colonies. When a committee of thirty-one, led by a few of the outstanding merchants, lawyers, and planters of the province, proclaimed in the name of the colony the usual statements of Whig principles and expressions of sympathy for Boston, one hundred and three equally prominent men published a protest against what they held to be the committee's presumption in im-

2. Because of these factors a Georgia historian observes, "It is not to be wondered that the Revolutionary spirit developed more slowly in Georgia than in the sister colonies to the north. Indeed, the surprise is rather to be found in the fact that Georgians joined the Revolution at all...." Albert B. Saye, *New Viewpoints in Georgia History* (Athens, 1943), 134.

3. Saye, *A Constitutional History of Georgia,* 69, 58-59.

4. Charles C. Jones, *History of Georgia,* 3 Vols. (Boston, 1883), II, 116-117; Saye, *A Constitutional History of Georgia,* 82.

plying mass support for its views. The one hundred and three asserted that only twenty-six persons had gathered at a tavern meeting in Savannah to vote the committee's resolutions, and that the doors had been locked in order to exclude representatives of several parishes known to be opposed to the radicalism of the Savannah group.[5] A few days later almost one-third of the inhabitants of the town and neighborhood of Savannah held a public meeting at the courthouse and signed a dissent from the committee's proceedings. Similar action was taken in several parishes. Governor Wright, with some justification, wrote to the Earl of Dartmouth that the committee's resolutions "were not the voice of the people, but unfairly and insolently made by a junto of a very few only."[6]

Undaunted by opposition, the Savannah radicals called a Provincial Congress in January, 1775, when the Commons House was scheduled to meet, in order to secure the adoption of the Continental Association and have delegates elected to the Continental Congress. None had been sent in the fall of '74 because of the strong reaction against the committee. But the indifference to the Whig cause again frustrated the plans of the Savannah radicals. Only five of the twelve parishes sent delegates, and the three men chosen by the gathering to represent the colony in Philadelphia refused to serve, realizing that they represented a small minority of the population. "Alas!" they wrote the President of the Continental Congress, "with what face could we have appeared for a Province whose inhabitants had refused to sacrifice the most trifling advantages to the public cause, and in whose behalf we do not think we could safely pledge ourselves for the execution of any one measure whatsoever?"[7]

5. Jones, *History of Georgia*, II, 149-155.
6. *Ibid.*, 156.
7. *Ibid.*, 173.

After arrival of the news of Lexington and Concord, however, radical sentiment burgeoned suddenly for reasons which have never been adequately explained. In view of the subsequent events, however, this reversal of opinion may well have been connected with a desire for democratic reform. In 1775 the parish of St. Andrews, inhabited by the descendants of New England Puritans, had accepted the Association while declaring that "encouragement should be given to the poor of every nation by every generous American." In the same resolves the people had testified to their abhorrence of slavery and urged general manumission.[8] The committee at Darien in January, 1775, denounced slavery as "a practice founded in injustice and in cruelty,... debasing part of our fellow creatures below men, and corrupting the virtue and morals of the rest...." St. Johns, a predominantly Puritan parish and likewise strong for the Whigs, sent its own representative to the Continental Congress in March, 1775, who participated in discussions but did not vote. By July radicalism had spread to the other parishes. All twelve of them were represented in the Second Provincial Congress, attended by over 100 delegates who were probably elected by mass meetings which disregarded suffrage qualifications.[9] A committee system was established and royal government disintegrated.

In Georgia as in Pennsylvania this sudden shift of power from conservatives to radicals signalized the beginning of an internal revolution. The lower classes appear to have become the mainstay of the radical movement. Governor Wright reported to the Earl of Dartmouth that the parochial committees were "a parcel of the lowest people, chiefly carpenters, shoemakers, blacksmiths," led by a few merchants and planters. "It is really terrible, my Lord," he complained,

8. *Ibid.*, 160-161.
9. Saye, *New Viewpoints in Georgia History*, 160.

"that such people should be suffered to overturn the civil Government and most arbitrarily determine upon, and sport with Other Men's lives liberties and properties." [10] A Loyalist lady of Savannah commented that in the revolutionary ferment "the scum rose to the top." [11]

The Congress gave the vote for future meetings to all taxpayers, divided the colony into districts, and reapportioned the representation.[12] In April, 1776, it adopted a temporary constitution called *The Rules and Regulations,* and a few days after the signing of the Declaration of Independence the President of the Council of Safety called a convention to draft a permanent instrument of government. All taxpayers could vote for members of the convention, but only freeholders could serve as delegates.

The instrument adopted by this body indicates that the yeoman farmers had won fairly complete control of the state, but that the merchants, lawyers, and planters were still strong enough to secure constitutional protection for their interests. The most outstanding victory for democracy was the establishment of a unicameral legislature. As in Pennsylvania, there was to be no upper house independent of the people's representatives which would accord special protection to accumulated wealth or give opportunity for the better-educated to review popular legislation. Again as in Pennsylvania, representation was weighted in favor of the poor and populous back country as against the metropolis dominated by a wealthy few.

The judicial process was carefully regulated in order to avoid the type of abuses which the Regulators had complained of in North Carolina. The impanelling of impartial

---

10. Quoted from Ethel K. Ware, *A Constitutional History of Georgia* (New York, 1947), 23-24.

11. Charles F. Jenkins, *Button Gwinnett* (New York, 1926), 62.

12. Saye, *A Constitutional History of Georgia,* 92.

juries was assured, all executions of judgment could be stayed until the first Monday of March of every year, court costs could not exceed £3 and cases could not remain on the docket for more than two sessions. One unique and tremendously important provision declared that special juries summoned on appeal to Superior Court would be the judges of law as well as of fact. If strictly adhered to, this would practically have emasculated the judicial power, for judges would be little more than moderators of popular tribunals. Another provision gave an opportunity for the special juries to exercise judicial review. In bringing in verdicts they were empowered to "judge" the "rules and regulations contained in this constitution." The importance given to juries by the framers of the Constitution suggests that they were designed as the instruments of popular sovereignty against judicial or executive tyranny.[13] Entail and primogeniture was abolished; sheriffs, constables, and all local officials except justices of the peace and registers of probate would be elected within the counties; free public schools were to be erected in each county; and the amending process could be initiated by petitions of a majority of the voters in a majority of the counties.

The Constitution contained certain conservative elements which to some extent qualified its generally democratic tone. The suffrage, given to all taxpayers in 1775, was now limited to those free, white, Protestant males with possessions worth £10, and a property qualification of 250 acres of land or £250 personalty was stipulated for representatives. The Executive Council, although denied a legislative veto, was privileged to recommend amendments to bills. The committee sent from the upper body was to read the proposed amendments "sitting and covered," while the members of the House remained "sitting and uncovered." The fact

13. For an interesting discussion of this point see Saye, *New Viewpoints in Georgia History*, 189-191.

that this piece of punctilio was written into the fundamental law seems to indicate a desire to attach a superior prestige to the Council even though it was in fact almost powerless. Sunbury and Savannah, the two principal seaports, were given two and four members in the House respectively "to represent their trade"—indication that the merchants were able to some extent to redress the discrimination against them in representation.[14]

These checks on pure democracy were probably of small moment, however. During the rest of the Revolution the common man held the whip hand in Georgia. The first House of Representatives, in defiance of the Constitution, refused to allow Savannah and Sunbury their individual representation. Joseph Clay, an influential Savannah merchant and a member of the original Whig group, complained that the new Constitution was "so very democratical that it has thrown power into such hands as must ruin the country."[15] Since the best people, in his opinion, were either Tory or too timid to participate in politics, government was being conducted by "those whose ability or situation in life does not entitle them to it." The Grand Jury of Chatham County, in which Savannah was located, complained of the absence of a check upon the legislature, and a Georgia correspondent of Henry Laurens charged that a strong faction in it, while "bellowing liberty," was doing everything it could to deprive "the best part of the community of even the shadow of it."[16]

Thus, although facts are so scanty that conclusions must be

14. Constitution printed in Francis N. Thorpe, *Federal and State Constitutions*, 7 Vols. (Washington, 1909), II, 777-785; discussed in Saye, *Constitutional History of Georgia*, 137-140 and Ware, *Constitutional History of Georgia*, 34-48.

15. Archie H. Jones, The Georgia Constitution of 1777 (MS in possession of the author, 1950), 26.

16. *Ibid.*, 27.

to a certain extent inferential, it appears that in Georgia as in Pennsylvania the Revolution brought a new class to power previously unidentified with colonial government. Although the Constitution did not bring the complete political equality inherent in the Pennsylvania Constitution, nevertheless the characteristics of the two governments were quite similar. In both states the single-house legislature was supreme and the basis of representation was designed to give dominance to the democratic hinterland as against the more aristocratic metropolis. The transition from colony to commonwealth in Georgia deserves thorough investigation, for apparently the break from Britain set a train of circumstances in motion which led to one of the first victories for American democracy.

BIBLIOGRAPHICAL NOTE

The general sources for a study of the American Revolution are sufficiently well known to make a detailed bibliography for this volume unnecessary. The books, pamphlets, documents, and newspapers noted in the following pages have been selected from the much larger mass of material cited in the text because they have the most direct bearing on the subject. This bibliography, then, may be considered primarily as a key for future students of Revolutionary democracy.

Historians covering the broader aspects of the Revolution have been slow to realize the importance of the struggles for reform of colonial institutions which took place within the states. Not until the last fifty years has much importance been attached to aspects of the war other than military and diplomatic events and the political struggles centering in the Continental Congress. Only in the last ten years or so has the significance of the democratic movement been recognized. The first work devoted exclusively to political affairs within the states, and one of enduring merit, is Allen Nevins, *The American States During and After the Revolution* (New York, 1924). Nevins considered the democrats as impractical radical theorists, and as a result his sympathies lay with the conservative Whigs. The reluctance of the colonial merchants to sanction independence for fear of arousing radical movements which might threaten their political and economic interests was revealed by Arthur M. Schlesinger, *The Colonial Merchants and the American Revolution* (New York, 1918). J. Franklin Jameson, in a provocative series of lectures entitled *The American Revolution Considered as a Social Movement* (Princeton, 1926), pointed to the significance of the Revolution as inducing change in the relations of social classes to each other, attitudes on slavery, methods of landholding, and in the currents

348

of business, intellectual, and religious life. Surprisingly, however, he failed to mention the democratic movement. But more recent works have corrected this omission. John C. Miller's well-written and incisive volumes, *Origins of the American Revolution* (Boston, 1943), and *Triumph of Freedom, 1775-1783* (New York, 1948), note some of the attempts of the politically unprivileged to take advantage of the Revolution to obtain political rights. Merrill Jensen, in *The Articles of Confederation* (Madison, 1941), sees the drafting of the *Articles* as a focus for conflict between conservative Whigs and those with more democratic inclinations. Philip Davidson, *Propaganda and the American Revolution* (Chapel Hill, 1941) is a good study of the methods and techniques of the Whig leaders. Daniel J. Boorstin, in *The Genius of American Politics* (Chicago, 1953), lays much needed emphasis on the conservative aspects of the Revolution.

Studies of political thought and constitutional history are important as background for any examination of democracy in the Revolution. One of the best of the works on political ideas is Charles E. Merriam's *History of American Political Theories* (3rd ed.: New York, 1936), but Moses Coit Tyler's *Literary History of the American Revolution*, 2 Vols. (New York, 1897), is far from outdated and sometimes shows deep insights. William S. Carpenter, *The Development of American Political Thought* (Princeton, 1930), examines a wider range of material and attempts a synthesis on a topical basis. Randolph G. Adams, *Political Ideas of the American Revolution* (Durham, 1922), is a distinguished study of such concepts as consent, natural rights, and popular sovereignty. Adams stresses the importance of James Wilson as a political thinker. Charles H. McIlwain, in *The American Revolution, a Constitutional Interpretation* (New York, 1923), like Wilson justifies the Whig conception of colonial rights by pleading the seventeenth-century British constitution against the eighteenth. The essays by Pargellis, Schneider, and Salvemini contained in Conyers Read., ed., *The Constitution Reconsidered* (New York, 1938), are illuminating and useful. Leonard W. Labaree's *Conservatism in Early American History* (New York and London, 1948) is an excellent study of the ideas of the colonial leaders who became Tories or who, if they supported the patriot cause, were looked upon as "aristocrats" by the Whigs. Clinton Rossiter, in his excellent *Seedtime of the Republic* (New York, 1953), gives the most comprehensive treatment yet available of the political ideas of the Revolutionary generation.

A few leading articles on special topics deserve particular mention. Max Farrand, "The West and the Principles of the Revolution," *Yale Review,* XVII (1909), notes the growth of protest on the frontier against the domination of the colonial governments by eastern aristocrats. Philip G. Davidson, *The Southern Backcountry on the Eve of the Revolution,* in Avery O. Craven (ed.), *Essays in Honor of William E. Dodd* (Chicago, 1935), shows how this antagonism drove many of the yeoman farmers toward Toryism. H. G. Webster analyses and compares the provisions of the first state constitutions in *A Comparative Study of the State Constitutions of the American Revolution,* American Academy of Political and Social Science, *Annals,* IX (1897). E. S. Corwin, in "The Progress of Constitutional Theory Between the Declaration of Independence and the Philadelphia Convention," *American Historical Review,* XXX (1925), notes a gradual shift from the acceptance of virtual legislative supremacy to a desire for the separation of powers. The extent to which the principle of fundamental law was written into the first state constitutions is discussed by B. F. Wright, Jr., *The Early History of Written Constitutions in America,* in *Essays in History and Political Theory in Honor of Charles H. McIlwain* (Cambridge, 1936).

A good many printed letters bearing on the democratic movement and other information unobtainable elsewhere will be found in biographies of leading Revolutionary figures. Among the more useful of these for the student of Revolutionary democracy are: Richard Frothingham, *Joseph Warren* (Boston, 1865); Theophilus Parsons, Jr., *Memoir of Theophilus Parsons* (Boston, 1859); Alvah Hovey, *A Memoir of the Life and Times of Isaac Backus* (Boston, 1858); Jared Sparks, *Life of Gouverneur Morris,* 2 Vols. (Boston, 1832); Frank Monaghan, *John Jay* (New York,

1935); William B. Reed, *The Life and Correspondence of Joseph Reed*, 2 Vols. (Philadelphia, 1847); Charles J. Stillé, *The Life and Times of John Dickinson, 1732-1808* (Philadelphia, 1891); Carl Van Doren, *Benjamin Franklin* (New York, 1939); Burton A. Konkle, *George Bryan and the Constitution of Pennsylvania, 1731-1791* (Philadelphia, 1922); Griffith J. McRee, *Life and Correspondence of James Iredell*, 2 Vols. (New York, 1857); Richard H. Barry, *Mr. Rutledge of South Carolina* (New York, 1942). Among the numerous biographies of Jefferson, the ones most useful for the historian are those by Randall, Chinard, Malone, and Schachner.

Much of the best writing on the Revolution dealing with the internal conflict is in volumes and articles devoted to particular colonies and states. Samuel E. Morison, *The Struggle over the Adoption of the Constitution of Massachusetts,* Massachusetts Historical Society, *Proceedings,* Vol. L, is perhaps the most important work of this type for the student of Revolutionary democracy. Morison analyses and classifies the objections to constitutional proposals made by the General Court appearing in the returns from the towns. In his article the outlines of the democratic program clearly emerge. The returns are so voluminous, however, that there is room for still further study of them. Harry A. Cushing, in *The History of the Transition from Provincial to Commonwealth Government in Massachusetts* (New York, 1896), made some use of this source, but he failed to recognize the tremendous significance of the returns, and the judgments and estimates in his book are dated. J. E. A. Smith, *History of Pittsfield* (Boston, 1869), contains much illuminating material on the progress of democracy in the back country of Massachusetts. Ellen E. Brennan, *Plural Officeholding in Massachusetts: 1760-1780* (Chapel Hill, 1945), is an important book insofar as it emphasizes the fact that the common people looked on the separation of powers as the abolition of plural officeholding. Chapter 1 of Oscar and Mary F. Handlin's *Commonwealth; a Study of the Role of Government in the American Economy: Massachusetts, 1774-1861* (New York, 1947), is a well-documented and generally excellent account of state politics in the Revolution which emphasizes sectional tensions and the desire for reform in many back-country towns. Richard F. Upton, *Revolutionary New Hampshire* (Hanover, 1936), contains a competent chapter on constitutional struggles in that state.

One of the best works dealing with the Revolution is Carl Becker, *The History of Political Parties in the Province of New York, 1760-1766* (Madison, 1909). Becker brilliantly describes class conflicts in New York City previous to independence. Irving Mark, *Agrarian Conflicts in Colonial New York, 1711-1775* (New York, 1940), contains an account of the "Great Rebellion of 1766," and E. Wilder Spaulding, *New York in the Critical Period, 1783-1789* (New York, 1932), describes the advance of democratic ideas during and after the Revolution.

Charles H. Lincoln, *The Revolutionary Movement in Pennsylvania, 1760-1776* (Philadelphia, 1901), like Becker's volume, gives a full account of class and sectional tensions. Lincoln did not realize the importance of the move for a change to royal government, however, and his sections dealing with the Constitution of 1776 have been superseded by J. Paul Selsam, *The Pennsylvania Constitution of 1776* (Philadelphia, 1936). Although well organized, this latter work lacks incisiveness and shows little recognition of the unique characteristics of the Revolution in Pennsylvania. Robert L. Brunhouse, *The Counter-Revolution in Pennsylvania, 1776-1790* (Harrisburg, 1942), describes the gradual collapse of the democratic movement in Pennsylvania from 1776 to 1790. Brooke Hindle, "The March of the Paxton Boys," *William and Mary Quarterly*, 3rd Ser., III (1946), appears to be the definitive treatment of the subject.

Philip A. Crowl, in a condensed and well-written monograph, *Maryland During and After the Revolution* (Baltimore, 1943), gives an insight into class and sectional tensions appearing during the formation of the first state constitution, and Charles A. Barker, *The Background of the Revolution in Maryland* (New Haven, 1940), provides an able introduction for a study of them.

The fullest and best-balanced description of the Carolina back country is in Carl Bridenbaugh, *Myths and Realities: Societies of the Colonial South* (Baton Rouge, 1952). There is no mono-

graphic treatment of the Revolution in North Carolina, but the
James Sprunt Historical *Publications* and the *North Carolina
Historical Review* contain articles covering many aspects of it,
and there are also several good institutional studies. Julian P.
Boyd, "The Sheriff in Colonial North Carolina," *North Carolina
Historical Review,* V (1928), describes in detail the corruption
of local government. Other articles on the same theme are, William C. Guess, *County Government in Colonial North Carolina,*
James Sprunt Historical *Publications,* XI (1911); E. Merton
Coulter, *The Granville District,* James Sprunt Historical *Publications,* XIII (1913). John S. Bassett, *The Regulators of North
Carolina,* American Historical Association Annual *Report,* 1894,
is still the standard factual treatment of the subject and will probably never be completely superseded. Hugh T. Lefler has made
a more judicious evaluation of the Regulation, however, in the
following recent works: Hugh T. Lefler and Albert R. Newsome,
North Carolina, the History of a Southern State (Chapel Hill,
1954); Hugh T. Lefler and Paul Wager (eds.), *Orange County*
(North Carolina), *1752-1952* (Chapel Hill, 1953). Elmer D. Johnson, in The War of the Regulation: Its Place in History (master's
thesis, University of North Carolina, 1942), has compiled figures,
which, although not conclusive, would seem to indicate that a
relatively small number of Regulators became Tories in the
Revolution. He has also examined in some detail the westward
migration of some Regulators after Alamance.

The beginning of the Revolution in North Carolina and the
formation of the Constitution of 1776 are treated in R. D. W.
Connor, *History of North Carolina; The Colonial and Revolutionary Periods, 1584-1783,* Vol. I (Chicago and New York, 1919);
and in Lefler and Newsome, *North Carolina.* Joseph S. Jones, in
*A Defense of the Revolutionary History of the State of North
Carolina from the Aspersions of Mr. Jefferson* (Boston and
Raleigh, 1834), apparently drew upon original material not obtain-
able today and reveals the extent to which the aristocracy controlled the course of the Revolution. Robert O. DeMond, *The
Loyalists in North Carolina During the Revolution* (Durham,
1940), is disappointing because the author never comes to grips

with the problem of motivation in the case of the various Loyalist groups.

The history of the Colonial and Revolutionary periods in South Carolina has been so ably written by Edward McCrady in *South Carolina under Royal Government, 1719-1776* (New York, 1899), and in *South Carolina in the Revolution, 1775-1780* (New York, 1901), that apparently no one has considered doing it again. There is a real need, however, for new volumes on the two periods which will utilize material unavailable to McCrady. The Regulator Movement of South Carolina has been ably described by Richard J. Hooker in his edition of Charles Woodmason's journal, *The Carolina Backcountry on the Eve of the Revolution* (Chapel Hill, 1953). The importance of sectional tensions as a leading factor of the state's history has been indicated in William A. Schaper, *Sectionalism and Representation in South Carolina; a Sociological Study,* American Historical Association Annual *Report,* 1900, I, 237-463.

The democratic revolution in Georgia and the equalitarian aspects of the first state constitution have been noted by Albert B. Saye, *New Viewpoints in Georgia History* (Athens, 1943), and *A Constitutional History of Georgia, 1732-1945* (Athens, 1948). Fletcher M. Green, *Constitutional Development in the South Atlantic States, 1776-1860* (Chapel Hill, 1930), is a work of enduring merit which shows insight into the intentions of the Whig leaders regarding domestic government.

Contemporary writings bearing on the democratic movement are profuse in the states which had printing facilities and almost nonexistent elsewhere. Therefore, pamphlet literature and newspaper editorials are extensive enough in Massachusetts and Pennsylvania to give some understanding of the issues between democrats and conservatives. *The People the Best Governors, or a Plan of Government Founded on the Just Principles of Natural Freedom* (1776)—probably published in Hartford or Worcester —contains the most complete statement of democratic ideas on state government to be written during the Revolution. (See above, note 12, p. 15.) The pamphlet has been reprinted as an appendix in Frederick Chase, *History of Dartmouth College*

(Cambridge, 1891). In Massachusetts, the pamphlets of Isaac Backus afford understanding of the campaign for religious freedom waged by members of the dissenting sects, and William Gordon's articles in the *Continental Journal* and the *Independent Chronicle* show the progress of democratic thinking. *An Address to the Inhabitants of the County of Berkshire Respecting their Present Opposition to Civil Government* (Hartford, 1778), reveals the hostility of the back-country farmers for the General Court. Other examples of this attitude can be found in the columns of the Massachusetts *Spy*, printed in Worcester. Theophilus Parsons' *Essex Result* (1778)—reprinted in Parsons, *Memoir of Theophilus Parsons*—illustrates the position of the more materialistic conservatives regarding constitutional issues. Political editorials are numerous in the following newspapers: Boston *Gazette*, Massachusetts *Spy*, *Continental Journal*, New England *Chronicle*, *Independent Chronicle*. The Boston Athenaeum has complete files of all these papers except the *Spy*, which may be found in the American Antiquarian Society, Worcester.

North Carolina was without a press during the Revolution and for most of the Colonial period. Comment on the Regulator movement appeared, however, in the Virginia *Gazette* and in the South Carolina and American General *Gazette*. The very important writings of Herman Husband, *An Impartial Relation,* and *A Fan for Fanning,* and the pamphlet by George Sims, *Address to the People of Granville County* are reprinted in William K. Boyd (ed.), *Some Eighteenth Century Tracts Concerning North Carolina* (Raleigh, 1927). Husband gives an eye-witness but biased account of the Regulator movement, and Sims reveals the extent of the corruption in local government.

Fortunately for the student of the democratic movement during the Revolution, there is a tremendous volume of printed documents of all sorts. The most important collection is, of course, the monumental *American Archives,* 4th and 5th Series, 9 Vols. (Washington, 1837-1853). The thousands of pages contain a miscellany of legislative journals, private letters, and newspaper editorials, arranged in chronological order. Fortunately also, the veneration for the Revolutionary fathers has resulted in the extensive printing of literary remains. The student should consult the works of John Adams, Samuel Adams, Thomas Paine, John Dickinson, James Wilson, and James Otis. Of great importance is the Princeton edition of Jefferson's works. The editors—Julian P. Boyd, Lyman H. Butterfield, and Mina R. Bryan—have brought together a tremendous amount of new material bearing on Jefferson's career. The first five volumes are an indispensable source for the history of Virginia during the Revolution. Mr. Butterfield's edition of *The Letters of Benjamin Rush* (2 Vols., Princeton, 1951), is compiled with the same care and insight which marks the Jefferson volumes and casts new light on the Revolutionary history of Pennsylvania.

Many of the states have printed all the documents bearing on their Colonial and Revolutionary history which could be found. Nathaniel Bouton and others (eds.), *The Provincial and State Papers of New Hampshire,* 40 Vols. (Concord, 1867-1943), contain the public documents indispensable for an understanding of constitutional struggles during the Revolution in that state. Unfortunately, however, the returns from the towns on the draft constitutions of the period have been lost. The contents of the archives in Massachusetts have not been published, but the proceedings of the Constitutional Convention of 1779-1780, together with related documents and the rejected constitution of 1778, have been printed in *Journal of the Convention, 1779-1780* (Boston, 1832). Many towns have published their archives. Most important are the *Boston Town Records, 1770-1783,* 2 Vols. (Boston, 1887-1891). *Acts and Resolves of the Province of Massachusetts Bay,* 21 Vols. (Boston, 1869-1922), V, contains session laws for the Revolutionary period supplemented by important documentary material. The public documents of Pennsylvania during the Colonial and Revolutionary periods have been published in *The Pennsylvania Archives,* Ser. 1-9 (Harrisburg, 1852-1935). The some 130 volumes are cluttered with genealogical material, no observable order or method was used in compiling, and the few indexes are faulty. Series 8 contains the journal or *Votes* of the Assembly. Since many more petitions and memorials were written into the *Votes* than into the journals of most other colonial legislatures, it is perhaps the most important single source for political history in the Colonial and early Revolutionary periods. The *Pennsylvania Magazine of History and Biography,* which started publication in 1877, is in itself a small archive of printed source material. Carl Van Doren (ed.), *Letters and Papers of Benjamin Franklin and Richard Jackson, 1753-1785* (Philadelphia, 1947), throws much new light on the Assembly's motives in desiring a change to royal government. Two indispensable sources for the study of the Revolutionary period are: Alexander Graydon, *Memoirs of His Own Time* (Philadelphia, 1846), and William Duane (ed.), *Extracts from the Diary of Christopher Marshall, 1774-1781* (Albany, 1877). The origins of the Whig party in Pennsylvania are described in a letter from Charles Thomson to William H. Drayton and in "Joseph Reed's Narrative," both of which are printed in volume XI of New York Historical Society, *Collections,* 75 Vols. (New York, 1868-1942). The journals of the North Carolina Assembly, petitions and memorials by the Regulators, and a large volume of important correspondence is printed in volumes VII to X of William L. Saunders (ed.), *The Colonial Records of North Carolina,* 10 Vols. (Raleigh, 1886-1890). This is the most complete publication of its type in any of the colonies, for most of the documents were copied from the originals in English archives.

The most important single manuscript source for a study of democratic ideas during the Revolution are the returns of the Massachusetts towns on constitutional questions between 1776 and 1780. They are contained, along with other pertinent material, in MS volumes 156, 158, 276, and 277 of the Massachusetts Archives, State House, Boston. There is no guide or index to the Archives and the titles of the volumes are sometimes misleading. The manuscripts are in good condition but difficult to read because of the limitations of the writers. The collections of correspondence in the Historical Society of Pennsylvania also contain information valuable for a study of the democratic movement in that state. The official correspondence of Governor John Penn and the letters of the Pemberton family cast light on the attempt of the Quaker party to transform Pennsylvania into a royal colony. The Burd and Shippen papers contain material bearing on the attitude of the West regarding the issue. Miscellaneous, but important, pieces of information on the beginning of the Revolution and the attitude of the upper classes toward the democratic constitution will be found in the Gratz collection (Charles Thomson's note book, George Clymer papers), Dickinson family papers, Thomas McKean papers, Richard Peters papers, and the Jasper Yeates papers. Most of the material bearing on the struggle for democracy in North Carolina has been printed in the *Colonial Records* or in Boyd's *Tracts,* but occasional important facts unobtainable elsewhere can be gleaned from the Hayes, Thomas H. Emmet, and Johnston collections, and from the Thomas Burke, Samuel Johnston, and Miscellaneous papers. All are housed in the North Carolina Department of History and Archives, Raleigh. The Regulator papers in the Southern History Collection, University of North Carolina, contain a few very important letters of Regulator leaders.

INDEX